MIMEKOR YISRAEL

SELECTED CLASSICAL JEWISH FOLKTALES

ממקור ישראל

In Assemblies bless God, the Lord,

O you who are from the

fountain of Israel

[PSALM 68:27]

MIMEKOR YISRAEL

SELECTED CLASSICAL JEWISH FOLKTALES

Collected by Micha Joseph bin Gorion

Edited by Emanuel bin Gorion

Translated by I. M. Lask

Prepared, with an introduction and headnotes,
by Dan Ben-Amos

INDIANA UNIVERSITY PRESS
BLOOMINGTON AND INDIANAPOLIS

Manufactured in the United States of America

LC number 88–46029

ISBN 0–253–31156–X (hardbound)
ISBN 0–253–20588–3 (paperback)

1   2   3   4   5   94   93   92   91   90

Contents

[v]

In the Days of the Second Temple

Talmudic Tales

Rabbinical Tales

In the Land of Israel

Forebears and Descendants

Kabbalists and Hasidim

Timeless Tales

Tales of Wisdom

Preface

Immediately upon its original publication in a six-volume set in German as *Der Born Judas*, during and shortly after World War I, *Mimekor Yisrael* attained the status of a scholarly and a literary classic. Micha Joseph bin Gorion (Berdyczewski) drew into this collection tales from traditional classical sources, medieval and later folk books that served as the basic staple of a narrative tradition that nurtured Jewish communities in Asia, Europe, and North Africa. Since most of these books were no longer accessible to the modern reader, the very anthology of tales that bin Gorion assembled became a classical collection. In that sense this volume of tales is true to its Hebrew title. *Mimekor Yisrael* means "from the fountain of Israel," and indeed, the tales in that volume had been selected from the fountainheads that fed the broad stream of Jewish tradition, turning *Mimekor Yisrael* itself into a new source of traditional tales for the modern reader.

After the original publication, Emanuel bin Gorion, Micha Joseph's son, prepared an edition that included the Hebrew texts that his mother, Rachel Ramberg, translated into German. The Hebrew version of *Mimekor Yisrael* appeared in three editions, in 1939, 1952, and 1956. It was the last of these editions that had been translated into English and published in a three-volume set by Indiana University Press in 1976. In preparation for an abridged edition Emanuel bin Gorion selected two hundred and sixty-five tales that are included in a revised abridged and annotated edition of *Mimekor Yisrael*. He passed away at the age of eighty-four, on June 10, 1987, before he could make the selection for the present edition of the book. Dan Ben-Amos, his collaborator in the preparation of the revised editions, selected the hundred and thirteen tales that constitute the present volume. The commentary in this edition is limited to interpretive remarks; further bibliographical information pertaining to individual tales is available in the headnotes of the abridged and annotated edition.

When Micha Joseph bin Gorion made his original selection of tales, from the hundreds of traditional books that he examined, he did not seek any allusive core of Judaism that the folk tradition might contain. Diversity rather than unity was for him the essence of the Jewish spirit. In keeping with his thought, the present selection of a limited number of tales does not necessarily represent any minimal canon of classical tales; rather, it reflects the diversity and variability that he perceived in the broad spectrum of Jewish folk tradition.

Introduction

Micha Joseph bin Gorion (Berdyczewski) (1865-1921) was one of the most prominent Jewish authors to emerge out of East European traditional life to embrace Western intellectual ideas and to foster modern literature in Hebrew and Yiddish. Controversial and passionate, he wrote fiction and essays, expressing his views on Jewish tradition, theology, philosophy, and literature. In his latter years he engaged in research, collecting Jewish legends, fables, and folktales from post-biblical, medieval, and even recent collections.

Mimekor Yisrael: Classical Jewish Folktales is the apex of his scholarship. He culled these texts from the popular literature that evolved in Jewish societies over a thousand years, appearing as biblical exegesis and homily, medieval narrative collections and popular chapbooks, historical accounts and tales of travel, translations of folklore classics of other nations, and literary renditions of fables. These books and manuscripts circulated in Jewish communities in the Near Eastern, Mediterranean, and European countries from the Middle Ages to modern times. The tales served to instruct children in Jewish history and religion, to entertain women in their hours of leisure, and to delight men during their learning and trade. These were stories of biblical events and heroes, the lives of rabbis, saints, and scholars, deeds of righteous and holy men, acts of the Jewish martyrs, and the miracles of Elijah the Prophet. They set models of behavior in situations of conflict between Jews and Gentiles and between Jews and Jews. They emphasized cultural values and religious precepts. Stories of demons and devils forewarned people of the hazards of straying from the rules and regulations of social and moral life and vividly portrayed the dangers awaiting man in the uninhabited countryside. In written texts and on storytelling occasions, these narratives were interspersed with tales of romance and wit, of humor and jest, of the world of the spirits, of fantastic countries in faraway lands and on the bottom of the oceans, tales which spur the imagination of young and old alike.

This narrative tradition enjoyed a long and continuous literary history. Though told and performed orally, many tales were written down as early as the fifth and sixth centuries. Out of the riches of Jewish literature, bin Gorion selected the most popular narrative versions, to demonstrate the religious, ethnic, and literary diversity in Judaism.

He viewed Jewish society and thought not as a cohesive integrated social and philosophical system, but rather as an arena for conflicting forces and tendencies. Judaism was, for bin Gorion, neither the religious synthesis that the rabbis constructed and sanctioned, nor the ideological system of modern Zionism. He conceived of Judaism as a social and religious reality abounding in contrasts, incongruities, and contradictions. To him the normative values of Judaism in the Hebrew Bible, in the Talmud, and in medieval rabbinical literature reflected just one aspect of Jewish religion and ethics. Equally important were the conflicting, or deviating, forces which existed in each period and each community and which contributed to the diversity of views in Jewish society.

Popular texts served bin Gorion as the most adéquate material to demonstrate his views of Judaism. He searched not for an ideal construction of traditional Jewish thought but for the actual multifaceted realities of Jewish life. The notion of diversity was fundamental in his conception of Jewish society, religion, and thought. In the face of awakening national feelings that considered the unity of the Jewish people as the central social ideal, bin Gorion's position demonstrated individualism, courage, and readiness to face reality. Moreover, for him the diversity of the Jewish people was not just a result of political, social, religious, and economic circumstances, but was an inherent quality of the people. Dissent was a basic Jewish quality. Therefore, there was no single period, trend, belief, precept, or text that could encapsulate Judaism.

Bin Gorion applied the notion of diversity in a nation not only to the ethnic but also to the religious domain. In that respect he extended the boundaries of Jewish society and at the same time the scope of Judaism itself. Historically, rabbinical authorities banned religious deviants and condemned dissenters. Splinter sects in Jewish society were the target of slurs and relentless smear campaigns. Social, economic, and religious pressures were exerted on any religious personalities and their followers who did not abide by the rules and regulations of the rabbinical authorities. Often such groups were expelled from Jewish society, or were not recognized as Jews to begin with. Yet consistent with his views, bin Gorion considered the religious dissenters as an integral part of Jewish society. Hence he included the narratives of such groups as the Samaritans, the Karaites, and the Hasidim among the popular expressions of Jewish tradition. Only the totality of ethnic as well as religious diversity could reflect the historical and spiritual creativity of Judaism.

In the formulation of his view of Judaism, bin Gorion also had to account for historical change. The diversity in Jewish society also had a temporal dimension. The essence of Jewish culture could not have been, according to bin Gorion, just the synthesis of the varieties of experiences distilled in time and examined from the perspectives of the present. Rather, it is necessary to account for the differences between historical periods, to explore incongruities between them, and to consider the accumulation of historical experiences as a process of both continuity and change.

Therefore he includes in his anthology biblical stories as medieval narrators rendered them and talmudic legends as subsequent generations retold them. Both narrative themes and narrators have their respective historical contexts. Bin Gorion assumed that traditional storytellers view the tales of the past anachronistically, from their own perspective. Hence, the understanding of traditional narratives requires that scholarship account for the historical context of the narrative subject, as well as that of the narrator.

While the notion of historical change might appear to be a commonplace, its application to Jewish folk narrative research was revolutionary. Previously, the study of Jewish popular narratives focused primarily on bibliography and history of manuscripts and books. The narrative themes themselves were considered part of the heritage of tradition, transmitted timelessly from one generation to another. Without ignoring thematic continuity in Jewish tradition, bin Gorion proposed to perceive popular narratives in the context of their time, place, and society. From this viewpoint, differences in language and style, personalities and events begin to emerge. Consequently, the narrative tradition appears as a dynamic cultural entity directly related to a historical period of a particular Jewish society.

Mimekor Yisrael bears testimony to the art of popular Jewish narrators throughout history. At the same time it carries the imprint of the literary taste and the philosophical and historical thought of Micha Joseph bin Gorion. It is a collection of Jewish traditional tales seen through the eyes of a great author. He selected the tales. In spite of his careful scholarly approach, occasionally he could not restrain his literary impulse and slightly modified the text. Often such alterations involve omission of a word or a line; at other times they are more substantial. Nevertheless, in spite of this intrusion of literary creativity into scholarship, *Mimekor Yisrael* is a monumental representation of the development of Jewish popular traditional literature, a cornerstone of the study of Jewish folklore in particular and comparative folktale research in general. Medieval and modern tales, religious legends and secular romances, historical events and mystical experiences form the web of folk tradition which appears to have passed away, yet is rediscovered anew in each generation.

DAN BEN-AMOS
University of Pennsylvania

MIMEKOR YISRAEL

YISRAEL

SELECTED CLASSICAL
JEWISH FOLKTALES

In Bible Days

I
THE FOUR GUARDIANS OF THE WORLD

This medieval midrash is an exegesis of the biblical verses The Lord by wisdom founded the earth; By understanding He established the heavens. By His knowledge the depths were broken up, And the skies drop down the dew *(Proverbs 3:19–20). This fragment relates directly to the phrase* by His knowledge the depths were broken up, *articulating a cosmology of balance between opposing forces, cultured and wild, in the created, animated world. The contrasting pairs are humans vs. demons, domesticated vs. wild animals, fowl vs. birds of prey, and small vs. large fish. In each case there are divine or mythical figures that in specific seasons protect the physically weaker of the two. Source: A. Jellinek, ed.,* Bet ha-Midrasch *5:64–66.*

The Holy and Blessed One created humankind, and as against them He created demons and evil spirits and set the terror of them among men. Had it not been for His manifold mercies and the rules He made for them, men would not be able to withstand these evil spirits and demons and monsters of the night even for a single hour. Now what were these rules? Year by year during the month of Nisan in the early spring the seraphim grow powerful and raise their heads on high, and they terrify the harmful spirits and demons and sprites, and cover humankind over with their pinions in order to spare them the harm that might be caused. "He shall cover you with His pinions. . . . You need not fear the terror by night," as it says in Psalm 91.

He created domestic beasts and gentle beasts, and as against them He created lions and leopards and bears. Had it not been for His manifold mercies and the special provision He made, the domestic and gentle beasts would never have been able to withstand the lions and the leopards and the bears. And what was His special provision? As against them He created Behemoth in the Thousand Mountains, and throughout the month of Tammuz in early summer the Holy and Blessed One gives strength to Behemoth, who grows mighty and raises his head and roars but once. Yet his voice passes through all settled lands and the beasts hear it; and the dread of him falls upon the lions and leopards and bears and all the evil beasts for a whole year. Otherwise the domestic and gentle beasts could never have withstood the evil beasts.

He created clean and unclean birds, some in settled places and others elsewhere, and as against them the vulture and the eagle, which are not in settled places. Had it not been for His manifold mercies and the provision He made, the birds would not have been able to withstand the vulture and the eagle. What was the provision He made? Whenever the month of Tishri comes in early autumn, the Holy and Blessed One gives strength to the great bird Ziz-Sadai, who grows powerful and raises his head and sets it between his wings and soars aloft and gives voice; and the birds hear his voice and the dread of him falls on vulture and eagle year after year.

In the sea He created fishes great and small. Now how vast is the greatest? Some of them are a hundred or two hundred or three hundred or even four hundred leagues long. Had it not been for His manifold mercies and the provision He made, the large ones would have swallowed the small. And what was this provision? He created Leviathan. Every month of Tebet which marks the onset of winter Leviathan raises his head and gathers his strength and breaks wind in the water and sets it seething; and the dread of him falls on the fish in the sea. Otherwise the little ones would never have been able to withstand the big ones.

Do you suppose they think highly of themselves when they rejoice? They do not think highly of themselves but give praise and laudation and glorify and exalt the One who spoke and the world came about. For they will end by being dust again and nothing will be left save the Holy and Blessed One in His Unity, may His Name be praised and the mention of Him be exalted. "For the Lord alone shall be exalted in that day" (Isa. 2:17).

2

THE BIRD MILHAM

Only in Jewish medieval sources is the mythical immortal bird called Milḥam; in the Babylonian Talmud it has an Aramaic name, Urshina, and in Palestinian midrashic literature it is called Ḥol or Ḥul. The latter appears as an exegetical interpretation of the biblical verse im kini egva ve-ka-ḥol arbeh yamim, *"I shall die with my nest and like Ḥol my days will be many" (Job 29:18). The Septuagint, and subsequent European translations, render the word Ḥol as "Phoenix"; yet it is not clear whether this is the original biblical meaning or an anachronistic meaning of the term. A city of immortals, which appears in the conclusion of the tale, is mentioned also in talmudic-midrashic literature, and its name is Luz. Source: M. Steinschneider,* Alphabetum Siracidis, *pp. 27a, 28b–29b.*

Nebuchadnezzar asked Ben Sira: "Why does the Angel of Death hold sway over all creatures save the offspring of Milham the Bird?" And he answered:

When Eve ate of the Tree of Knowledge and gave to her husband so that he ate with her, she grew envious of the other creatures and gave them all to eat. She noticed Milham the Bird and said to him: "Eat of what your comrades have eaten." But he told her: "Is it not enough that you have transgressed before His Blessed Name and have been the cause for the future death of others, but you come to me and try to entice me to disregard the commands of the Holy and Blessed One so that I should eat and perish? I shall not listen to you."

A Divine Echo immediately resounded and said to Eve and Adam: "You received a command and did not keep it but sinned, and came to Milham the Bird to cause him to sin as well, yet he would not do so but feared Me even though I gave him no command, but he observed My decree. Therefore he shall never know the taste of death, neither he nor his offspring."

In due course the Holy and Blessed One told the Angel of Death: "You have authority over all creatures and their seed except the offspring of a bird whose name is Milham, who are not to taste death." Then the angel said to him: "Lord of the Universe! Keep them far away because they are righteous, otherwise they will learn from the behavior of the remaining creatures and sin before You, though they are not supposed to know sin." Thereupon He gave the angel permission and he built them a great city and declared: "It has been decreed that neither my sword nor any other sword shall rule over you, and you are not to taste death till the end of all ages."

3
LEVIATHAN AND THE FOX

This story, a tale from the Indian collection of tales known as the Pancha-tantra, *is an example of the influence of Oriental narrative tradition upon medieval Jewish folk literature. Source: M. Steinschneider,* Alphabetum Siracidis, *pp. 27b–28b.*

Nebuchadnezzar asked Ben Sira: "Why are the images in the world to be found in the sea as well save the likenesses of the fox and the mole, which are not in the sea?" "Because," said he, "the fox is shrewder than all other creatures."

When the Angel of Death was fashioned and raised his eyes and saw the many creatures found in the world, he promptly said to Him: "Lord of the Universe, give me authority to slay them." And the Holy and Blessed One answered: "Fling a pair of each of the creatures into the sea and you shall hold sway over those who are left." This he did at once and flung a pair of each species into the sea, where he drowned them. When the fox saw this, what did he do? He promptly stood stock still and began to weep. "Why are you weeping?" the Angel of Death asked him; and he answered: "Because of my companion whom you have flung into the sea." "And where is your companion then?" asked the angel. Thereupon the fox went over to the seashore and the Angel of Death saw the fox's reflection in the sea, so he thought that he had flung some other pair instead of him and said to him: "Clear away from here." Thereupon the fox fled and saved himself.

The mole met him and he told her what had happened and what he had done. She went and did the same and also escaped.

A year later Leviathan gathered all the creatures in the sea together. The only ones missing were the fox and the mole, which had never entered the water. He sent to inquire and was told what the fox had done in his wisdom, together with the mole. And they told him that the fox was exceedingly wise. When Leviathan heard that the fox was clever, he became envious of him and sent big fishes after him and commanded them to mislead him and to bring him to his place.

They went and found him strolling by the seashore. When the fox saw the fishes playing there, he was surprised and joined them. When they saw him, they asked him: "Who are you?" "I am a fox," said he. "Why," they told him, "do you know how greatly you are held in honor, for it is to you that we have come." "How is that?" he asked them. "Leviathan," they explained, "is sick and on the verge of death, and has ordered that none may reign in his place save the fox; for he has heard that you are wise and more understanding than all creatures. So come with us, since we have been sent in your honor." "How can I enter the sea without perishing?" he asked them. "Ride upon one of us," they said, "and he will carry you above the surface so that the sea does not touch you with a single drop even on the tip of your paw until you reach the kingdom. There we shall bring you down, though you will feel nothing, and you will reign over them all and be king and rejoice all your life, and you will no longer need to go in search of food, nor will savage beasts that are larger than you come and strike you and consume you."

When he heard their words he believed them and rode on one of them, and they set out across the sea. When he reached the waves, he began to regret it. He felt uneasy and said: "Woe is me! What have I done? These fish have mocked me more than all the mockery I have ever made of other creatures, and now I have fallen into their hands and how can I be delivered?" So he said to them: "Since I have now come with you and am in your power, tell me the truth. Why do you desire me?" "We shall tell you the truth," they answered. "Leviathan has heard that you are exceedingly wise, so he has declared: 'I shall rip his belly open and eat his heart and then I shall be wise.'" "Now why did you not tell me the truth earlier?" said he to them. "For then I would have brought my heart with me and I would have given it to King Leviathan and he would have honored me. But as it is you are going wrong." "You do not have your heart with you?" they cried. "Oh no," said he, "for it is our practice to leave our hearts in our own places when we go hither and thither. If we need it we take it, and if not, we let it remain in our own place."

"Well then," said they, "what shall we do now?" "My place and dwelling," he informed them, "are by the seashore. If you like you can take me back to the spot where you found me, and I shall take my heart and come with you and give it to Leviathan so that he honors me and you, too. But if you conduct me thus without a heart, he will be angry with you and consume you. As for me, I do not need to be afraid, because

I shall tell him: 'My lord, they did not tell me to begin with, and when they did tell me I advised them to go back with me so that I could take my heart, but they did not wish to.'" Thereupon the fishes said: "He speaks well." And they turned back to the spot whence they had taken him on the seashore. There he climbed off the fish's back and began dancing and rolling in the sand and laughing. "Come, take your heart quickly," they said to him, "and let us go." "Clear off, you fools!" said he. "If my heart had not been with me, I would not have entered the sea with you. Or do you have any creature that moves about and does not have its heart with it?" "You have tricked us," said they. "Oh, you fools!" he answered. "I laughed at the Angel of Death, and can most certainly laugh at you."

Shamefacedly, they returned and told the tale to Leviathan. "Indeed," said he, "he is cunning and you are silly, and of you the verse was uttered: 'The waywardness of the silly shall slay them'" (Prov. 1:32). And he ate them up.

Ever since, every species of all creatures, and even of Adam and his wife, is to be found in the sea with the exception of the fox and the mole. You will not find them there.

4
NOAH'S VINEYARD

The application of animal metaphors to stages of drunkenness occurred in the literature of the late antiquities and was popular in Europe in the Middle Ages and the Renaissance. The association between wine and Satan suggests an Islamic influence, since in the Koran wine is considered the work of Satan (5:92). Source: Midrash Tanḥuma, "Noah," No. 18.

Our sages of blessed memory told this tale:
When Noah began to plant a vine, Satan came and stood before him and said to him: "What are you planting?" "A vine," said he. "And what is that?" asked Satan. "A vine," explained Noah, "has fruit that is sweet both wet and dry, and from it men will make wine that makes their hearts joyful." "Come," said Satan, "and let us both share in this wine." "Let it be so," said Noah.

And what did Satan do? He fetched a sheep and slew it under the vine. After that he fetched a lion and slew it, and after that he fetched a swine and slew that. After that he fetched an ape and slew that under the vineyard. And the blood of all these beasts dripped through that vineyard and watered it.

By this Satan wished to let him know: Before a man drinks wine, he is as innocent as any sheep that knows nothing, and silent as a ewe lamb before her shearers. If he takes a good drink, he is as brave as a lion and declares: There are none to compare with me in the world. But once he drinks too much he becomes like a swine, messing himself with urine and ordure. When he is properly drunk, he becomes like an ape that stands and dances and plays and utters all kinds of filth in the presence of all people and does not have the slightest idea what he is doing.

Now all those things happened to Noah the Righteous. And if it happened so with Noah the Righteous, whom the Holy and Blessed One Himself praised, how much more does it befall the rest of mankind!

5
WHO HOLDS THE FORTRESS?

This legend belongs to a narrative cycle about Abraham's discovery and confirmation of the existence of a single God in the universe. In all of the narratives of this cycle, Abraham reaches this religious awareness in childhood and through being intellectually inquisitive, rather than in adulthood and through mystical revelation. Source: Mordecai Margulies, ed., Midrash Haggadol on the Pentateuch: Genesis, *pp. 210–211, 12:1.*

"Y ou love righteousness and hate wickedness; therefore God, your God, has chosen to anoint you with oil of gladness, over all your peers" (Ps. 45:8). This verse was said in respect of our Father Abraham, who loved the Holy and Blessed One and came under the wings of the Shekinah and hated the idolatry of his father's household.

He used to meditate and thought to himself: "How long are we going to prostrate ourselves before our own handiwork? It is unfitting to serve and prostrate oneself to anything except the earth, which brings forth fruits that keep us alive." But when he saw that the earth requires rains and that if the heavens did not open and permit the rain to fall, the earth would grow nothing, he changed his mind and said: "There is nothing worthy of worship except the heavens." Then again he saw the sun give light to the world and make the plants grow, and he said: "This alone is worthy of worship." But when he saw that it sets, he said: "This cannot be a god." Then in turn he considered the moon and the stars, which give light at night, and said: "These are worthy of worship." Yet when the morning star arose, they all faded away; and he said: "These cannot be gods either." And he used to worry and say: "If these have no leader, why does one set and the other rise?"

This can be compared to a person who was on the road and saw a great and lofty fortress. He wished to enter it and went all around it, yet could find no entry. He shouted and shouted but none gave him answer. He raised his eyes and saw red woolen garments stretched on the roof. Then he saw white linen cloth. Said he to himself: "There must certainly be somebody within this fortress, for if there were no person here, why would these be taken away and those put in their place?" When the keeper of the fortress saw that he was puzzled and grieved by this, he said to him: "Why do you worry? I hold the fortress!"

So it was with Abraham. When he saw that these were setting and those were rising, he said: "If they had no controller they would not be like this. Therefore it is not fitting to bow and worship them but rather the One who rules over them and controls them." And in his mind he pondered in order to understand this thing truly. When the Holy and Blessed One saw that he was puzzled and disturbed, He said to him: "'You love righteousness and hate wickedness.' As sure as you live, I shall anoint you out of all the generations that are before you and after you."

6

ABRAHAM AND ISHMAEL

Hospitality has been a basic value in Jewish society throughout history. Both biblical (Genesis 18:1–8) and post-biblical traditions sanction it by attributing to Abraham the Patriarch hospitable behavior. In this story he is not the host but rather the guest, testing the hospitality of his daughter-in-law. Source: Anon., Sefer ha-Yashar, *pp. 41a–42b.*

Ishmael was a sharpshooter and bowman and dwelt in the wilderness for many a day. Thereafter he and his mother went to the land of Egypt and dwelt there. And Hagar took a wife in Egypt for her son, and her name was Meriba. And Ishmael's wife conceived and bore four sons and one daughter to him. After that Ishmael set out with his mother, his wife and children, and all his belongings and returned to the wilderness. They made themselves tents in the wilderness and dwelt in them and used to journey and encamp continually, month by month and year by year. God gave Ishmael flocks and herds and tents for the sake of his father Abraham, so that the man spread far and wide with his cattle. He dwelt in his tents in the wilderness, traveling and sojourning for many a long day, but never saw his father Abraham.

Now the day came when Abraham said to Sarah his wife: "I shall depart and see my son Ishmael, for I long to see him very much, since I have not seen him all this while." So he rode on one of his camels and set forth for the wilderness to seek his son Ishmael, for he had heard that he was dwelling in tents out in the wilderness, together with all that was his.

Traveling through the wilderness, Abraham at length reached Ishmael's tent at noon. He asked for Ishmael and found Ishmael's wife seated in the tent with her children; but Ishmael, her husband, and his mother were not with them. And Abraham asked the woman: "Where has Ishmael gone?" And she said: "He has gone into the field ahunting." Now Abraham was still riding on the camel and had not descended from it, for he had sworn to Sarah his wife that he would not descend from the camel or set foot on the ground. And he said to the wife of Ishmael: "Daughter, give me a little water to drink, for I am weary and tired from the journey." And Ishmael's wife answered Abraham: "We have neither water nor bread." She sat there in the tent and did not look at Abraham and did not ask him who he was. All she did was beat her children in the tent and curse them, and she cursed also Ishmael her husband, and reviled him.

When Abraham heard what Ishmael's wife was saying to her children, he grew very angry and it seemed evil in his eyes. So he called her to come out to him from the tent. Out came the woman and stood facing him where he still sat on the camel, and he said to her: "When your husband Ishmael returns here, this is what you should tell him: A very old man came here from the land of the Philistines to seek you and this and that was his appearance, but I did not ask who he was. When he saw that you were not here, this is what he said to me: When your husband Ishmael returns, tell him that this is what the man said: Upon your return remove the tent peg upon which you have set up this tent and put some other tent peg in its place." Therewith Abraham made an end of his words to the woman and turned the camel about and went his way.

When Ishmael returned in due course from his hunting with his mother and came to his tent, his wife told him: "A very old man came here to seek you from the land of the Philistines, and this and that is what he looked like, but I did not ask who he was. He saw that you were not here and he told me: When your husband comes back tell him this is what the old man said: Remove the tent peg you have here and replace it with another." Ishmael heard his wife's words and understood that it was his father whom his wife had not honored. Also he understood the meaning of what his father had said, and he hearkened to his father's counsel and sent that woman away and she went. After that, Ishmael came to the land of Canaan and took another wife and brought her to his tent in place of the one who had been there.

Three years later Abraham said again: "I shall go once more and see my son Ishmael, for I have not seen him this many a day." So he rode on his camel into the desert and reached the tent of Ishmael at the noon hour. He inquired for Ishmael and the woman came out of the tent and said: "He is not here, good sir, for he has gone into the desert to hunt and herd the camels." And the woman said to Abraham: "Come into the tent, good sir, and eat bread here, for you must be weary to the soul from your journey." But Abraham answered: "I cannot descend, for I must hasten on my way. But I pray you, give me a little water to drink, because I am thirsty." Then the woman hurried into the tent and brought water and bread out to Abraham and placed it before him and entreated him to eat. He ate and drank and felt better at heart and then blessed Ishmael his son.

After eating, he blessed the Lord and said to Ishmael's wife: "This is what you should tell Ishmael when he returns: A very old man came here from the land of the Philistines, looking like this and that, and he said to me: When Ishmael comes here, tell him that this is what the old man said: The tent peg you have placed here in the tent is very good, do not remove it from the tent." And Abraham made an end of his words and went riding back to the land of the Philistines.

Ishmael came to his tent, and his wife came out happily and cheerfully to meet him and told him: "A certain old man came here from the land of the Philistines and he asked about you, but he has gone away. I brought bread and water out to him, and he ate and drank at his ease and this is what he said to me: When your husband Ishmael returns here, tell him: Your tent peg is very good indeed, do not remove it from the tent."

Then Ishmael knew that it had been his father and that his wife had shown him proper honor, and Ishmael blessed the Lord.

That was the time when Ishmael rose and took his wife and his children and his cattle and all his belongings and set out from there and went to his father in the land of the Philistines. And Abraham told his son Ishmael exactly what the first wife he had taken had done. And Ishmael and his children dwelt in the land together with Abraham for many a day.

7
THE TENTH GENERATION

The following tale, current in popular tradition from the Middle Ages to the present time, has an international distribution. While Moses is the tale's hero in Jewish tradition, Peter appears in the same role in Christian narratives and Jesus in Islamic tradition. Source: S. Krauss, "A Moses Legend," pp. 339–363.

In due course Moses went to Mount Horeb, and in his hand was a staff he had taken from the home of Jethro. While he was following the paths through the wilderness, he reached a parting of the ways. There a certain old man met him. "Peace be with you, master!" said Moses. "Peace be with you!" said the other. Then Moses asked: "Where are you going?" "Wandering far and wide," said he. "Have you food to eat in the desert?" asked Moses. "For it is not a place of seed and figs and vines—otherwise you may be weary and exhausted and thirsty." "I have two cakes," said the man to him. "And I," said Moses, "have three cakes." "Come then," said the other, "and let us put them together and we shall have provision for the way." Then each of them took out the number he had mentioned, and the old man took them and placed them in his wallet together and put it on his shoulder. "Bear them in mind!" said Moses to him.

They walked some four or five miles. Then one said to the other: "Let us eat in order to restore our souls from hunger." They took out two cakes, one for each, and ate them. Then they went on, with the old man keeping the other three, until they were very hungry. "Let us eat," said each of them to his companion, "in order to restore our souls." So they took out two cakes and ate, and one cake was left.

When they had been walking about half a day in the wilderness, Moses said to the old man: "Give me the cake that is left." At this the old man denied that there had ever been such a cake, and swore a mighty oath that there had never been more than four. When they had walked a little farther, the Holy and Blessed One directed two deer to them. "Go and get one of the deer," said Moses to the old man. And the old man answered our Master Moses: "Am I a fool to go after the deer when there is nothing faster?" "Take my staff in your hand," said Moses to him, "and brandish it at them!" So he took the staff in his hand and brandished it, and the deer could not move from their place. Then Moses took them and slaughtered them at once and broiled them. "Be careful," said Moses to the old man, "that you do not break any of the bones!" When they had eaten their fill of the venison, Moses placed bone to bone and took the staff and put it on them and prayed a full prayer to his Creator, and the Holy and Blessed One brought the deer back to life and they rose to their feet. And Moses said to the old man: "Swear to me now by Him who revived the deer when they had neither flesh nor sinews that you have not been deceitful about the loaf!" And he swore that he had not eaten it or touched it.

They went on through the wilderness and were thirsty. Moses took the staff and brought forth water with it from the flinty rock, so that they drank and their thirst was quenched. Then Moses said to the old man: "Swear to me by Him who brought forth water from the rocky flint that you did not touch the loaf!" He swore an oath as before, that he had not touched or eaten it. And Mosess aid: "Let us go farther!"

They went on and came to a city. They found the townsfolk weeping, because an elder, who had been as a father to them, had died. Said Moses to them: "Why are you all weeping?" Said they: "We would give our souls for his!" Then Moses took pity on them and prayed for the dead man and rested his staff upon him. The dead man breathed heavily and came to life. Then Moses said to the old man: "Swear to me by Him who brought the dead to life—what happened to the loaf?" He swore by a great oath that he had neither touched it nor eaten it. Then Moses said: "This must clearly be one of the tenth generation" (cf. Deut. 23:3–4).

When they went on in the desert, Moses proceeded about his affairs. And he said to the old man: "Here is this staff in your hands, while I go and cleanse myself at this well." When Moses went away, the man said to himself: "Now here is this stick with which Moses did all those miracles. I will go and take it and revive the dead with it." So he took it and went off. On the way he came to a village. And what were the deeds of the villagers? They dwelt there and they had a child with them who had money. The old man came and slew the child and took the money. Then he took the staff and placed it on the child, thinking that he would do the same as Moses. Yet it is with reason that they say: "All creatures are not equal."

But Moses came pursuing him and found him in great distress with the villagers wishing to slay him, for as the Torah says: "Life for life" (Exod. 21:23). But Moses prayed and brought the youngster to life and saved the old man from death; according to the words of our sages of blessed memory: "Whosoever walks four ells with his companion—the Holy and Blessed One makes the sentence lighter for them."

As they went, they found a brook on their way. There Moses made three mounds of earth and prayed over them; and they became gold. And Moses said to the old man: "See what the Holy and Blessed One has done!" Then the old man said to our Master Moses: "Who is that for?" And he said: "Let the one who ate the loaf take two and the other is for the one who did not eat it." Then the old man said: "I am the one who ate the loaf." When he confessed, Moses said: "By all means take the lot." And our Master Moses went his way, and the other did not know where he had gone. Afterward the old man grieved and was in distress about the gold. At last men came with camels, and the old man said to them: "Come and carry the gold, and two-thirds will be for me and one-third for you." "We are hungry," said they, "so you go and fetch food from the city yonder so that we should restore our souls." As he went to the city, he thought to himself that he would put poison in the food. And they in turn planned that when he came back to them they would cut his head off. When he came, they cut off his head. Then they ate the food and died, and the gold remained hidden away.

And all this is told in order that you should know that the tenth generation are unbelievers, as we have said, that they swear false oaths, deceive, lie—deniers and wicked and evil. May the Holy and Blessed One deliver us from them for the sake of His Name and His loving-kindness.

8

At the Well

This tale has been known in Jewish tradition since the fourteenth century. It belongs to a theodicy narrative cycle that is common in many Jewish traditions and which has a variety of heroes who wonder about the ways divine justice manifests itself in human society. Source: M. Grünbaum, Judisch-deutsche Chrestomathie, pp. 215–218.

It was the habit of Moses our Master to stay alone in the fields in order to receive the spirit of the Lord. One day he was resting under a tree, and there was a well of fresh water nearby. As he looked around, he saw a man coming to the well. He drank and went his way, not knowing that his pouch full of gold had dropped from his hands in forgetfulness. Meanwhile another man came to the well and drank its water and turned aside to rest, and there the pouch was before him. He picked it up most joyously and went his way. After that a third man came to the well and also drank of its water. While he was still there, the first man came hurrying in great excitement to seek his money, and he claimed: "You found it." The other answered him very innocently: "I have not found anything and all I did was to drink a little water and I ate some food and I turned aside to rest. Now I am about to go my way." The first man began quarreling with him, and in his fury he rose and slew him.

When Moses saw this act of violence, he cried unto the Lord from his heart: "O Lord, why do You show me such misdeeds and gaze unmoved on such distress?" And an answer came from the heavens: "Be it known to you that the forgetful man is a saintly person but his father was a wicked evildoer who stole the pouch from the father of the one who found it. Here the latter man came in to his rightful heritage. As to the case of the victim, let Me tell you that he had slain the brother of the murderer, and now I have avenged innocent blood consciously and in order to show that the ways of the Lord are upright. As for you, you have no right to cast a doubt on My dispositions."

9
THE HEADSMAN

Although Abraham ben Elijah of Vilna (1750–1808) refers to earlier books as his sources, scholars could not verify the occurrence of this Jewish version of the Oedipus legend in any earlier writings. It is possible that he drew upon Jewish oral rather than literary tradition. This tale indeed bears the hallmark of oral narration; the episode of a baby discovered in a fish's belly is an anachronistic etymological tale, explaining the name of Joshua bin Nun by the Aramaic meaning of his patronymic. Source: Abraham ben Elijah of Vilna, Rav Pe'alim, p. 12a.

The Eminent and godly Kabbalist, our teacher and master Rabbi Nathan Nata, wrote that he found a reason given on the authority of a midrash as to why Joshua was called "bin Nun," while the spies said of him: "Yon's the headsman."

For the father of Joshua dwelt in Jerusalem, and his wife was barren. Now this saint used to pray for his wife, and the Lord acceded to him. After she conceived, the saint used to fast and weep day and night without ceasing. His wife took this ill and she said to him: "You ought to rejoice, for the Lord has answered your prayers!" And he never answered her.

When she went on speaking to him day after day, pressing him with her words, he told her all that he had on his heart. He had been told from heaven on high that his son who would be born to him would cut off his head. She believed his words, for she knew that he always spoke the truth. So when she gave birth and saw it was a son, she took a little ark and smeared it with mortar and pitch and in it she placed the child and let him float away on the stream. But the Lord appointed a great fish to swallow the ark.

But it came to pass that the king made a great feast to all his ministers and servants. A fisherman captured the fish which had swallowed the little ark and brought it before the king. They cut it open, and lo and behold! a little boy was weeping within. The king and all his ministers were astonished, and the king ordered a woman to be brought to suckle the babe. Now the boy grew up in the king's household, and he appointed him to be his executioner. And long after all these things, his saintly father transgressed before the king of Egypt, and the king ordered his executioner to cut off his head and take his wife and children and property for himself, as was their practice in those times.

Now when he drew near to his mother to come to her, the whole bed filled with milk from her nipples. He grew exceedingly alarmed and took his lance to slay her, thinking that she was a witch. But his mother remembered the words of his saintly father of blessed memory, and this is what she said to him: "This is not witchcraft but milk on which you were suckled, for I am your mother." And she told him the whole tale.

And he at once withdrew from her, for he too remembered how he had been told that he was found in a fish. Indeed, he could not know that this was his father, but now he repented and changed his ways.

That was why they called him "bin Nun," meaning son of a fish, for he was found in a fish, which in the Aramaic language is *nun*. And the spies called him "headsman," on account of his first deeds—what he had done to his own father.

10
THE JARS OF HONEY

This story is part of the medieval narrative midrashim, which elaborate upon biblical themes and figures in medieval literary Hebrew. It first appeared in print in the beginning of the sixteenth century in a collection known as "Parables of King Solomon." In several versions young Solomon, the archetypical wise king in Jewish tradition, rather than David is the hero of the tale. The basic themes of the story occur in both Oriental and European folklore. Source: A. Jellinek, ed., Bet ha-Midrasch 4:150–151.

I n the days of Saul, king of Israel, there was a very rich man who had an exceedingly beautiful and gracious wife. This man was very old and his time came to depart and go to his eternal home. Now since the woman was beautiful, the lord of the city cast his eyes on her and wished to take possession of her by force. But she did not so desire for any reason, and she grew very much afraid. And she took all her money and placed it in jars. Into these jars she poured honey and then entrusted them to a certain man who had been the acquaintance and close friend of her husband. She did this in the presence of witnesses, and then she fled from the city.

Time passed and that lord died so that she could come back home. But meanwhile the man to whom she had entrusted the jars gave a betrothal banquet for his son and needed honey. He went and found the jars with the honey and took the little honey that was on top. Trying to pour out more he found that all the jars were full of gold. And he took the money at once and filled the jars with honey.

When the woman returned home, she went to the man and said: "Give me the deposit I left with you." "Go," said he, "and fetch me the witnesses in whose presence you gave me the honey and then take what is yours." So she went and fetched the witnesses, and he took out all the vessels and returned them to her in the presence of the witnesses. When she went home she found that all the jars were full of honey, and she began to weep and wail. She went to the judge of the city and complained to him. "Have you any witnesses?" asked the judge. "No," said she. "Daughter," said he, "what can I do for you? Go to King Saul and let him judge your case."

So she went to Saul, and he sent her to the Sanhedrin. They too asked: "Have you witnesses that you entrusted the money to this man?" "I have no witnesses," said she, "for what I did, I did cunningly because I feared the lord of the city." "Daughter," said they to her, "we have authority to judge only if there are witnesses, for we are unable to judge or know what is in the heart."

She went away from them in misery. As she set out to return home, she met David, king of Israel, who was then still a little shepherd boy and was playing with the other boys. As soon as she saw them, she cried: "Children, I have complained, yet I could not receive any judgment against the man who has deceived me. Listen to me and judge you in your kindness!" "Go to the king," then said David, "and ask him to give me authority, and I shall bring your case to the light."

She went back to the king and said: "My lord, I have found a young lad who says that he can bring my case to the light." "Go and bring him before me," said the king. So she summoned him, and Saul said to him: "Is it true that you can show what really happened?" "If I but have permission from you," answered he, "I have trust in my Lord." "Go with him," said the king to her. And David told her: "Fetch out the vessels which you entrusted to that man." She brought the vessels out, and he said to her: "Do you recognize that these are the same vessels that you entrusted to that man?" "Yes, sir," said she. Then he asked the man too, and he agreed that they were the identical jars.

"Now, go and fetch me other empty vessels," said David to her. She went and fetched them and at this instructions emptied the honey into them. Then David took the first jars and smashed them before all those assembled. He felt around and in the broken pieces of the jars he found in one place two gold pieces which had been stuck to the sides of the vessel. Then David said to the man who had held the pledge: "Go and return what you took to the woman!"

As soon as Saul and all Israel heard this, they were very much astonished and knew that the Holy Spirit rested upon the lad.

11
The Spider and the Hornet

The theme of a man being saved by a spider web has been part of both Christian and Islamic escape legends. In Jewish tradition the tale first appears in the Middle Ages, but translation tradition indicates that it was known even earlier. Source: M. Steinschneider, Alphabetum Siracidis, *pp. 24a–25b.*

Nebuchadnezzar, the king, asked Ben Sira: "Why did the Holy and Blessed One have to create hornets and spiders in His world? They just cause waste and bring no benefit." And he answered:

On one occasion David, king of Israel, may he rest in peace, was seated in his garden and saw a hornet eating a spider. And David asked the Holy and Blessed One: "Lord of the Universe! What benefit is there in these creatures that You have created in Your world? A hornet just eats honey and is wantonly destructive and brings no benefit. A spider spins all the year round, yet who can wear what he spins?" And the Holy and Blessed One answered: "David, do you mock at things created? The time will come when you will need them, and then you will know why they were created!"

Now when David hid in the cave because of King Saul, the Holy and Blessed One sent a spider that spun a web over the entrance to the cave and closed it. Saul came and saw the web and said: "Nobody can have entered here, otherwise he would have torn the web to shreds." So he went on and never entered. When David came out and saw the spider, he kissed it and said to it: "Blessed is your Creator, and you, too! Lord of the Universe, who can do deeds like Yours, as strong and fine as Yours, for all Your works are splendid!"

Then there was the occasion when David found Saul sleeping at noon, and Abner was lying across the entrance to the tent with bent legs. David entered between his legs and took the cruse of water. When he was about to pass between his legs, Abner stretched them out and held him between them as between two great pillars. Then David begged mercy of the Lord, saying: "My God, my God, why have You forsaken me?" (Ps. 22:2). At that moment the Holy and Blessed One performed a wonder for him and sent a hornet that stung Abner's legs so that he straightened them out; and David departed, praising the Holy and Blessed One.

So it is clearly not fitting that any man should belittle the works of God.

12
The Compassion of a Father

*This is a midrashic-narrative resolution to an apparent contradiction be-
tween a biblical text and cultural assumptions about maternal qualities.
Compassion is a quality the people of Israel attributed to God as one of the
attitudes He had toward them. The appellation of God as a father occurs
only in post-biblical prayers and poetry; yet the scriptural simile that serves
as a textual basis for this present tale already employs compassion as a
shared attribute between God and father. Indirectly the verse denies this
feeling to the mother, and the story offers a justification for the implicit
negative attitude toward mothers. Source: A. Jellinek, ed., Bet ha-
Midrasch 5:52–53.*

"As a father has compassion on his children, so You have compassion
on us" (Ps. 103:13).

They say that when Joab heard David say this, he wondered and said:
"Is a father more compassionate to his children than a mother? Surely the
mother has greater compassion for her children, for she toils for them and
brings them up! And yet David has said this?" Then Joab told himself:
"I shall go and see how people behave in order to know whether his words
are true or not."

So Joab made the rounds through all parts of Israel in order to see,
and he reached a certain place and visited an old man who had twelve sons.
Now this man was hard at work every day in the field and in the evening
he bought bread with his wages and barely maintained himself and his wife
and his children. Yet although he was old and poor, there was no need
for the sons to exhaust themselves working, but he toiled for them and
nourished them. This is what he did every night: He used to cut the bread
into fourteen pieces and gave each of them one piece while to his wife
he gave one piece and ate one himself.

When Joab saw this, he wondered and said: "I cannot test anyone better
than this man." Next day when the old man went out to work in the field,
Joab said to him: "Why is it that an old man like you should labor all
day long and feed your sons? Would it not be better for you if they were
to work and you were to eat? If you take my advice, you would sell one
of them, and in that way you would be able to sustain yourself and the
other children." But when the old man heard Joab's words, he rebuked
him and went his way.

Then Joab went to the mother, and this is what he said to her: "You have grown old at your work yet you have twelve sons, and still you are the one who toils and they merely eat!" "It is the custom of the world," she answered, "that mother and father maintain the children." Then Joab said to her: "Instead of having to work to exhaustion all the time, would it not be better if you were to maintain them without toil or weariness from some other earning?" "What could it be?" she asked him; and he answered: "Sell one of your children, and you will receive plenty of money for him and maintain yourselves and your children in ease." "Tell that to my husband," said she, "and maybe he will agree." "You tell him," said he. "Maybe he will not agree," she demurred. Then he said to her: "You sell the son and your husband will not even know, because there are so many children." "I fear to do so," said she, "for if he gets to know and I cannot change the situation, he will kill me." "Sell the child to me," said Joab, "and I shall give you a hundred gold dinars for him; but if your husband should be angry, I shall return him."

When she heard this, she took his money and gave him one of the sons. And then Joab went away from that place to see what would happen.

When the old man sat down to eat at his table that evening, he took the bread and divided it into fourteen portions. When he saw that one portion was left over, he cried aloud: "Where is he?" And his wife whispered to him: "He is with his friend." "Go and call him," said the father, "for I shall not eat until he comes." "Let us eat first," said she, "and afterwards I shall call him." "We shall do nothing of the kind," he insisted, "until he is here."

When she saw this, she said to him: "Why should I hide from you that I have sold him to the man who was in the house, and here are the hundred dinars in gold that I took from him; and I did this all in order that you should not be hard-pressed in his upkeep."

When he heard this, he grieved very much and neither ate nor drank that night. In the morning he rose and took the hundred dinars and took his weapon, so that if he found the man who purchased his son and if this man were not prepared to return him and take the money, he would slay him. He went after Joab, who was standing along the road waiting for him. Raising his eyes, he saw the old man run toward him, and he waited for him.

"Give me back my son," said the old man to him, "and take your money." "His mother sold him to me," said Joab, "and now shall I return him to you?" "Does she not have the same share in your son as you? And even if you say that you also have a share in him—after all you have twelve sons and each of you owns half of each one of them, and she only sold one. So now you take one of the others as your own to make up for him."

"Stop talking like that," said the old man. "If you do not return him, I shall kill you, or else you can kill me!" When Joab heard this, he laughed, took his money, and returned the child to him.

And Joab said: "David was quite right when he said 'as a father has compassion on his children,' and not as a mother has compassion on her children. For with this boy—his mother sold him to me, even though she did not have to toil about his upkeep, while his father, who did toil for his upkeep, was ready to be slain for his sake. And that shows that it is the father who is compassionate toward his children."

13
THE BORROWED EGG

Dating back at least to the second half of the thirteenth century, this story is part of a narrative cycle about the cleverness of King Solomon in his childhood. While in European tradition the peasant's daughter often exhibits wit and wisdom that solves riddles, problematic litigation, and incongruous tasks, in Jewish narrative tradition often the child Solomon serves in this role. Source: I. Lévi, "Un recueil de contes juifs inédits," pp. 65–67.

The tale is told that the servants of King David were seated one day at a feast at which they ate eggs. One of them was exceedingly hungry and ate the portion that had been given to him before his companions. He felt ashamed because there was no food before him, and he said to the man sitting next to him: "Lend me one egg." "I shall lend it to you," said he, "if you take a vow about it before witnesses that you will return it to me, with all the profit that a man can earn from a single egg, at the time when I shall demand it back from you." "I agree," said he; and the man gave him the egg in the presence of witnesses.

After a very long time he came and demanded it back. "All you can claim from me," said he, "is a single egg." They appeared before King David and found Solomon sitting in the gateway, for it was the custom of Solomon to be seated in the king's gateway; and whenever anybody came to the king for judgment he would ask him: "What are you doing before the king?" And the man would say: "This and that is what happened between that fellow and me." Now when the man who had borrowed from his companion came, Solomon said to him as well: "Why have you come to the king?" And he answered: "This and that is what happened." "Appear before the king," said Solomon to him, "and when you return tell me what the king said."

They appeared before King David. The claimant brought witnesses of the condition they had agreed to; namely, that he should pay him whatever profit a man can make from a single egg from that time until the time that the claim was presented. "Go and pay him," said King David. "I do not know how much," said he. Then they presented an account to the king: One chick in one year; in the second year that chick can beget up to eighteen chicks; in a third year those eighteen chicks can each produce eighteen chicks, and so in the fourth year—so that the account finally came to a vast sum. And the man went out greatly distressed.

Solomon met him and said: "What did the king tell you?" "The king," he answered, "found that I owe this, and that it amounts to a very great sum." "Listen to me," said Solomon, "and I shall give you good counsel." "Long life to you," said he. And Solomon went on: "Go and buy yourself beans and boil them. On such and such day the king wishes to stay at this and that place. Now you stand at the wayside, and whenever the king's men pass before you, you sow the beans in some plowed field by the road. If anybody asks you what you are sowing, answer him: 'I am sowing boiled beans.' And if he asks you whoever saw boiled beans being sown, you tell him: 'Whoever saw a boiled egg from which a chicken came?'"

The man went at once and did this and stood sowing the boiled beans. When the king's forces passed, they asked him: "What are you sowing?" "I am sowing boiled beans," he told them. "And who," said they, "has ever seen boiled beans growing?" "And who," answered he, "has ever seen a boiled egg from which a chick came out?" And this he said to each company in turn until it was reported to the king.

When the king heard this, he said to him: "Who taught you to do so?" "I myself," said he. But David said to him: "Solomon has been helping you!" "As sure as you live, my lord king," said the man, "he told me to do this from beginning to end." Then the king sent for Solomon and said to him: "What do you have to say about this?" And Solomon answered: "How can he owe for something that never came about? The egg he borrowed was boiled and could not produce any chick!" "Then," said the king, "let him go and pay the other fellow one egg!"

And it is because of this that we find: "To Solomon. O God, give Your judgment to the king and Your righteousness to the king's son" (Ps. 72:1–2).

14
THE TRUE HEIR

This story is part of the medieval cycle of "Parables of King Solomon." It is an extremely popular tale in Jewish tradition, occurring in medieval literary tradition and current oral tradition of several ethnic groups. Sometimes it is related to, or confused with, a different test of paternity in which brothers are asked to physically abuse their father's corpse; the person who refuses is declared the true heir. Source: A. Jellinek, ed., Bet ha-Midrasch 4:145–146.

A certain man who lived in the days of David, king of Israel, was very rich indeed. He had men-slaves and women-slaves and much property; and he had a single son. And what did that man do? He bought many wares and gave them to his son. The son took ship and set out for Africa, where he stayed for many years. During those years his father died and left his possessions with a certain slave who was in charge of his treasure. Now this slave began to oppress all the members of the household with fiendish punishments until they ran away from him, and he remained alone with all the money that his lord had left him; and he used to eat and feel happy because of his desire for money.

A long time after, the young man came back from overseas and went to his father's home where he found that his father had passed away. He was about to enter his house when the slave came out and pushed him away and said: "What are you doing in my home, you worthless fellow!" What did the youngster do? He took his stick and began to beat him over his head and said to him: "Slave, you have seized all my belongings and the belongings of my father and teacher, and you are happy with that money!" There was a great quarrel and nobody interfered, but at last the old man's son fled and went to the king to complain of the slave, saying: "O king, live forever! This and that man has taken all the money my father and teacher left me, and he says: 'You are not the old man's son but I am.'" "Have you any witnesses?" asked the king. "No," said he. Then the king summoned the slave and said to him: "Have you any witnesses?" "No," said he. Then the king said to the slave: "Depart in peace! You do not have to return anything."

When the old man's son heard this, he began to weep and cry aloud before the king a second and a third time, and he went on until the king rebuked him and said: "If you go on, I shall have you punished. If you have witnesses, well and good, but if not, what can I do for you?"

Solomon, the king's son, heard of this, and called the man aside and said to him: "Cry out again before the king, and if he is angry, say: 'My lord the king, if you do not give me justice, give the case to your son Solomon!'"

He handed the case over to Solomon his son, and Solomon said to the young man: "Do you know where your father is buried?" "No," said he. Then he summoned the slave and asked him: "Do you know your father's grave?" "Yes," said he. Then the king's son said to him: "Go and fetch me your father's arm." Off he went and cut off the old man's arm and fetched it. "Both of you draw blood," said he to them, "and each of you let your blood flow into his own cup." He said to the slave: "Dip the bone in your blood." He dipped it, but it did not become colored. Then he said to the old man's son: "You too dip it in your blood." And the bone assumed the color of the blood, and he showed it to all the people. Then he said to them: "See, this blood came out of this bone!" And all Israel was astonished, and all the money went back to the young man, and he became master of the slave against the slave's will.

That is why the Bible says of Solomon: "And he was wiser than all men" (I Kings 5:11).

15
THE MERCIFUL WIDOW

Although the following tale belongs to the narrative cycle about the judicial wisdom of King Solomon, it is an illustration of divine rather than human justice and of God's control of worldly events. The tale has appeared in the traditions of Jews who lived in Islamic countries. Source: S. B. Ḥuẓin, Ma'asim Tovim, pp. 18–19, No. 13.

Once there was a woman who was accustomed to practice charity all her days; and even though she was not rich, she still gave charity in spite of her own need. Every day she used to bake three loaves; two she gave to the poor and one was for herself. One day a poor man came and stood at her door and said to her: "My lady, I was on board a ship, and it was wrecked and everything that was within it was lost together with its sailors, but the sea flung me out at a port, and there I was at ease. Yet the trouble is that my soul sighs within me, since for the last three days I have eaten nothing because I have lost my way."

She took out the bread that she had left for her own food and gave it to him at once. Then she sat down to eat the second loaf, and another poor man came and raised his voice and cried: "My lady, take pity on me and give me some bread to restore my soul, for the slave traders captured me, and this is the third day since I escaped from them, but I have found nothing whatever to eat in my flight." She gave him the second loaf and said: "Blessed is the Lord who enabled me to perform this commandment, and God aiding, may all things go well with me!"

She took out the third loaf to eat, and yet another poor man came and said to her: "My lady, I was on the road and robbers in ambush came out against me, and I ran away from them to the forest, and several days have now passed and I have eaten nothing but grass and have forgotten the taste of bread. So I pray you, favor me with a piece of bread that satisfies the hungry."

She gave him the third loaf and remained without anything and was hungry. Then she said to herself: "Let me go and see whether I have any flour left to knead and bake, and then I shall return." She went and found that she had nothing left at all. Then she said to herself: "I shall go and take some wheat in my sack and grind it and restore my ravenous soul." So she filled the sack with wheat and went to the mill and ground it and put the meal on her head and walked off bearing the sack. Suddenly a great wind from the sea blew them away. At that the woman felt that her hope had been in vain, and she began to grieve and weep bitterly, saying: "What sin have I done that this should happen to me today!"

On her way she went to King Solomon, may he rest in peace, and to the Sanhedrin. And she said to them: "Tell me what sin I can have done that caused me not to have even a dry piece of bread." And while she was still talking with the king and telling her tale, three merchants came who had become friends on a ship. And they said to him: "Lord king, take these seven thousand gold pieces, and let them be dedicated to poor people of good family.'"

Then King Solomon asked them: "Why are you donating such a large sum?" And they answered: "We were in a ship with many wares and precious stones when a great rent was torn in the ship's side and we could not block it, and the ship was about to be wrecked together with all that was in it. Then we said: 'Lord of the Universe! Transport us even to the wilderness and the desert, and we shall give the money in our possession to the poor and we shall repent our ways!' When we saw that we were all but lost, we flung ourselves on our faces so that we should not see the death of our companions, and we were so grieved that we were out of our minds. Then suddenly we saw that we were at the mouth of the river, and we assessed our wares at once, and here is a tithe of it, seven thousand gold pieces. That is what we vowed to dedicate."

Then King Solomon, may he rest in peace, said to them: "Do you know where the hole was and who filled it?" "We do not know," said they. "Go and see," he told them, "whether there is anything in that place." They went and found the woman's sack and brought it to Solomon. Then he said to the woman: "Can you make known the signs and seal of your sack?" "Of course, I know it," said she. And when she saw it, she said: "That is mine." Then he told her: "The Holy and Blessed One did all this only for your sake, for whosoever walks in the ways of the Lord has God with him."

And then the Sanhedrin and the people recognized the wisdom of Solomon.

16

ZIZ-SADAI AND THE QUEEN OF SHEBA

The present text, a translation of a story that occurs in "Targum Sheni" ("Second Translation") of the Book of Esther, dates from the seventh and the early eighth centuries, and is the earliest narrative articulation of the Queen of Sheba story in Jewish tradition. While the account of the royal meeting occurs in the First Book of Kings and in Second Chronicles, the talmudic tradition seems to suppress any reference to the Queen of Sheba. The deliberate avoidance of any reference to her may reflect the existence of a narrative tradition that the rabbis would rather not record. Indeed, in later Jewish as well as Islamic and Ethiopian traditions the stories about the Queen of Sheba teem with sexual and demonic themes and allusions. The story is part of the narrative traditions of all the religions in the area, but has a central position in the Ethiopian national tradition. Source: M. David, Das Targum Scheni zum Buche Esther, *pp. 8–10 (Aramaic).*

Now it came to pass when the House of David began to reign over the whole world that his son Solomon arose, and the Holy and Blessed One caused him to reign over all the beasts of the field and the birds of heaven and all the creatures that crawl upon the ground. And he knew the languages of them all while they knew his language, and that is why it is written: "And he spoke of trees" (I Kings 5:13). Now when the king's heart was merry with wine, he commanded that harps, cymbals, drums, and lyres upon which his father David used to play should be brought. And while the king was still merry with wine, he ordered that the birds of the air, the beasts of the field, and the vermin that crawl on the earth should be brought and dance and leap and bound before him. For he wished to show the kings who were seated with him all his glory and his greatness. And the king's scribes called all of them by name, and all of them came and gathered before him, not in fetters and not in iron chains and with no man leading them.

At that time there was a searching for Ziz-Sadai, which is the wild cock, among all the birds of the air, but he was not to be found. Then the king in his wrath commanded that he should be brought and chastised. But Ziz-Sadai answered the king and said: "Be still and hear, my lord, king of the whole world, and permit my words to enter your ears. Why, three months ago I took counsel with myself and admonished myself wisely. I ate no food and drank no water, but I said: 'Let me fly and look out over the whole world to see whether there is a kingdom or a realm that does not obey my lord the king.' I gazed and saw one country, and its city is called Kitor, in the eastern lands. Its earth is more precious than gold, and the silver is like ordure in the streets, and the trees of the fields have been planted there since the six days of creation, and they drink the waters of Eden. There is a great host and army within it and they wear golden crowns. They are unable to wage war and they cannot smite or shoot the bow, and there is no falsehood in their land. Likewise, indeed, I saw a certain woman ruling and queening it over them, and her name is the Queen of Sheba. And now, if I have found favor in your eyes, and my lord the king sees it fitting, I shall gird my loins like a warrior and fly and depart to the city of Kitor in the land of Sheba. There I shall bind their kings in fetters and their honored ones in chains of iron and fetch them to my lord the king."

This found favor in the king's eyes; and the royal scribes were summoned and they wrote a letter and they folded it and tied it to the wing of Ziz-Sadai. Then he rose and mounted to the lofty heavens and flew off amid the fowl. And as he swooped and flew, all the other birds flew after him. And they went to the city of Kitor in the kingdom of Sheba.

Now before dawn the Queen of Sheba came forth to prostrate herself before the sun as was her practice. And lo and behold! the sun grew dark because of the birds; and she set her hand on her garments and rent them and was astounded. As she stood astonished, Ziz-Sadai came down before her, and she saw that a letter was bound to his wing. She opened the letter and read, and this is what it said: "From Solomon the king, peace to you and peace to your princes! Do you not know and have you not heard that the Holy and Blessed One has made me the ruler of the beasts of the field and the birds of the heavens, and all the kings of the East and the West and the North and the South come and ask my weal. Now, if you wish to come to me and ask my weal, I shall give you greater honor than all the kings who are seated before me. But if you refuse and disobey and do not ask my weal, I shall send kings, soldiers, and horsemen against you. And if you ask: Who are the kings, the soldiers, and the horsemen of King Solomon? Then know you that the beasts of the field are the kings, the birds of heaven are the horsemen; the beasts of the field will slay you in the field, and the birds of heaven shall consume your flesh from upon you."

Now when the Queen of Sheba read the words of this epistle, she took hold of her garments and rent them afresh, and she commanded that the elders and the princes should be summoned. And she said to them: "Do you know and have you heard what Solomon the king has sent to me?" And they all answered in unison: "We do not know Solomon the king, nor do we desire his rule." But she paid no attention to their words and disregarded them. Instead, she went and summoned all the oarsmen and captains of the sea that she had and commanded them to load and prepare the ships with cypress wood and every kind of precious jewel. And she sent King Solomon six thousand youths and maidens, all born in the same year, in the same month, on the same day, indeed, at the same moment; they were all of one height, all of one manner of movement, and all of them clad in purple. And she wrote a letter and at their hands she sent it to King Solomon: "From the city of Kitor to the land of Israel is a seven years' journey. Yet now I seek to see you face to face, so I shall appear before you when three years are done."

So at the end of the three years the Queen of Sheba came to King Solomon in Jerusalem. And when King Solomon heard that the Queen of Sheba had come to him, he sent Benaiah ben Jehoiada to meet her. And Benaiah was like the light that comes at the end of the morning watch, and like the Hind of the Dawn, which is the morning star, that stands flashing amid the stars, and like the rose that dwells by streams of water. When the Queen of Sheba saw him, she descended from her chariot. But Benaiah ben Jehoiada descended and said to her: "Why did you come down from your chariot?" And the queen answered: "Are you not King Solomon?" and Benaiah ben Jehoiada answered her: "I am not King Solomon but one of his servants who is seated before him." Then she turned her face about and said in a parable to her princes: "If you have not seen the lion, you have seen the place where he crouches; and if you have not seen King Solomon, you have seen the likeness of the handsome man that stands before him."

And Benaiah ben Jehoiada conducted her to King Solomon. And when he heard further that the Queen of Sheba had arrived and had come to his royal mansion, the king departed from his palace and went and took his seat in his glass house. Now when the queen saw this, she thought to herself: "King Solomon is seated in water." Then she raised her skirts in order to pass and he could see the hair on her legs. And King Solomon said to her: "Your beauty is the beauty of women but your hair is the hair of men, and hair is fitting for men but a reproach for women."

But the queen responded: "My lord king, I shall ask you three riddles. If you answer them, I shall know that you are indeed a wise man, but if not, then you are like all other men to me." And she began with her parable and said: "Wooden well and iron pail that draws up stones and watery flow. What is it?" And the king answered: "This is the little vessel in which kohl is kept." (For kohl, which is hard as stone, is taken with an iron spoon from a wooden container, and when it is applied to the eyes, the tears flow.)

Then the queen responded again: "Dust came out of the earth and its food is dust from the earth, it is poured out like water and it looks homeward. What is it?" And the king responded and said: "It is naphtha." (Crude petroleum is dug out of the earth and spills like water and clings to the walls of the house.)

Then the queen said again: "A tempest goes ahead and cries loudly and bitterly, bows its head like a reed. It is the praise of princes and the reproach of the needy, the glory of the dead and the grief of the living, joy for birds and sorrow for fishes—what is that?" "That," replied the king, "is flax." (For from flax it is possible to make fine linen, sackcloth, shrouds, a rope for hanging, linseed, and nets.)

This is what the queen then said to him: "I never believed it until I came and saw with my own eyes, yet indeed, I was not told the half of it. You have added wisdom and goodness to the tidings I have heard. Happy are your men and happy are these your attendants!"

And the king conducted her to his royal palace. When the Queen of Sheba saw the greatness of his glorious wealth, she uttered praises and thanksgiving to the One who created him and said: "May the Lord your God be blessed, He, who set his desire on you and placed you on the royal throne in order to do right and justice!" And she gave the king much gold and silver. And the king gave her all that she desired. And when the kings of the West and the East and the North and the South heard of his fame, they all rose and set out together and came from their places in great deference and with vast wealth, with gold and silver and jewels and pearls.

17
THE CASE OF THE LETTER YOD

While Aēshma is but a minor destructive deity or a negative force in Zoroastrian religion, in Jewish folk tradition and mysticism he has become, as Ashmedai, Asmodeus the King of the Demons. In apocryphal literature he is associated with wickedness, plotting in particular against newlyweds. As King of the Demons he is pitted, in this story, against King Solomon, who represents the ultimate of reasoned judgment. The tale has been extremely popular in Jewish traditions since the talmudic period. Source: L. Grünhut, Sefer ha-Likkutim 1:20–22.

"Thus said the Lord: Let not the wise man praise himself with his wisdom" (Jer. 9:22).

That applies to King Solomon. While he sat on the throne he became overweeningly proud and transgressed the words of the Torah: "And he shall not multiply wives to himself" (Deut. 17:17). Now, what did the letter Yod in the word *yarbeh* (he shall multiply) do? She stood before the Holy and Blessed One and said: "Lord of the Universe! Have You written even a single letter in Your Torah that was not necessary?" "No," said He. Then she said to Him: "Yet Solomon makes nothing of me and has wedded a thousand wives and has transgressed against Your Torah." And the Holy and Blessed One said to the Yod: "I must take up your quarrel and judge your case."

Thereupon the Holy and Blessed One said to Asmodeus, king of the demons: "Go to Solomon and take his seal away from him and assume his form and sit on his throne." Asmodeus went and took his seal away from his hand and assumed his form and sat on his throne, and Israel believed that he was Solomon. As for Solomon, he went wandering through all the towns and villages declaring: "I am Solomon! 'I, Kohelet, was king over Israel!'" (Eccles. 1:12). And three years passed in that fashion. All the time people were saying to one another: "What an idiot that fellow is! The king is on his throne, yet he declares: 'I, Kohelet, was king!'" And he went wandering, and fugitive. Then the Holy and Blessed One said: "I have already carried out the sentence of the Yod."

And what did Asmodeus do during those three years? He passed through all the wives of Solomon until he came to one of them who was in her courses. When she saw him, she said to him: "Solomon, why have you changed the way you have been treating us?" He made no answer. Then she said to him: "You are not Solomon."

That was not all. He went to Solomon's mother and said to her: "Mother, this and that is what I want of you." "My son," she answered, "do you think to find any pleasure in the place from which you came? If you do this, you cannot be my son!" And she went at once to Benaiah ben Jehoiada and said to him: "Benaiah, this and that is what Solomon demanded of me." As soon as he heard this, he trembled and shook and rent his garments and tore his hair and said: "Assuredly this cannot be Solomon but it must be Asmodeus, while that young fellow who is wandering round declaring, 'I am Kohelet,' must be Solomon himself."

He sent at once and summoned the young fellow and said to him: "My son! Tell me who you are!" Then he said: "I am Solomon, the son of David." "What happened to you, my son?" asked Benaiah. And he told him: "I was seated in my palace one day, and a kind of tempest swept about me and flung me far away. From then until now I lost my mind, and that was why I was wandering."

"Have you any sign?" asked Benaiah.

"Yes, indeed," said he. "When I was made king, my father David took one hand and placed it in your hand and he took the other hand and placed it in the hand of Nathan the Prophet, while my mother stood and kissed my father's head. That is the sign I have."

When Benaiah heard his words, what did he do? He summoned the

Sanhedrin and told them: "Go each one and write the Expressed Name and place it on your hearts." They went and then returned to him and said: "We fear that name which is engraved over the heart of Asmodeus." "Can one name overpower seventy names?" he asked them. "It means that you do not have the grace of the Lord!" And what did he do? He dealt Asmodeus one single blow and took the seal and wished to slay him. But a voice came from heaven and said: "Do not touch him because it came from Me, since Solomon transgressed against what is written in the Torah."

Benaiah at once set the seal on Solomon's hand again, and he appeared in his proper form and returned to his kingdom.

Then Solomon said: "Where was my kingdom and where was my bravery, that they were to no avail? Yet whoever degrades himself in this world is raised on high by the Holy and Blessed One, for in this world there is nothing to compare with meekness and humility, as it is written: 'True sacrifice to God is a contrite spirit'" (Ps. 51:19).

18
LIFE AND DEATH ARE IN THE POWER OF THE TONGUE

The theme of the debate about priority between the body members occurs in classical and medieval fable traditions. In Jewish folklore biblical characters figure in the story though it remains fictive in nature, being framed by a request from an anonymous "King of Persia." The set of personalities that appear in the narrative frame clearly indicates the fictive nature of the tale, since, in the basic biblical story, King Solomon has no dealings with any King of Persia. Source: S. Buber, ed., Midrash Tehilim, *p. 39b.*

The tale is told that a king of Persia was near death and became exceedingly gaunt. His physicians told him: "The only remedy for you is to drink the milk of a lioness, for that will cure you." He sent messengers to King Solomon son of David, and they took much money with them. And Solomon sent and summoned Benaiah ben Jehoiada and asked him: "How can we find the milk of a lioness?" Then Benaiah told him: "Give me ten nanny goats." Then he and the king's attendants went to a lion's den, where they found a lioness suckling her cubs. The first

day he stood at a distance and flung her one nanny goat, and she ate it.
The second day he came a little nearer and flung another. This he did every
day. By the tenth day he was playing with her and milking her udders
until he had taken enough of her milk, and then he went his way. He
and his men returned to Solomon, who bade the Persian king's messengers
farewell, and they departed.

When they were halfway back the leading messenger, who was himself
a physician, dreamed that all his limbs and organs were arguing with one
another. The legs said: "There are none to compare with us, for if we had
not walked, the body would not be able to fetch the milk." And the hands
responded: "None can compare with us, for if we had not done the milking,
there would have been no milk to fetch." As for the eyes, they said: "We
come first, for if we had not shown him the way, nothing could have been
done." And the heart chimed in: "I am more than all of you, for if I had
not given this counsel, none of you would have achieved anything." And
now the tongue responded: "I am better than any of you, for were it not
for speech, what would you have done?"

At that all the limbs and members together answered the tongue: "How
do you dare to compare with us when you are in a dark and gloomy spot
and have no bone in you like all the limbs?" And the tongue told them:
"You will soon admit that I am the ruler of you all!"

When the messenger awakened from his sleep, he marked the dream
in his mind and went on. When he presented himself to the king, he said
to him: "Here is the bitch's milk we sought for you, and now drink it."
The king promptly flew into a rage at him and ordered him hanged. While
he was waiting for the execution, he dreamed again. All his limbs were
quivering and trembling, and the tongue said to them: "Did I not tell you
that none of you are good for anything! If I save you, will you admit
that I am the ruler of you all?" "Most certainly," they answered.

The man woke up and his tongue said to the executioners: "Lead me
back to the king! Lead me back to the king!" They did so; and he asked
him: "Why did you order that I was to be hanged?" Said the king to him:
"Because you fetched me bitch's milk." "And what difference would it make
to you," asked the man, "as long as you are cured? And what is more,
the lioness is called bitch."

The king took the milk and drank it and was cured; and having found
that it was indeed the milk of a lioness he let him depart in peace. Then
all the limbs said to the tongue: "Now we admit that you rule over all
the limbs and members of the body!" And that confirms the verse: "Life
and death are in the power of the tongue" (Prov. 18:21).

19
ONE MAN IN A THOUSAND I FOUND

This is a translation of a text that originally appeared in the sixteenth century narrative midrash of "Parables of King Solomon," but the story itself has been known since the eleventh century. By the twelfth century it was the subject of a literary rendition. The tale belongs to a cycle of misogynistic medieval narratives that occurs in several books of the period. Source: A. Jellinek, ed., Bet ha-Midrasch *4:146–148.*

The tale is told of King Solomon, may he rest in peace, that he said through the Holy Spirit: "One man in a thousand I found, but a woman among all these I did not find" (Eccles. 7:28). When the people in the Sanhedrin heard this, they were astonished. And Solomon told them: "If you so desire, I shall show it to you." And they all said: "Yes."

Then he said to them: "Seek a woman who belongs to the best folk of the city and also a man who is better than anyone else." They investigated and found a man who had a good and beautiful wife. The king summoned him, and he was brought before him. Then the king said to him: "Know that I wish to show you honor and make you a lord of my palace." "I am your servant," answered the man, "and shall behave toward you as befits one of your servants." Then King Solomon said to him: "If so, go and slay your wife and fetch me her head tonight, and tomorrow I shall give you my daughter and shall set you in office over the greater number of Israel." And the man said: "I shall do as you desire."

Home he went, and he found his wife handsome and beautiful, and she had little children by him. This pierced his heart, and he wept and wailed. When his wife saw that he was upset, she turned to him and said: "What ails you, husband, that your face should be so fallen?" "Let me be," said he, "for I am worried at heart." She went and fetched him food and drink at once. He did not wish to eat but thought to himself all the time: "What shall I do? Shall I slay my wife when I have little children from her?" So he said to her: "Go and lie down with the children."

When she went to bed and fell asleep, he drew his sword to slay her, but found her little baby sleeping between her breasts while one little boy was lying with his head on her shoulders. Then he said to himself: "Some devil has entered Solomon's heart!" And he went on thinking: "Woe is me, what shall I do? If I slay her, these little children will perish, too." And he sheathed his sword at once and said: "May the Lord rebuke you, O Satan!" A second time he thought: "I shall slay her and tomorrow the king will give me his daughter and much of his wealth." At once he brandished the sword over her, but he saw her hair spread out over the two babies, and sudden pity entered his heart, and he said: "Even if the king should give me all his household and all his wealth I shall not slay this wife of mine." And he sheathed his sword at once and lay beside his wife until morning.

Then the king's messengers came for him and led him to the royal presence. "Have you done it?" the king asked him. "Have you carried out what you said you would?" And he answered: "If it be good in the king's eyes, let him not discuss this matter with me. I wished to perform this deed once and again, but my heart would not permit me to do it." Then Solomon declared: "Indeed, one man in a thousand I have found!" He let the man depart and left him alone for thirty days.

After thirty days had passed, the king sent secretly to his wife and had her brought before him and said to her: "Have you a good husband?" "Oh, yes," said she. "I have heard of your beauty and your radiant countenance," said the king, "and I have come to love you enough to take you to wife. And we shall set you to reign over all the princesses in the kingdom and garb you in gold from head to foot." "Indeed," said she to him, "I shall do whatever you desire." Then he said to her: "One thing can harm us and prevent me from doing anything, the fact that you have a husband." "Then what shall we do?" she asked him; and he said: "Slay your husband, and afterwards I shall take you to wife." "That we shall do," she agreed. But Solomon said to himself: "Indeed, this one is about to slay her husband. Let us do something to make sure that he does not die." And what did he do? He gave her a tin sword. When she saw that it shone, he said to her: "Slay him with this, for as soon as you lay it against his neck, it will be cut."

The woman returned to her home and her husband with the sword. When her husband came, she went and embraced him and kissed him and said to him: "Be seated, my lord, crown of my head!" When he heard these words, he was very happy. And he sat at ease and had no evil thought in his mind. And she fetched the table, and they ate and drank; and her husband said to her: "Wife, what do you wish to do tonight?" "I wish to rejoice with you," said she, "and to have you drunk tonight." He laughed with her cheerfully and drank until he was drunk and fell asleep. When she saw this, she rose and girded her loins and brandished the sword that the king had given her and began to cut the skin. Her husband promptly awakened from his sleep and saw his wife about to slay him.

"Tell me the whole matter," he said to her, "and who gave you the sword, and how it has happened—otherwise I shall cut you to little pieces." "This and this," said she, "is what King Solomon told me to do." And he told her: "Have no fear."

Early in the morning the king's messengers came for them, and he and his wife went to the king. There they found the Sanhedrin in session, too. When the king saw them, he laughed and said to them: "Please be good enough to tell me what happened. "This and that," they said, "is what came about." And he said: "I woke up and found my wife standing ready to slay me. If it had not been a tin sword, I would long since have been dead. I took pity on her, though she had no pity for me."

Then Solomon said: "I knew indeed that there is no pity among women. That was why I gave her a sword of tin."

And when the Sanhedrin heard this, they said: "Indeed, there is truth in the king's saying: 'One man in a thousand I found, but a woman among all these I did not find.'"

20

A WOMAN AMONG ALL THESE I DID NOT FIND

This tale also belongs to the cycle of medieval misogynistic narratives (see the previous story). It is a translation of a text that originally appeared in the sixteenth-century book of "Parables of King Solomon." Unlike the former story, here King Solomon serves only as a temporal reference and does not take an active part in the plot. This tale validates King Solomon's condemnation of women that appears in Ecclesiastes 7:28. Source: A. Jellinek, ed., Bet ha-Midrasch 4:146.

In the days of King Solomon a certain man went from Tiberias to Bethar to study Torah. And a very handsome young man he was. A certain maiden saw him and said to her father: "I beg you, give me that young man for a husband." He went and chased after him and said to him: "If you are prepared to wed a wife, I shall give you my daughter." "I agree," said he. And he went and wedded the maiden and returned home and rejoiced with his wife for a whole year.

After the year was over, his wife said to him: "Please take me to my parents so that I shall see them." Thereupon he took horses and gifts and food and drink and went with his wife to visit her parents. On the way an armed robber came out against them. When the woman saw him, she fell in love with him. And the woman and the robber seized the young man and bound him with ropes, and the robber seduced the woman with idle words, and afterwards the robber went to eat and drink with her. As for the young fellow, he was tied to a tree and saw it all.

Then the robber went to sleep with the maiden, and took the pitcher and placed it at his head and fell asleep. Now a serpent came and drank the wine and spewed deadly venom into it. When the robber woke up, he took the pitcher and drank and perished; and the young man saw the miracle that was wrought for him. Said he to his wife: "Please be good enough to untie me and release me from the ropes." "I fear that you will slay me if I do," said she. "I take oath," he answered, "that I shall not put you to death." She put her hand on the robber and found that he was dry wood (dead). Then she released her husband, and they both went to the home of her father.

When her parents saw her, they were very happy and arranged for a feast. But he said to them: "I shall neither eat nor drink until I tell you what has happened to me." And he told the whole tale. And what did her father do then? He slew that wicked daughter of his.

That is why Solomon could say in his wisdom: "And a woman among all these I did not find" (Eccles. 7:28).

21
THREE WISE WORDS

This tale is a part of a larger narrative complex known in Jewish tradition since the Middle Ages and still alive in the folklore of many Jewish ethnic groups. Most of the narratives in this group are Jewish renditions of internationally known tales concerning the "wise words" of a king or a dying father. King Solomon, the archetypal wise king in Jewish tradition, appears in this tale as an adult ruler rather than a "clever child," serving both as a dispenser of wisdom and as a judge. The Hebrew original text appeared in the sixteenth-century "Parables of King Solomon." Source: A. Jellinek, ed., Bet ha-Midrasch *4:148–150.*

There were once three brothers who went to study Torah with King Solomon. The king said to them: "Stay and serve me, and I shall teach you wisdom." Furthermore, he appointed them officers of his court. They stayed with him thirteen years, and at the end of that time they said to one another: "What have we been doing? We have abandoned our homes and all that belongs to us for ten full years and three, and we have come to study Torah and we have served him, yet we have learned nothing. Let us request persmission and return home."

One day they came to Solomon and said to him: "Your majesty, thirteen years have passed since we left our homes. Grant us permission to go and see our households." The king at once summoned his treasurer to bring him three hundred gold pieces. And he said to them: "Choose one of these two: either I shall teach each of you three words of wisdom or I shall give each of you a hundred gold pieces." They consulted with one another; then they took the money, obtained permission and departed.

When they were about four miles away from town, the youngest suddenly said to his brothers: "What have we done? Did we come here for gold or to study Torah? If you wish to hear my counsel, let us return the money and learn wisdom from King Solomon." "If you wish to return the gold," said his brothers, "in order to learn three wise words, go and do so; but we shall not go back to buy such things for the money."

Back went the youngest brother to Solomon and said to him: "My lord king, I did not come here for gold. If it pleases you, take the gold and teach me wisdom." And there and then the king began to teach him, and said: "My son, when you are on the road, be careful to be ready to depart when the sun rises in the morning, while in the evening make your camp while it is still daylight. That is the first. When you see that the river is full, do not enter it but wait until it descends and goes back to its old bed. That is the second. And never reveal any secret to any woman, not even to your own wife. That is the third." He asked for permission to leave at once and mounted his horse and chased after his brothers. When he reached them, they said to him: "What have you learned?" And he answered: "What I have learned, I have learned."

He began to journey on with his brothers. By the ninth hour of the day (in the afternoon) they came to a place which was suitable for camping. Then the youngest brother said: "This is a good place for stopping, for here there is water and trees and grass for the horses. If you agree, let us spend the night here, and when the morning star rises, if His Name has decreed that we live, let us go on in peace." But his brothers answered:

"Oh, you fool! When you gave away your money to buy the words, we knew there was no wisdom in you. We can go another eight miles before evening, and you say that we should stay here!" "Do what you desire," said he to them, "But I shall not move from here."

They went on while he stayed there and began to lop branches and started a fire and made a kind of encampment for his horse and himself. He allowed the horse to graze until evening and then he gave it barley, and he and the beast ate and lay down at ease that night. As for his brothers, they went on until evening fell, but they could not find any grass for their horses and no trees for a fire. Then a heavy fall of snow came down on them so that they perished from the cold. But the snow did not harm the younger brother because of the shelter and the fire and the food and drink. When the morning star arose, he prepared himself and mounted his horse and took up the way and followed his brothers, only to find them dead. When he saw them, he fell beside them and wept bitterly. Then he buried them, took their money, and went on.

The sun rose, the snow melted, the rivers filled to overflowing, and he could not cross the river that was before him. So he dismounted and waited till the spate had passed. As he was pacing about on the riverbank, he saw Solomon's servants leading two horses that were laden with gold. "Why don't you cross?" they asked him. "Because the river is full to overflowing," said he. They paid no attention but began to cross. When they came down into the riverbed, the current swept them away and they perished. As for the youngest brother, he waited until the river went down; then he crossed, took the money, and went to his home in peace.

His sisters-in-law saw him and asked about their husbands. "They are still staying to learn wisdom," said he to them. And meanwhile he began to purchase fields and vineyards and build fine houses and buy cattle and property. His wife used to ask him: "Tell me, where is all this money from?" He grew very angry and gave her a thorough beating, saying: "Why must you ask that?" But she enticed him again and again until he told her the whole tale.

On one occasion he vexed his wife, and she began to shout: "Is it not enough that you murdered your two brothers and now you want to murder me as well!" When his sisters-in-law heard that their husbands were dead, they went and complained about him to the king. And the king ordered that he should be brought before him and be executed.

Before they led him forth to execution, he said: "Please permit me to make a statement to the king." They took him to Solomon at once, and there he fell on his face and said: "My lord, I am one of the three brothers who stayed with you for thirteen years in order to learn wisdom. I am the youngest who returned the gold pieces in order to learn wisdom from you, and the wisdom you taught me was my protection."

At that Solomon recognized the truth and said: "Have no fear. The money you took from your brothers and from my servants was yours, and the wisdom you acquired has delivered you from death and from that woman. Now depart and be glad!"

It was then that Solomon said: "How much better is it to acquire wisdom than gold" (Prov. 16:16).

22

THE TALK OF BEASTS AND THE CHIRPING OF BIRDS

Originally this text was written in a rhymed prose, an Arabic literary form known as maqāmā, *that many medieval Jewish poets employed. Ibn Ḥasdai of Barcelona, a thirteenth-century poet, recorded the present tale in his translation from the Arabic of an originally Hindu book, "The Prince and the Hermit," describing the youth of Buddha and known in European languages as* Barlaam and Joasaph. *The idea that King Solomon understood the animal languages is based on the biblical verse . . .he spoke also of beasts, and of fowl, and of all creeping things, and of fish (I Kings 5:13). In a variety of forms, this theme occurs in modern Jewish folklore. Source: Abraham ben Samuel ha-Levi ibn Ḥasdai,* Ben ha-Melekh ve-ha-Nazir. *"The Prince and the Hermit" (Mantua, 1557), ch. 24, pp. 71–73.*

This is a tale that was told by the Nazirite to the king's son:

They say that in a distant land King Solomon had a friend who used to visit him year by year, when the year comes to an end. The king used to give him gifts when back to his land and his people he did wend. And one year the friend brought him a precious gift, as much as a strong man could lift, and when he prepared to depart from him, the king in return wished to give him something that was worth even more, but he refused to take it and on it would not set any store, saying: "My lord king, I do not desire any gifts from you, for thanks be to God and your kindness, too, I already have all that I need and to spare, and there is nothing that I require. Yet if my lord king wishes to do me some kindness at least, then teach me the chirping of birds and the talk of the beasts."

"Surely," the king said, "I shall not refuse you your request, my brother, and I shall let you have what I would not give to another; yet what you ask is very perilous, for in it there is a secret deep which to yourself you must keep. If you should tell one thing of all that you hear, death will reach you that day and no ransom of yours can keep it away." "Whatever befalls," said the friend, "give a little of your wisdom to me, and God aiding, I shall abide by your decree." And when the king saw how great was his desire, he imparted the secrets most dread and most dire, and then the man returned to his home.

Now one day as he sat with his spouse, his ox came from the field and passed by the house, and they tied it beside the ass and gave it some food, but they gave the ass none for it did not feel good. And the ass said to the ox: "Brother, how do you stand among all these men?" And the ox replied: "By our master's life, brother, all I do is to toil and to moil, both when day is bright and also at night." "I wish you some ease," said the ass, "and I shall give you good advice, and then you can rest and be at your ease." "Brother," said the ox, "if only you would pity my plight, I shall heed your advice and not turn away, neither to left nor to right." And the ass said: "The Lord knows that out of my innocent heart and pureness of thought I am speaking my part. And this I tell you is what you should do: Eat nothing at all here tonight, not straw and not fodder, not even a bite. When our master sees that you do fast, he will think you are ailing and so cannot last, and he will not exhaust you but leave you to rest. In that way your fate will be of the best as mine is today in quiet and ease, and I have surcease of all my toil, because they see that I must be ill." And the counsel found favor in the ox's eyes, and he did what was told him by that donkey wise.

But the man rose by night and saw that while the ox was asleep the ass went to his crib and ate what he could, till his belly was full. And since he had heard their talk, he could see what the donkey was doing with such trickery. In his surprise he opened his mouth and he burst into a hearty laugh. And his wife said to him: "Why are you laughing so loud, there is no one here but you, good-for-nothing and proud!" "I just remembered," he said fast, "an amusing thing of the past."

In the morning he went to the crib of the ox, where he found the fodder the ass had left, and he said to his man: "See how the poor ox does peak and does pine. He will not work today; take the ass in his place." So he worked for the ox and did his own work as well. When evening came, the ass returned drooping and weary, and the ox said to him: "Brother, did you hear what those cruel men were saying of me?" And the ass replied:

"I heard them say that if the ox does not eat his fodder tonight, they will slaughter him next day, and then they will eat him up anyway." When the ox heard this, he was very disturbed and set his mouth to the crib like a lion to the prey and kept his head there until he finished the fodder and the crib was empty and bare.

Now the man had heard the words of the ass and his wiles, and he laughed aloud, and his wife said to him: "That was the way you laughed yesterday. Then I said that it may be sheer chance, but now that you again laugh out when there is no one here, you must be laughing at me or see something wrong about. Now by God I swear that you will not come near nor touch me till you will tell what is true." And he implored her with love and with honor as well: "Do not ask, wife, for this is something I cannot tell." "Now indeed," said the woman, "indeed, I do swear, you shall never see me any more—so there—until you have told me the whole of the truth." And the man said: "Alas, I know it full well—I shall perish if ever this secret I tell." But the woman replied: "I shall not abide it, and I shall not eat or drink, but shall nag and shall wheedle and persuade you, I think."

Said the man: "I swear by my soul to do things great and things small, I would far sooner die than let a single hair fall from your head, for what would be left me if you starve till you are dead? But now let me be and hope for the best while I make my will. Then I shall obey your behest!" And he summoned all his kinsfolk and friends to make his will before them.

Now he had a dog in his home, and he had bread to eat and fat meat and a bone, but he would not touch a thing or make use of his teeth because of concern for his master and grief. And the cock came and took the meat and the bread, and ate it all up with his hens without dread. Then the dog like a lion went over to him; and he said: "Alas, you cruel and worthless fool, how shameless you are and from decency far! Your lord is preparing and ready to die, yet you cheerfully eat all the while and have no concern for him and his fate."

But the cock replied: "If your lord is a fool and a sot, am I to blame—because I am not? Why, I who have ten wives, rule them all with a will. Not one will gainsay me for good or for ill. Yet your master indeed, he only has one, and he cannot rule her or treat her the way it should best be done!" And the cock opened its mouth and crowed:

"Netted for life and all through a wife—
When a woman rules man—what worse can there be?

So hearken to wisdom, to my words give ear,
And learn understanding from old chanticleer!"

"What should he do?" asked the dog. And the cock answered: "He ought just to take a thick stick and beat her and whack her, licking and lick, and I remain certain and sure as I am here, she will beg him not to tell her any secret whatever, not now or forever."

And the man heard this, and he did so and he was saved.

23
THE CRAFTSMAN'S WIFE

The feminine image in this tale contrasts sharply with the misogynistic view that was common in medieval tradition. The craftsman's wife is loving and faithful, warding off all attempts to dissuade her from the path of honesty, with cleverness and boldness. The theme of the faithful wife is current in the folk traditions of several Jewish ethnic groups and has been known in European narrative tradition since classical times. Source: Israel ben Sasson, Likkutei Ma'asiyyot, pp. 11–15.

This is a story of the time when King Solomon, may he rest in peace, began to build the Temple. He sent missives to the kings of all the different countries where there were important and expert craftsmen requesting that those men come to Jerusalem and do their work there and be well paid. And because of the honor and fear and dread of King Solomon, the kings sent messages to all the outstanding craftsmen in each of the different countries.

Now in a certain city there was a truly distinguished craftsman who used to work in his own city and came home with his wages every evening. He would never go beyond the city wall to work, even if they offered him all the riches in the world. For he would not leave his wife alone at home, fearing that violent men might come and sport with her, even seduce and lie with her. For his wife was so exceedingly comely and beautiful that her like would scarcely be found anywhere in the whole world.

Now when the missive of King Solomon, may he rest in peace, reached the king of the city where the aforesaid craftsman lived, the king sent for him at once. He appeared and bowed and prostrated himself and asked: "What does the lord the king command his servant?" "It is my desire," answered the king, "that you should go to the city of Jerusalem and engage in the work of your craft for King Solomon. He is so mighty and powerful a monarch that I cannot reject his requests." Then the craftsman told him: "My lord king, I cannot go there and abandon my house without its owner."

This angered the king very much indeed, and he told the craftsman that whether he wished to or not he would have to go there, for if he did not go he would certainly be put to death.

He left the royal presence very upset and returned home unhappy when evening fell. There he neither ate nor drank and did not converse happily with his wife as he usually did. So his wife asked him: "Why is this night different from all other nights, and why are you so disturbed and unhappy as though you were in mourning?" "How can I be other than unhappy and disturbed?" answered he. "For the king has commanded me to go to Jerusalem and work there for King Solomon. Yet how shall I forsake my wife and household when men may come and endeavor to entice and seduce you?"

"What answer did you give the king?" asked his wife. "I did not agree," said he, "to go up there, and the king was very angry with me and said to me: 'If you do not go you will be put to death!'"

At this his wife laughed and told him: "So it is because of me that you are afraid? You need not be afraid at all or have the slightest doubt in your heart. Believe me, indeed, that I shall not be enticed or seduced by any other man except you, even if it should be a king. Besides, I shall give you a sure sign, and as long as you see that it is unchanged, you will know that there is no change in me either. And tomorrow, God willing, get up and go quietly and in peace with all the other craftsmen and do everything precisely as the king has told you, and then your path will be assured. Have no fear or apprehension, and rest assured that I shall not be polluted by any other man." After that they sat and ate and drank and rejoiced all night long. Early in the morning he went to the king and informed him that he wished to proceed to Jerusalem in compliance with the royal behest.

When the man rose to depart, his wife gave him a little glass vessel the mouth of which she closed and sealed. In it was a wick of cotton and a glowing coal. And she told her husband: "Hang this round your neck. As long as you see that the fire does not burn the wick, you may rest assured that I too have not been burned by the fire of wrong desires, and that its heat has not possessed me, and I have not been polluted by any other person. But if you should see that fire spreads from the coal and burns the wick, then you may know that I have been polluted by others. Guard this sign and do not forget it. But rest assured that as long as my breath is within me, I shall not make myself free or destroy my soul wantonly by polluting myself with other men. Have no fear and go secure." And the craftsman promptly departed together with the others, and they went to the city of Jerusalem to do their work.

Now King Solomon came day after day to observe the work being done by the craftsmen in accordance with his wishes. And he promised to pay them many times their usual rate. And one day his eyes fell on this craftsman who had the glass vessel hanging round his neck; and he saw that within the vessel there was a cotton wick and a glowing coal and nothing else. This astonished the king exceedingly, and he asked himself what made this craftsman different from all the others; and he promptly summoned him and asked him about the glass vessel: "Why do you hang it round your neck when there is nothing in it but those two items? What is the reason for it?"

"My lord king," answered he, "my wife hung this glass vessel with the two items in it round my neck, because she is exceedingly comely and beautiful and there is scarcely any other like her in the world. And in order that nobody may set his eyes on her and try to mislead her to evil deeds, I have always refrained from working in any other city, so that she should not remain without her husband even for a single night.

"Now I did not wish to leave the walls of my city when I was at home, even though the king ordained that he would have me slain if I did not go to Jerusalem. I was prepared to accept death rather than depart from my city on account of my wife, who would remain alone without a husband, and maybe somebody would mislead her to evil deeds in my absence. But my wife gave me permission to go in order to escape from the royal threat; and she promised me that I had no reason to be in fear of this. Then she gave me this glass vessel to keep as a sign before my eyes by day and night. And she told me: 'As long as this cotton wick is not burned by the coal, you may rest assured that I have not been polluted either. But if you should see that the wick is burned, then you can know that I too have been burned by the heat of evil desire and have been polluted, and you can despair of me. But I would have you know in all truth and faith that as long as the breath is in me, and I am alive on earth, I shall not permit myself to fall into this transgression; and you may have complete faith in me.'

"With that promise I left my home and my city and came to work for your royal majesty here in the city of Jerusalem, where I have never been before."

Now when King Solomon, may he rest in peace, heard the tale of the craftsman, he was astonished and startled and wondered whether such a great and remarkable thing could ever be? And being wiser than all men and given to pursuing matters to their very end, he made up his mind to make a trial of this matter and see whether things would actually be as the woman had declared to her husband. Was it possible that if she should be so wanton as to sleep with another man, the cotton wick would really be burned?

So what did the king do? He ordered his attendants to fetch him two handsome and comely young men with fine eyes, without the knowledge of the craftsman. When the young men appeared before him, he ordered them to depart at once to the city of the said craftsman and take up a lodging in his home and stay there until they had succeeded in seducing his wife and sleeping with her by any means whatsoever; and he also gave them much money in case that might seduce her. Meanwhile the king would observe the glass vessel hanging round the neck of the craftsman in Jerusalem and see whether the wick really was consumed or not.

Well, the king sent them off, and they arrived at the town of the said craftsman and took lodging in his house. The woman received them with all courtesy and honor and set the table for them and brought them a feast that was fit for a king. When they wanted to sleep, she prepared their beds in one of her rooms, and the woman's servants led them to that chamber where they lay down. Then she ordered the servants to lock the door so that they should not be able to open it by day either, and there she left them for many a long day. Every day they were brought ample food and drink and they did whatever they required there, but they did not leave that chamber and remained there for a full month.

Meanwhile, King Solomon came to the workers and craftsmen every day and from time to time would steal a glance at the little vessel hanging from the craftsman's neck in order to see whether the cotton wick had burned yet. Yet whenever he did so he could see that it was still there. This went on for about a month. He saw that there was no change, and everything remained as it was, nor had the two young fellows come home. Then he said to himself: "This cannot be an accident. There must be some good reason for it. Maybe something has happened to them, and I had better go and see for myself."

So King Solomon himself went off to the craftsman's city with two attendants, divesting himself of his royal attire so that no one should recognize that he was a king. And he too went and took up lodging in the craftsman's home. Now the woman sensed at once that this was King Solomon, and she welcomed him with the utmost honor and all possible courtesy. That night she made a feast that was truly fit for kings; and after they had eaten and drunk, she prepared the best bed for him, as well as beds for his attendants in a building all their own. As for herself, she went and slept in one of her rooms, and rose with the dawn and went to the entrance of the place where they were sleeping in order to serve them. And she also prepared them a noon meal, and they ate and drank. All this she did the next day as well.

The third day she brought them a feast. After they had eaten and were satisfied, she brought the king a dish filled with boiled eggs, each of which was painted in a different color; one being green, another red, a third yellow, and a fourth black. Then she took one egg of each color and said to him: "My lord king, eat these eggs." "Who is a king here?" he asked her. "Which of us are you calling king?" Then she answered: "When you entered my house, I knew that you must be King Solomon, for your regality looks out from your eyelashes and now I, your maidservant, entreat you to taste each of the eggs just to know the difference and find out which of them is better and has a finer flavor."

Now when the king heard this, he did not refuse but tasted each of the eggs. And the woman asked him: "Which of them had the better flavor?" To which the king answered: "They all have the same taste, and there is not the slightest difference in their flavor, even though they do differ in their appearance."

Thereupon she promptly said to him: "My lord king, precisely as these eggs all have different appearances and one does not look like the other, one looking fine and handsome from the outside while another looks ugly and bad, and just as eggshells are thrown away, no matter how finely they are colored, and what is inside is eaten, and in that respect all eggs are the same—so it is with women. Although the face of one may be fine and bright just like the colored eggshells, yet for the use of what is within the body there is no difference between a beautiful woman or an ugly woman, and they are all equal. That is how it is with me, too. Although I am comely and very beautiful, more so than other women, yet for actual use I am the same as all the other women; they and I are identical.

"Now since that is the case, it was not befitting and proper for your majesty to go to the bother of coming all this distance in order to sleep with me on account of my appearance. And since you had already sent two handsome young fellows, I already knew your royal purpose and intention, and that they had come to seduce me. For that reason I closed them into one of my rooms and locked and bolted the door on them and have not let them out either day or night, but I have sent them food and drink as much as I have had. And I knew for certain that you had sent them to seduce me, and that was why I kept them in my house until now, a full month. For I knew that when you would see that they did not come back, you would be very upset and wonder what delayed them and whether some harm had befallen them, or possibly they had been unable to seduce me and therefore had stayed in order to try to succeed in the purpose for which you sent them.

"And I knew that then you would decide: I myself have to go there in order to know what has happened to them, and what is more, maybe they cannot do anything with her and she disregards them, but I shall find some clever device and succeed. I saw quite clearly that all this must occur to you. Yet, my lord king, you are the king of kings, and who am I and what is my life to withstand you when I have no words to utter or things to say to you and I shall not be even as one of your handmaidens. But you have the power to do whatever you will with me and whatever is fit and proper in your eyes. But know, my lord king, that you are a wise man, and the praises of your wisdom have spread far and wide through all lands and cities. It cannot be hidden from your majesty's eyes that all the desires of this world are vanity and unhappiness of spirit and no more than a will-o'-the-wisp. And you can see the proof in these eggs which have been painted in all those different colors that I set before you."

Now when the king heard her pleasing words, he said to her: "Blessed are you before the Lord and blessed is your good sense. When I saw the glass vessel hanging from your husband's neck, I asked him in my surprise what it was; and he told me, my wife hung it round my neck, and that you promised him that you would not come to sin. That was why I wished to test you. Now I know most clearly that you are a wise woman and your mouth and heart are equally pure and clear of all deceit and wickedness. Henceforth I undertake that you shall be as one of my sisters to me, nor shall I forget to keep your love fresh in my memory and treat you with all respect and honor to the best of my ability."

She promptly released the two lads from the room and brought them before him, and made them a great feast and they ate and drank. And meanwhile the king gave her a present worthy of a king, and they all returned to their city Jerusalem in peace. There he told her husband, to wit, the craftsman, all that had happened, and the king showed her craftsman husband much esteem and honor and also said this to him: "I have made a covenant with her that she shall be like one of my own sisters." And the king ordered him to honor her more than ever, because she was a worthy and intelligent and faithful woman. Then he paid him many times the amount of his wages and said: "Go, enjoy your possession!" And he sent him away, and he went home in peace.

His wife also told him all that had happened, and her words and those of the king were identical. Then he kissed her on her brow and rejoiced with her and honored and esteemed her tenfold more than ever he had done before. And everlasting affection likewise continued between them and King Solomon, may he rest in peace.

24
SOLOMON'S DAUGHTER

Salomon Buber discovered the present version of this tale in a manuscript of Midrash Tanḥuma *in the Bodleian Library of Oxford University. The tale appears in Jewish medieval tradition, and its principal themes have occurred in nineteenth century European Jewish oral traditions and are current in the twentieth century oral tales of several Jewish ethnic groups. The Hebrew poet Ḥayyim Naḥman Bialik (1870–1934) rendered the tale, which he partially learned from oral sources, in a literary form. Because of Bialik's central position in modern Hebrew literature, his two versions stimulated literary scholars to explore the sources of the various themes of the tales in Jewish traditional literature. However, the theme of marital predestination has wide distribution in the folktale traditions of many peoples. Source: S. Buber, ed.,* Midrash Tanḥuma, *"Introduction," p. 68b.*

I t is told that King Solomon had a most beautiful daughter whose like could not be found in the whole land of Israel. He watched the stars to see who was her appointed spouse and who would wed her, and saw that this would be a certain poor man, and none would be poorer than he in Israel. What did he do then? He built a lofty tower in the sea and had walls around it on every side. Then he took his daughter and set her in that lofty tower and placed seventy eunuchs of the elders of Israel with her. In that tower he made no entrance in order that no man should be able to enter, but in it he placed ample provender and said: "Now let me see the acts and workings of His Name!"

In due course that poor man who was the maiden's destined spouse set out on a journey by night. Now he was ragged and barefoot, starving and thirsting, and had nothing on which to lie. He saw the carcass of an ox flung away in the field and crept in between the ribs to keep himself warm. There he fell asleep, and a huge bird came and took that carcass and bore it away to the roof of the tower above the maiden's room. There the bird consumed the flesh of the carrion, and there it stayed on the roof.

At daybreak the maiden left her room to go and walk on the roof as was her daily fashion, and there she saw that youth. "Who are you," she asked him, "and who brought you hither?" And he answered: "I am a Jew of the city of Acco, but a bird brought me hither." What did she do then? She took him to her room and clothed him and washed him and anointed him, and then he was shown to be so handsome that his like could not be found in all the regions of Israel.

Now the maiden fell in love with him with all her heart and soul, and her soul was linked to his, and the young man was keen and shrewd and witty and a scribe. One day she said to him: "Are you prepared to hallow me as your wife?" "Would that I might!" said he to her. And what did he do? He let some blood and wrote her a marriage contract with a bride price stated therein, all with his blood, and he hallowed her to him and said: "Witness is the Lord this day and witnesses are Michael and Gabriel the angels!" And he joined with her after the fashion of all men, and she conceived from him.

When the elders saw that she was pregnant, they said to her: "It seems that you are bearing a child within you." "True," she told them. "And from whom have you conceived?" they asked her. "What business is it of yours to know?" she answered. At that the faces of the elders fell, because they dreaded King Solomon and feared that he might bring charges against them. So they sent for him to come and speak to them. Solomon took ship and came to them. And they told him: "Your majesty, this is how things are, and do not put any blame upon your servants!" When he heard this, he summoned his daughter and asked her what had happened. And she answered him: "The Holy and Blessed One brought me a good and handsome youth, a scholar and a scribe, and he has hallowed me to him for wife." She summoned the youth, and he came to the king and showed him the marriage contract he had made for the princess. Then the king asked him details of his father and his mother and his family and the city from which he came; and from his answers he understood that this was the one whom he had seen in the stars. Then he rejoiced very much indeed and said: "Blessed is the Ever Present who gives a man his own!" And that is the point of the verse: "God sets the single ones to dwell in homes" (Ps. 68:7).

25

THE STORY OF TOBIAH

Ibn Zabara, a twelfth-century physician and Hebrew writer from Barce-
lona, is best known for his Sepher Sha'ashu'im, *a book of rhymed prose,*
which is the source of the present text. The tale is a literary rendition
of the apocryphal Book of Tobit. This book itself could have incorpo-
rated oral narratives that were in circulation in antiquities, since the theme
of the grateful dead man has worldwide distribution, which, of course,
could have been effected by its incorporation into the Septuagint and
into the Catholic and Orthodox Church canons. Scholars debate the time
and place of the original Book of Tobit, dating it from the fifth or fourth
centuries B.C.E. up to the first century C.E. Fragments of the book have
been found in the Dead Sea Scrolls. The tale was popular in medieval
Jewish tradition and was included in nineteenth century folk books.
Source: I. Davidson, ed. and trans., Sepher Shaashuim: A Book of Medieval Lore by Joseph ben Meir ibn Zabara, *pp. 55–59.*

I n the days of old when men were better than gold there dwelt in
this town a most upright man, one of those who does good wherever
he can. Great and wealthy indeed was this man and his name was Tobiah
ben Ahiah of the tribe of Dan. He always followed the righteous way and
served poor and needy as prop and as stay. If a man passed away, he would
make him a shroud, bury him at his own pay, and attend to all other array.

Now in the city were worthless men who denounced all the Jews to
the king, saying: "Lord king, the Jews do open our graves and from there
take out the bones of our dead and in place of burial burn them instead,
in order to make medicine and witchery." The king grew very angry at
their words and ordered that they must be punished and fined, saying: "Let
this be the pay they have gained: If any Jew perishes throughout all my
land, let him be flung into the great pit which is close to the city, and
let not one of them be brought to the grave, and any who bury will be
hanged on the tree!"

Now it came to pass that a stranger died, and there were none him
to bury, and the pious Tobiah arose and washed him and clad him in cere-
ments and brought him to earth. And worthless men saw him and caught
him and brought him before the judge and said: "Lord judge! This Jew
has transgressed the king's commands and buried one of his people." And
the judge ordered him to be hanged because he had disobeyed, all the Jews
to bring fear and awe because he had broken the king's command and his

law. So they led him out of the city to hang him on a tree they prepared, yet when they approached it they all grew blind, great and small, and nobody there could see him at all.

So Tobiah slipped away from them and returned to his home and summoned all his friends and kin who were mourning because of what happened to him, and told them what had befallen and the kindness of God. And he said to them: "Give thanks to the Lord for He is good and forever His mercy endures, and there is no other God who keeps watch, be assured, and blessed be His glorious Name, who wishes His servants cured." Now when the king came to the city, they told him all that befell with the Jew whom they had wished to hang. And the king trembled greatly and in his heart he felt many a pang, and he ordered the word to be spread in his land that any who touched a Jew's body or goods or belongings, you see, was as good as striking the royal eye, and any who injured them would be hanged from the tree, no matter how noble or wise he might be, and would certainly die. And he ordered the Jews to bury their dead with honor and took and held them in high esteem all the days of his life, while all those wicked people of strife saw no brightness or light for the rest of their days.

Now one day that pious man was lying on his couch, and there was a swallow's nest in the house. He opened his eyes to look at the nest, and the swallow's mutings fell in his eyes and he could no longer see, for his eyes were covered and as white as could be. Now all that he and his wife had was one single son, and he summoned him and to speak he began and this he said: "My son, when I was engaged in trade, I used to wander from land to land and from state to state, and once I traveled to the Indian strand where I trafficked and earned a very great sum. But because I feared the roads and the seas I left my wealth in the hands of a good faithful man whose name is Bestintheland. And now my son, listen to me and go and hire me a caravaneer who knows the way to the land of India, and I shall send you with him to the faithful friend with whom I left my silver and gold, and I know that when he sees you, my son, and my handwriting comes to behold, recording what was between him and me, he will give you all my wealth, you will see, for he is faithful and my loving friend, and will take pity on me again when he hears of my sickness and pain."

So the boy went to the place where the hired men were and found a certain man who knew the whole land of India and all its roads and ways and countries and places. And he brought him to his father and said to him: "See, I have found this man who knows the whole of India and all its roads as he knows this city and the way for anyone who comes and who goes." And the righteous Tobiah said to him: "Do you know a certain city in the land of India which is called Tubat?" And he answered: "Good sir, I know it and dwelt there for two full years, and a great city it is with sages that have no fear." Then he said to him: "What shall I give you to go there with my son?" And he answered, "Fifty gold pieces." Then the pious man said: "I shall give them to you gladly and in all good cheer." And he wrote his letter to his faithful friend and in it he set the appointed sign. Then he embraced his son and kissed him and said: "Go now in peace and the Lord of my fathers preserve me till you return."

So off the young fellow went with the hired man till they came to the city of Tubat and brought him to the faithful friend whose name was Bestintheland, and the young fellow said to him: "Good sir, are you the faithful man whose name is Bestintheland?" And he answered him: "Why do you ask my name?" And the young fellow said: "My father Tobiah of the tribe of Dan sent me to you, and he seeks your weal and asks how things are with you and all those with whom you have whatever to do." And he gave him his father's letter, and when the man saw the letter and the signs therein, he ran his eyes over them and believed that the lad was the son of his friend and embraced him and kissed him and gave him to eat of the finest and best and asked: "Is all well with my worthy and faithful friend?" "All is well," said he. And the man rejoiced with his son and attendant, and his fragrant love was like a fine scent, and he said to him: "My son, spend a full month with me and I shall enjoy having you and your words wise and witty." But he answered him: "Good sir, let me go and return to my place and my land, for that is my father's wish and also my own as you may well understand. For since I left that old man, my sire, my heart is full of a fear that is dire. For my father has no child excepting for me, therefore with God's aid I must go home speedily." Then the faithful friend satisfied all his desire, and gave him the wealth that was earned by his sire, as well as many more garments and gifts and other such things. And he gave him two youths to go and to serve him, and let him depart in gladness with many a hymn.

Now on the way they proceeded along the seashore, and the waves rose because of a wind stern and sore that flung a fish before them upon the dry land. Then the hired man swiftly took it and cut the belly open and took out its liver and gall and the young fellow said to him: "Upon your soul! Why did you leave the rest and just take those parts?" And he answered: "Know that these two have a value most rare, for they can be made into remedies that are good anywhere. For wherever this liver is burned to a smoke, no mischievous demon will ever dare to come in, and the dwellers will always be safe and sound. As for the gall, if a blind man rubs it on his eyes, they will open so that he can begin to see." Then the young fellow entreated him to give them to him, and he did so, and he bound them in the end of his robe.

So the young fellow gladly came home where he found his father quiet and sick, and he rejoiced with his son and the wealth he had won. And his father said to him: "Go with this hired man to the banker and give him a hundred gold pieces and more if he desires, and pay him whatever he wishes!" So the young fellow went with the man but looked away a moment and no longer saw him, and he searched for him all over the town but he was not to be found. Then he went to his father and said: "I went with the man but when I looked back, he was no longer there, and I have sought him throughout the city but could not find him anywhere." Then his father told him: "My son, know that God sent him to us for an aid and a sign, for he was really Elijah, the godly and fine."

Then the young fellow told him of the liver and gall and set them before in filial wise, and rubbed the gall on his eyes, and God opened them then and there, and he began to look again and to see and to stare. Then he said to his son: "My son! Since the Lord has led you in the true way and has not deprived you of anything and has delivered you from any evil sending, and hearkened to our voice and restored you to us in peace—now hearken to me and do a kindness and fulfill a great commandment and take my brother's daughter to wife, for she sees all her friends wedded, while she feels nothing but shame in her life."

Now with regard to this maid, there was a wonder to make any person afraid, for she had been wedded to three men in turn, yet she was a wonder among women-born, for any who lay by her was found dead on his bed in the morn. And the young man said: "Father, tell me how I can draw near to her when I fear that the bed is my bier, when her three husbands have all of them perished?" Then he said to him: "Know for a truth, my dear son, it must be a mischievous demon that slew them one by one and took their souls from them. Now take the liver the man gave you and burn it all over the house as he said, and trust in the Lord and you will not be dead!"

So the young fellow took his soul in his hand and did not reject his father's command but took the girl to be his wife, for her indeed he did love. But at night he burned the fish liver all through the house within and without, and also his bed and its cover and their clothes, and the girl entered the room and he followed her.

Now his God-fearing old father wept before the Lord and did pray, while the heart within him throbbed and it quivered away, but the young fellow lay until the light of the day. And when they all arose in the morn, they found him standing happy and gay without any ailing or ache or disease. And both of them lived without fear and dread and spent their days well and their years in ease.

26
The Story of Susanna

True to his conception of Jewish tradition, Micha Joseph bin Gorion (Ber-dyczewski) included specifically a Samaritan rather than any other version of this popular tale. The earliest version of the story appears in the apocry-phal Book of Daniel. Revolving about the youth of Daniel, it belongs to the "clever child" theme, which in Jewish tradition has most commonly King Solomon as a hero. The story was popular in the talmudic-midrashic and medieval Jewish literary traditions, and has enjoyed visual, musical, and literary treatments in Europe since the Middle Ages. Source: E.N. Adler and M. Seligsohn, eds. and trans., Une novelle chronique Samari-taine, pp. 42–44.

Amram the High Priest had a daughter of beautiful shape and ap-pearance, who was wise at heart, and she wrote the Torah in her own hand and could explain it well. Now in those days there were two men who used to come to the House of God on Mount Gerizim because of a vow they had made, and they persisted in this vow for five and twenty years. Now the aforementioned daughter of Amram the Priest wished to be a Nazirite woman at the House of God on Mount Gerizim, and her father built her a house there. And she went up the mountain where she dwelt alone in Nazirite fashion in her house. And after all these things hap-pened the aforesaid two men went up on the roof to read the Holy Torah by the light of the moon, and they called to the daughter of Rabbi Amram to go up with them. So she went up on the roof.

Now when they saw the resplendent beauty of her face on the roof, they felt a desire for her and said to her: "Lie with us!" But she refused; so they seized her. Then she said to them: "Let me be while I go to my house and change my clothes and put on better clothes that I have there, and I shall soon come back to you, and then you can do to me whatever you see fit." And they rejoiced at her words and answered her: "Go and do that." So she went down from the roof and entered her house and closed the door behind her and prostrated herself to the ground and said: "O

Lord, if indeed I find favor in Your eyes, I pray You deliver me from these two men whose evil instincts are so great that they have forgotten Your commandments." And God gave ear to her.

Now the two men saw that the daughter of Rabbi Amram would not return, so they went down from the roof to enter her house and lie with her, but they failed to find the entrance to the house. So when the morning star arose, they went down from the mountain and entered the city of Shechem and gave evidence against her before her father, saying that they had found a stranger with her. And Rabbi Amram made a trial about this matter, but their wickedness was revealed before all the townsfolk. And after that they admitted at the place of the trial that they had brought false witness against her. Then Rabbi Amram ordered and they were burned with fire, as the Lord had said through His servant Moses in the Holy Torah: "And, behold, if the witness is a false witness, if he has testified falsely against his brother, then you shall do to him as he schemed to do to his brother!"

27
Zerubbabel and King Darius

In Jewish tradition there are three basic interrelated versions of this tale. It first appeared in the apocryphal I Esdras, dated probably from the second or third century B.C.E.; later it was reported by Josephus in his Jewish Antiquities; and finally it appeared in the tenth century popular rendition of Josephus's book, known as Josippon, which is the source of the present text. Although the tale reflects the social life and values in the court of the Persian kings, the story and its riddles are known in the folk-narrative traditions of many peoples. Source: J. H. Breithaupt, ed., Josippon, pp. 45–46.

Zerubbabel was a capable and successful man, wise and understanding and full of the spirit of comprehension, for Daniel had rested his hands upon him. He found favor in the eyes of the king, who loved him as much as he had loved Daniel and set him over all the nobles and made him the head of the two generals of the army who were the king's guard. In due course all the nobles gathered together to appear before the king after their fashion, and the king said to them: "Have you seen anywhere in the land a man like this Zerubbabel who is wise and understanding after the fashion of Daniel?" And they said: "The words of the king are true."

Now at noon the king used to lie down after his meal and sleep on his bed. The two guards would take up their posts as required, and Zerubbabel was with them and in charge of them. They stood round the king at attention, waiting till he awakened, but this time the king slept heavily because he was drunk with wine. The three young men grew weary of standing and said to one another: "Let us test one another with wise and riddling questions, each one according to his own cunning, and then we shall write our questions in a book and set it under the king's head, and when he wakes up and sees the scroll, he will understand what we were doing. And if any man has his words appear wiser than those of the other two, and his question preferable to the others, let him be second to the king, both in his throne seat and in the chariot, and also in coming and going before the great king; and let all the dishes at his table be of gold, and let there be a gold rein for his horse, and the diadem of the king's chief counselor be on his head, and let him receive that gift of office from the king; and let the king give him whatever he asks, and let him be the king's friend and companion." "Be it so," said they all, and they drew up a covenant and gave it proper form according to the laws of the Medes and Persians that cannot be altered. So they brought the scribe's inkhorn and the scroll; and they cast lots for all three of them and the lot fell on one, and he wrote: "There is none so mighty in the world as the king." And the second wrote: "There is none so mighty on earth as wine." But the third, who was Zerubbabel, wrote: "There is nothing in the world so mighty as woman."

When they finished writing their themes, they placed the scroll at the king's head; and meanwhile, the king was lying awake but with closed eyes, listening to their whispered conversation. When they placed the scroll under the pillows at his head, he rubbed his eyes with his hands and tumbled about at his head and found the scroll that the three young men had written. He opened it and read it but said nothing until all the viceroys and the officials and the satraps and the heads of the cities and states had arrived. Then he summoned the three young men and said: "Let each of you take his book and theme and explain the reasons for your maxims. And as for me, I shall take the one who is best and clearest of you three and carry out all that was written in your agreement and honor him and raise him high."

Then the first approached and read his sentence and said: "Let the king and the princes hearken to my words: There is none so mighty on earth as the king!" And the second approached and said: "There is nothing so mighty on earth as wine!" And the third, who was Zerubbabel, said: "There is nothing so mighty on earth as woman!" And the king and the princes said: "We have heard your themes. Now give your reasons and we shall listen to them."

Then the first explained: "By permission of my lord the king and you mighty princes and nobles, surely you know the king's strength and the might of his reign over the land and sea and islands and over all the peoples and the languages, with power to put to death or permit to live. If he orders them to send forth an army, they will all set out and not turn away even though they advance to death. If he orders walls to be destroyed, they are destroyed. If people plow and sow and harvest the yield of the earth, they set aside the king's measure before they eat of the crop. For they fear the king, and all of them tremble and are overawed by him, since he is lord and master over them all, and none of them may turn against his word or his commandment. Therefore my words are true and none on earth is as mighty as the king." And all those present were struck by his statement.

Then the second one said: "By permission of my lord and by permission of all you sage princes, it is true that you all know the might of the king and the power of his government, that he holds sway and rules over the world and he is feared by all mankind who stand in awe of him, as you have heard with your own ears. And yet wine is mightier than the king. For great and true though the might and valor of the king may be, yet when he drinks, the wine rules over him and will divert his heart to other matters, to sing and chant and dance and even to beseem himself foolishly. For the wine changes his heart and leads him to drive the near ones away and bring the distant near, to slay the loved ones and honor strangers, and to show no respect for father or mother or kindred. Surely you know that this is how strong wine is. If a man drinks it, an ignoramus will utter slander, a silent man will shout and reveal secrets, and things that should be kept private he will declare, while unhappy people grow glad. Mortal men who sorrow and are sad need but to drink a bit, and they will rejoice and be happy, while worried men will burst into melody, and those who are beaten with the rope's end before being led to death need but to drink of wine and they will laugh. A drunkard will flash a sword against his friend, and shamefaced people grow impudent. Yet when the wine departs from within them, they forget all that they have done and no longer comprehend or remember. Once the wine has departed from them, they say: 'We have done nothing.' So who can do other than believe, after all, that wine is stronger than the king when it can rule over him? For it can prevent a man's legs from walking and cause his eyes to see what is not there while his mouth will utter things he never learned. So surely you must agree that wine is stronger than the king if it can achieve all this." And the listeners all gaped and wondered.

Then the king called on Zerubbabel, who was the third, and said to him: "You too come and explain the reason for your statement as your friends have done with theirs." And he responded: "I shall tell you." Then he began: "Give ear and hearken to my words, O king and princes, nobles and satraps, and all you people who stand by.

"It is true that the king is mightier and greater than all, and that the wine can weaken the might of the king when it rules over him, so there can be no denying the power of the king or the might of the wine. And yet woman is stronger than wine and king and all the plantings of the vineyard from which the wine is pressed. And how can woman not be stronger than the king?

"For it is she who has given birth to the king and has suckled him and nursed him in her bosom and brought him up and fed him and dressed him and washed his excrement from off him, and she has punished him and ruled over him as a mother rules over the child of her womb, and he has been in awe of her and has trembled at her rebuke, since sometimes she may beat him and sometimes she may scold him. If she took the rod to him, he fled away from her into the open, because he feared her, until such time as the boy grows up and becomes a young man. Yet he does not forget his awe of her and nothing can change the honor in which he holds her, and he shows his respect for her at all times as a son should to his parent.

"Now thereafter, let him but look around and see a beautiful woman, and he will be filled with desire at her beauty and long for her, and his soul will cleave to hers and his heart inclines toward her, nor would he exchange his love for any wealth. While as for his mother who bore him and his father who begot him, he will abandon his father and mother and betray them because of his love of the beautiful woman and her comeliness. Indeed, many have been beguiled by love of woman and her beauty, and many have grown foolish and mad on her account. Many sages have been trapped in her net, and wise men taken in her trap. She can rouse hatred between brothers and separate those who love one another, so that one will betray the other.

"Surely you know that if a woman beautiful to behold passes before a man, no matter how well arrayed he may be, his eyes will follow her and her beauteous appearance, because his heart inclines toward her. Likewise she needs but to say a word, and he will abandon all that he has, with his mouth open as he stares at her, because she has led him and drawn his heart toward her.

"Who is there that does not believe this and would not admit the power and might of women? Tell it now for yourselves: For whom do you toil to weariness? And why do you rob and steal and gather up much wealth? Is it not for women and to purchase them anything they desire, gold and silver and jewels and every precious thing set in gold, and myrrh and aloes and all other kind of fragrance and balsam and fine unguent and pleasant incense. Why, you prepare all these only for women. And if a man breaks away and takes to waylaying in the wildernesses or the mountains or the forests or to piracy on the seas, and fights and murders and pillages and despoils and snatches what he can and sheds blood for his own profit, to whom does he bring the spoils and the booty that he has taken? Surely he brings it all to the woman.

"Indeed, I have seen the king seated on his throne wearing his crown of glory, with Aponiah his concubine, daughter of Abshiush the Macedonian, sitting opposite him, and I have seen her stretch out her hand and take the royal crown from his head and place it on her own; and the king smiled at her. When she grew angry, the king could not direct her or calm her or make an end to her anger. So who does not believe that woman is mightier than all? For a woman brought Samson's strength to naught, and as for David, he was misled, and women misled and seduced Solomon. Many are those she has entrapped, and those she has slain are beyond all telling, for numerous and plentiful are her victims.

"And this, too, you should learn to know. If a man rules over the whole world and even though its inhabitants are numberless beyond counting, they will all tremble and fear because he rules over them all. And a lord and king may rule over every woman; but once her desire is set on him, he will not be able to subdue her and rule over her. And so it was with Adam, father of all who dwell on earth. His wife inclined him to transgress the word of God, and so death was decreed for him and his offspring after him.

"Now I have assessed the mightiness of woman, and there are none who will not believe this, since it has not been unknown from the beginning of the world until its end, and I speak the truth. And now let me inform the king, and all you who listen, that the king who rules over the earth is vanity and mist, and the wine that rules over the king is likewise vanity and mist, and the woman is vanity and mist with all her powers and capacity as the ruler of all three. For it is Truth that rules and holds sway over all things in heaven and on earth, in the seas and the deeps; Truth will hold its own before men and God. For where there is Truth, no falsehood can stand, and it is on truth that heaven and earth are established, and Truth is the Lord our God forever."

Then all those present there said to the king: "It is Truth." And the king said to Zerubbabel: "Come to me." So he approached, and the king held out his hand and drew Zerubbabel to him and embraced him and kissed him in the presence of all the people standing there and said: "Blessed is the Lord God of Zerubbabel, who set the spirit of truth in him, for the God of Truth is He and establishes His throne on truth, and everything else is vanity." And all the princes and the deputies and the satraps and all the people responded: "Indeed, Truth is greater than all, and nothing in the world can stand before it, for it rules over heaven and earth and everything depends upon it, and Truth is the God of Zerubbabel, who set the spirit of truth in his mouth, to glorify and praise the truth before God and king and man."

Then the king ordered that the writ of agreement that had been written on a scroll by the three should be carried out, and he fulfilled it all to Zerubbabel; for he found more favor in the eyes of the king and the princes than his two friends. And the king said to him: "Ask whatever you have in mind according to what is written in the scroll, and I shall do it for you, even half of the kingdom and I shall give it to you."

But Zerubbabel answered the king: "Let my lord the king but remember the vow which you and King Cyrus vowed to the God of heaven, to build His House and restore His holy vessels to their place with the exiled people of the God of heaven, sending them in peace to serve Him in His Temple in which His Name is called and wherein He caused His presence to rest. In order that they may pray there unto the Great God, God of heaven, for the king and his kingdom, for the fulfillment of the vow that was vowed to the God of heaven should not be delayed."

Then the king gave his order, and the king's scribes swiftly wrote down all that Zerubbabel requested of the king concerning the rebuilding of the ruins of Jerusalem. And King Darius sent unto Cyrus, king of Persia, in order that he might act together in this matter, and pay his debt and reestablish the House of the Lord which is in Jerusalem.

In the Days of the Second Temple

28
ALEXANDER IN JERUSALEM

Alexander the Great (356–323 B.C.E.) conquered Palestine in the summer of 332 B.C.E., after a seven-month siege of Tyre, and began the historical encounter between Jewish and Hellenistic cultures. While his conquests in the area and his military itinerary are described in detail by Greek and Roman historians, his advances toward Jerusalem appear in the historical literature only in Josephus's Jewish Antiquities. *Because of this discrepancy between historical testimonies, the historical core and the symbolic meaning of the present story have been a subject of scholarly debate. The supernatural theme of the legend occurs in several tales about Alexander and is not specific to the story of his conquest of Jerusalem. Source: D. Günzberg and A. Kahana, eds.,* Josippon, *pp. 60–63.*

Now when the people of Macedonia rose against the kingdom of Persia, Alexander departed from Macedonia with a vast host and came to make war against Darius. He smote all the peoples who were in alliance with Darius including the land of Egypt and the land of Edom. Then he came to the seashore where he smote Acre and Ashkelon and Gaza and prepared to go up against Jerusalem and smite her, because she was in alliance with Darius.

So he set out from Gaza with all his host, advancing until he came to some resting place on the road where he encamped together with all his army. That night as he lay on his bed in the tent, he saw a man standing at his head garbed in white linen and an unsheathed sword in his hand. The sword, furthermore, looked like the lightning that flashes on a rainy day; and he raised his sword over the king's head. The king was greatly alarmed and said to him: "My lord, why should you smite your slave?" And the man answered: "Because God sent me to subdue great kings and peoples a-many before you, for I am the angel that goes ahead of you in order to aid you. Now I would have you know that you will most assuredly perish because your heart has led you to go up to Jerusalem and do evil to the priests of the Lord and His people."

But the king said: "I pray you, bear with the transgression of your servant! I entreat you, my lord, if it seems evil in your eyes, I shall turn about." But the man answered: "Have no fear, for I respect you and bear with you, go your way to Jerusalem! When you come to the gateway of Jerusalem, you will see a man garbed in white like me, and he will have precisely my appearance and form. Fall to the ground and prostrate yourself before him, and do whatever he may tell you, and do not transgress his words, otherwise you will assuredly perish on that day."

So the king rose and proceeded to Jerusalem as he had planned but in a state of fury. Yet when he approached Jerusalem with his hosts, the priest and all the people feared greatly, and they cried out unto the Lord and proclaimed a fast. After the fast the Jews went out to meet him and make entreaty before him that he should not destroy the city.

So they went forth from the gateway, all the people and the priests, with Hananiah the High Priest advancing at their head garbed in white linen. As soon as King Alexander saw the priest, he swiftly descended from his vehicle and fell on his face, prostrating himself before the priest. All the kings who served Alexander were astounded and annoyed at this and said to him: "Why are you prostrating yourself to a man who has no power for waging war?" And the king answered his royal servants: "Do not be surprised or angered at this. For the angel who goes before me to aid me among all the peoples has the likeness and appearance of this man to whom I have just prostrated myself."

After this the priest and King Alexander came to the Temple of our God. There the priest showed him the Temple building and the courtyards of the Temple and its treasures and halls and the place of the Holy of Holies and the place of the altar and the place of the burnt offering. And the king said: "Blessed is the Lord God of Israel, God of this House, and happy are you His attendants who serve in His presence at this place! Now I shall make myself a memorial and give much gold to craftsmen, so that they shall construct my image and erect it between the Holy of Holies and this building, so that my statue may be a memorial in the House of the great God."

But the priest said to the king: "As for the gold which you so generously offer, give it for the sustenance of the priests of our God and of His people who come to prostrate themselves in this House, and I shall make you here a memorial that is far better than the one you propose."

"And what can that memorial be?" asked the king. And the priest answered him: "Your memorial will be that all the children of the priests who will be born during this year in the whole of Judah and Jerusalem will be given your name Alexander, and that will be a memory of you when they come to perform the service of our God in this House. For in the House of our God you are not permitted to accept any statue or picture." And the king was astonished at the priest's words, but they seemed fit and proper to him. So he did so and gave the gold to the priests.

Then the king requested the priest to question God on his account whether he should go to war against Darius or refrain? And the priest said to him: "Go, for he will certainly be given into your hands." And he brought the Book of Daniel before him and showed him what was written there regarding the ram with the horns that was victorious in all directions, and the he-goat that charged at the ram and trampled upon him (Dan. 8). Then the priest said to him: "You are that he-goat and Darius is the ram, and you will trample him to the ground and take his dominion from him." So the priest strengthened the king's heart, and Alexander departed from Jerusalem rejoicing and cheerful, and went on to go to war against Darius.

29
A FAIR JUDGMENT

This tale was extremely popular in the talmudic-midrashic literature, appearing in many sources. It is possible to attribute its popularity to the anti-Hellenistic—and, by extension, any other anti-foreign government— tendencies that it conveys. Source: I. Lévi, "Sefer Alexandros Mokedon," p. 149.

King Alexander set out across the Mountains of Darkness led by a certain pearl which gave light before him. Now the king (of those lands) came to meet him and honored him greatly and did whatever he desired for him. One day as the two kings sat together with their crowns on their heads, two men appeared before the king. And one of them said to him: "By your leave, my lord, I purchased a certain piece of land from this man and wished to erect a building on it. When I began digging, I found a very great treasure hidden there. So I said to him: 'Take you the treasure because I only purchased the land from you, but the treasure I did not buy.'"

Then the other said to the king: "By your leave, my lord, when I sold my land I sold him all that was to be found therein from the nethermost deeps to the heights of the sky. And just as he does not wish to rob or steal, so I too do not wish to rob or steal."

Then the king said to one of them: "Have you a son?" "Yes, my lord," said he. And he asked the other: "Have you a daughter?" And he answered: "Yes, my lord."

Then the king said: "Give your son to his daughter, and give the whole treasure to both of them!" And so they did.

Alexander laughed, for it seemed strange to him. "Why are you laughing?" the king asked him. "Have I not judged well? Have I not done well?" Then Alexander answered: "You have judged well and done well. But in my kingdom I would not have judged in that way." "And how would you have judged?" asked the king; and Alexander said: "If it had happened in my kingdom, the king would have slain them both and taken all the money."

Then the king of those lands said to him in astonishment: "Does the sun shine in your kingdom?" "Yes," said he. And the king asked again: "Do you have cattle and sheep and goats in your kingdom?" "Yes," said he. Then the king said to him: "It is only because of the cattle that the people live and find sustenance." Just as it is written: "Man and beast the Lord will aid" (Ps. 36:7).

30
Tribute from Eden

This story, known as Iter ad Paradisum, *was very popular in the medieval "Romance of Alexander." Scholars consider the Jewish version that appeared in the Babylonian Talmud* Tamid *32b to be the earliest known rendition of the tale. Source: I. Lévi, "Sefer Alexandros Mokedon," pp. 155–156.*

"Fetch me my own statue and image," said Alexander. And the king swore by it that he would not return until he reached a place where it is impossible to pass either to the right or to the left and where he would not find any way of continuing. And he set out with all his host and crossed the river and came to a great gateway that was thirty ells high. The king was astonished at this height and he raised his eyes and saw letters engraved upon the gateway. Then he summoned Menahem the Scribe, who read the letters. And this is what was written: "Lift up your heads, O you gates, and be raised on high, you portals of the world, and let the King of Glory enter" (Ps. 24:7).

From there the king went on and passed amid the mountains with all his host for six whole months during which the mountain road did not end. At the end of the six months the mountains ceased, and there were no mountains left but only a plain. Upon this plain there was a most beautiful and lofty gateway the height of which was beyond human vision. Large and exceedingly beautiful letters were written on the gateway and Menahem read the letters, and this is what was written: "This is the gateway to the Lord—the righteous shall enter through it" (Ps. 118:20). "Clearly," said the king, "this is the Garden of Eden." And he shouted aloft: "Who is appointed over this gateway?"

Then a voice came back to him: "This is the gateway of the Garden of Eden, and no uncircumcised person may come hither!" Now that self-same night Alexander circumcised himself, and his physicians came and healed him at once with the best of herbs. Nothing was known to his camp, for the king commanded the physicians not to report it.

Next morning the king called to the keepers of the gate: "Give me tribute, and I shall go my way." They gave him a little box and in it was what seemed to be a piece of flesh and an eye. The king stretched out his hand to raise it from the ground but could not. Then he shouted: "What have you given me?" And they answered: "This is a single eye." "Why do I need it?" said he, and they answered: "Let it be a sign for you that your eye will never be sated with riches and likewise your spirit will never be sufficed with your wanderings on earth." "And what shall I do," asked Alexander, "in order to be able to lift it from the ground?" And they said: "Place a little earth on the eye and you will control it as you desire. And let that be a sign to you that your eye will not be sated with riches until you return to the dust from which you were taken."

The king did so, placing earth on the eye, and raised it from the ground. He placed it in his treasure house with all his most precious belongings to serve him as a sign and memorial that he had demanded tribute from Eden.

31
THE STORY OF JUDITH

This story is a medieval rendition of the apocryphal Book of Judith, presenting an amalgamate of accounts, figures, and dates. In the apocryphal book, Judith saves the Jews of the fictional city Bethulia, which is under siege, surrounded by King Nebuchadnezzar's Assyrian troops commanded by Holofernes. In the present version she saves the people of Jerusalem itself from the menacing forces of King Seleucus. The reference is apparently to Seleucus IV, who ruled over the Seleucid Empire between 187 and 175 B.C.E. According to an account that combines historical narration with supernatural explanation that appears in the Second Book of Maccabees chapter 3, Seleucus IV sent his minister Heliodorus to confiscate the Temple treasury. An awesome vision frightened Heliodorus and prevented him from accomplishing his mission. Later, on September 3, 175 B.C.E., Seleucus IV died or was murdered in a plot that might have involved Heliodorus. The date does not correspond to the Hebrew date of eighteenth of Adar that is mentioned in the text. In fact this date has no significance in the Jewish calendar; yet it is possible that narrators or scribes have confused it with the thirteenth of Adar, on which Jews commemorated the defeat of Nicanor, the Syrian officer defeated by Judah Maccabee in his last victory in 161 B.C.E. While there is no commemoration of the apocryphal Judith in the Jewish calendar, in folk tradition she is often associated with the holiday of Hanukkah. Source: M. Gaster, The Exempla of the Rabbis, No. 251, pp. 166–167.

O ur rabbis taught: The eighteenth day of Adar is the day when Seleucus went up.

As we learn: When he invested Jerusalem, Israel put on sackcloth and fasted. Now there was an exceedingly beautiful woman there named Judith daughter of Ahitub, and she used to prostrate herself before the Holy and Blessed One daily in sackcloth and ashes. The Holy and Blessed One put it into her heart to perform a miracle through her. She went to the keepers of the gate and said to them: "Open for me, since a miracle may possibly be done through me." "Maybe you are going over to the other side?" said they to her. "Heaven forbid!" she answered. So they opened before her.

Then she and her maidservant went to the camp of Seleucus and said to them: "I have a secret matter for the king." They went and told the king: "A beautiful maiden has come from Jerusalem, saying: 'I have a secret matter for the king.'" "Let her in," said he to them.

She came before the king and bowed low before him. Said the king to her: "What do you want?" And she answered him: "My lord king, I belong to a large family in Jerusalem, and my brothers' and father's household are kings and high priests. Now of you I heard them saying that the time has already come for this city to fall into your hands. Therefore I wish to find favor with you in advance."

When the king saw her beauty and heard her words, she found favor in his eyes. He rejoiced about the tidings she brought him and commanded his servants to prepare him a great feast. While they were engaged with this, he ordered all the royal retinue to withdraw from him and stayed alone with that maiden and demanded something improper of her. But she answered: "Indeed, my lord king, I have come here only for this single purpose. But at this present hour it is impossible, for I am in my courses, and only tonight do I bathe. But I wish your majesty to proclaim: If anybody sees a woman and her maidservant proceeding to the spring by night, let him not touch them. And when that woman returns, then she will be in the king's hands, and he may do with her whatever he sees fit."

The wicked fellow did so, and that night he summoned all the royal kin and his princes and servants and they shared in that feast with great joy and became drunk with wine. When the royal retinue saw that the king's head was drooping, they said: "Let us go out, for he wishes to be alone with the Hebrew woman." So out they went, and the king remained with the maiden and her servant. Then they took the sword and cut off his head and took it and went out. When they went out, the sentries noticed them but said to one another: "No man may touch these, for that was the king's order."

They went out and came to Jerusalem at midnight and said to the guards: "Open to us, for the miracle has already happened." "Are you not satisfied with having done wrong," said the gatekeepers to her, "but you also wish to betray the blood of Israel!" She swore to them, but they would not believe her until she showed them the head of that evildoer. Then they believed and opened before her. And they turned that day into a festival.

When the second day began, Israel went forth and raised their hands against those forces and slew away until they annihilated them completely. The others left their horses and their money and fled, and the Children of Israel captured everything.

32
The Daughter of Mattathias

This story does not occur in any of the books of the Maccabees, nor is there any reference to a sister the five sons of Mattathias might have had. The first reference to the tale appears in the chronicle "Seder Olam" ("The Order of the World"), attributed to a sage of the second century C.E. Later the story occurs in the scholium to "Megillat Ta'anit," which dates back to the seventh century C.E. Source: A. Jellinek, ed., Bet ha-Midrasch *6:2–3.*

When the Greeks realized that the Jews were not paying attention to their decrees, they went and imposed a very bitter and ugly law upon them whereby the first night of a bride after her wedding was to be spent with the local ruler. When the Jews heard this, they felt weak and helpless and simply refrained from betrothals. As a result, the Jewish maidens grew to maturity and aged as virgins, thus fulfilling the verse: "Her virgins are melancholy, and for her it is bitter" (Lam. 1:4).

As for the Greeks, they ravaged the virgins of Israel and continued to do so for three years and three months until the incident with the daughter of Mattathias the High Priest who was being married to a Hasmonean named Eleazar.

When her joyous day arrived, they set her in a litter. All the great men of Jewry came to the marriage feast in order to honor Mattathias and the Hasmonean, for there were no greater men in that generation. When they sat down to eat, Hannah, the daughter of Mattathias, rose from her litter and beat her hands together and ripped the purple robes off her and stood naked before all Israel and before her father and her mother and her bridegroom. And when her brothers saw this, they were shamed and looked down at the ground and rent their garments. Then they turned to her with the intent of slaying her.

But she said to them: "Listen now, brothers and dear friends! You feel shamed and jealous of me, because I stand naked yet blameless before good and righteous men, yet you feel no jealousy about handing me over to be ravaged by an alien and a stranger! Surely you ought to learn from Simeon and Levi, the brothers of Dinah. They were but two in number, yet they were jealous on account of their sister and slew the inhabitants of such a great city as Shechem, devoting their souls to the Unity of the Ever-Present One; and the Lord aided them and did not hold them to blame. And now you are five brothers, Judah, John, Jonathan, Simeon, and Eleazar, and more than two hundred youthful priests. Put your trust in the Ever-Present One, and He will aid you, as the Book of Samuel says: 'For there is nothing to hinder the Lord from aiding and saving, whether by much or by little!'" (I Sam. 14:6). Then she burst out weeping and cried: "Lord of the Universe! If You feel no pity for us, take pity on Your great and holy Name by which we are called and avenge us this day."

Then her brothers turned to one another and said: "Come and let us decide what we should do." They took counsel together and decided: "Let us take our sister and lead her to the great king and tell him: Our sister is the daughter of the high priest, and there is no one greater in all Israel than her father. It does not seem fit to us that our sister should spend the night with the governor rather than with the king who is of a standing like our own. Then we shall come together against him and slay him and come out and afterwards begin on his attendants and ministers, and may His Name aid us and make us strong."

And the Holy and Blessed One gave them a great victory, and a voice was heard echoing from the Holy of Holies: "The lads have been victorious in Antioch!"

Thus may the Ever Present bring victory also in these days of ours!

33
THE MOTHER

This is one of the earliest legends of collective martyrology in Jewish tradition, possibly relating to the period of religious persecutions during the reign of Antiochus IV Epiphanes (175–164 B.C.E.). It first appeared in the second and fourth books of Maccabees, and later it became one of the few Maccabean legends that entered the talmudic-midrashic literature. In rabbinic sources the mother's name is Miriam daughter of Tanḥum, but in current folk and literary tradition she is known as Ḥannah, a name that first appeared in a twelfth-century version of the medieval history book Josippon. *Source: Anon., Ḥibbur Maʿasiyyot, No. 2.*

I t is told that Miriam daughter of Tanhum was taken prisoner together with her seven sons; and she was brought before the emperor, who said to the oldest of them: "Worship the idol!" Said he: "I do not reject the Holy and Blessed One who wrote for us: 'I am the Lord your God!'" (Ex. 20:2). They promptly took him out and slew him. Then he summoned the second one and said to him: "Serve the idol!" And he answered: "I do not reject the Lord who wrote for us: 'You shall have no others gods before me!'" (Ex. 20:3). Him they slew as well. He summoned the third and said the same to him; and the young lad answered: "I do not deny the God who wrote for us: 'You shall not bow down to them!'" (Ex. 20:5). They slew him. Then he called the fourth one and said the same thing to him; but he answered: "I do not reject that God who wrote for us: 'You shall not prostrate yourself before any other god!'" (Ex. 34:14). They slew him, too. Then he summoned the fifth and said the same to him; and he answered: "I do not reject the God who wrote for us: 'Hear, O Israel! The Lord our God, the Lord is One!'" (Deut. 6:4). So they slew him. Then he summoned the sixth and said the same to him; and he answered: "I do not reject the God who wrote for us: 'The Lord is God; there is no other!'" (Deut. 4:39). And him they slew as well.

He summoned the seventh and said the same to him. "I shall go and ask my mother," said he. He went and took counsel with his mother, asking her: "What shall I do?" And his mother told him: "My son, do you wish your brothers to sit close to their Creator while you sit outside the confines? Pay no attention to the wicked man and do not differ from your brothers!" Then he returned to the emperor; and the emperor asked him: "What are you going to do?" He answered: "I do not deny the God who wrote for us: 'You have affirmed this day that the Lord is your God!'" (Deut. 26:17). Then the emperor said to him: "I am going to fling my ring to you, and it has an image on it. And you kneel down and pick it up, so that people should say that you have done what I ordered." "Alas for you, emperor," said the boy, "if that is what your honor means to you, how much more does the honor of the Holy and Blessed One mean to me who am required to honor him!" Then they took him out at once and slew him.

Then the woman said to him: "If it pleases you, permit me to kiss my sons." And they did so. And she said to her slain children: "Tell your father Abraham that he should not be proud of the one son whom he bound on the altar to be offered to heaven. For I have seven sons who have all been offered up and slain!" After that she flung herself from the roof and perished. And a heavenly voice was heard, saying: "Blissful is the mother of sons!" (Ps. 113:9).

And thus all Israel are admonished to fear the Holy and Blessed One so that their share will be with the righteous in Paradise.

34
PAULINA, OR THE DEED OF SHAME IN THE TEMPLE

In Josephus's Jewish Antiquities *this story occurs immediately after the Testimonium Flavianum, in which Josephus recounts the crucifixion of Jesus, and hence the story could be viewed as an indirect narrative parody of the Christian claim for the divine origin of Jesus. Josephus relates the incident to the cult of Isis, rather than Osiris as in the present version. Historically, the narrative has a dual significance: first it offers an account of the Isis and Anubis cults in the Graeco-Roman world, and second, as Josephus employs it, the tale suggests the cause for Tiberius's expulsion of the Jews and the Egyptians from Rome in 19 C.E. Current scholarship doubts the historicity of the Paulina incident and tends to view the story as a mock narrative romance. Source: D. Günzberg and A. Kahana, eds.,* Josippon, *pp. 358–361.*

Now I shall relate one of the shameful incidents which occurred in the days of the Emperor Tiberius. In his time there was a most beautiful and comely woman in Rome, a woman who was full of charm and grace so that all who saw her would abandon their work and stand looking after her. Many desired to lie with her but could not, because she was chaste and wedded. Her name was Paulina. Now this woman constantly used to go to her house of prayer. And a certain young man named Mundus saw her; he was one of the cavalry officers of the Emperor Tiberius. His love flamed up within him like fire because of the woman's beauty, and he asked her to lie with him for a sum of twenty thousand gold drachmas. But the woman refused to listen to him and revealed the secret to her husband.

When Mundus saw that she would not listen to him, he went to the priest who was in charge of that temple in Rome in those days. In that temple there were two images, one called Osiris and the other Anubis, Anubis being held more important than Osiris in the opinion of the people. So this young fellow went to the priest and gave him a thousand gold drachmas to entice and mislead her and bring her to the temple. The priest in turn went and said this to the woman: "Thus says Anubis the great god: Come to my temple and lie before my altar so that when I rise at night, I may converse with you in secret, since because of my love for you I shall make you my prophetess." The woman rejoiced very much and told her husband, who said to her: "Who can withhold what the gods request?" So the woman went to the temple, and her maidens prepared her a most sumptuous bed before the altar, and she lay down there. After that the maidens left the temple by order of the priest.

As she lay there, the young fellow in the guise of Anubis rose from behind the altar and went beneath her covers and fell upon her with an insatiable kiss. The woman woke up and asked him: "Who are you?" And he answered: "I, Anubis, have come because I love you." Then the woman said: "If you are a god, why should you desire a woman? And can a god have commerce with a woman?" To which the young fellow answered: "With a beautiful woman like you he can, for another woman accepted a god upon her and she bore him Jove, who is a god like me, while many other women have given birth to many gods." The woman, believing this, said: "I am the happiest of womankind to have a god loving me!" Therefore the woman did not withhold that which the young man desired, and he lay with her until the morning.

In the morning she went to her home exceedingly happy and told her husband all that had befallen her in the temple. He too rejoiced exceedingly, saying: "Happy are we that the god has visited us!" And all the other women declared her praises, telling her: "Happy are you, Paulina, for having companied with the god!"

But after all this Mundus went and told Paulina: "Happy are you for having companied with Anubis the great god. Now learn from what you have done, and as you did not refuse the god that which he requested, likewise do not refuse the request of any man. And as you were not sparing of your hidden parts with the god, so henceforth do not keep them from man. For the great god gave me what you refused to give me. He gave me all my desire, and also brought you into the temple and gave you to me in order that I should fulfill my desire with you! See, what you did not do willingly at my wish when you could have taken the twenty thousand gold drachmas I brought you, the god has done for me free and without any silver or gold. As for me, when my name was Mundus you did not wish to do what I desired, but when I changed my name to Anubis you did whatever I wished. So learn from that, Paulina, to fulfill all my desires henceforward!"

When the woman heard this, she grieved exceedingly since she had been misused by a man, and went and told her husband. He could say nothing and could not complain about her since she had gone with his approval and he had told her to go to the temple. The emperor also heard of all this and slew the priests and destroyed the temple and sank the images in the River Tiber. The young fellow he did not slay because, said the king, his love enflamed him and his desire overcame him; but he banished him to distant parts.

This shameful deed which was done in Rome in the days of Tiberius Caesar we have now written down; and in his times many more such shameful deeds were done.

35
ABBA GOLISH

This is a rare story in Jewish tradition; it appears in medieval European and Yemenite manuscripts that were discovered only in the nineteenth century. Micha Joseph bin Gorion has proposed that the tale represents a Jewish tradition which is analogous to the Christian narrative of Paul that appears in The Acts of the Apostles Chapter 9. Source: M. Gaster, The Exempla of the Rabbis, No. 131, pp. 84, 90–91.

Rabbi Pinhas related:

It is told that in Damascus there was a temple for idolators wherein there was a *komer* (priest of idols) named Abba Golish who served that idol for many a year. Now it came about that some painful distress befell him, and he cried out to his idol for a long time but to no avail.

After that, he went out by night and said: "Lord of the Universe, hearken unto my prayer and deliver me from my distress!" God heard his prayer at once and he was cured. Then he stole away to Tiberias and became a Jew. And he pursued good deeds and was appointed a charity warden for the poor. But once money came his way, those hands that had been accustomed to grope about in the idol-house groped about in the holy funds. He felt pain in one eye at once and it became blind. Once again he set hands on the dedicated funds, and the second eye grew blind as well.

Now the people of his original home came to Tiberias and saw that he was blind, and they said to him: "Abba Golish! What reason had you to mock at the idol and forsake him? If you had not done so, he would not have exacted this from you." And so said many more and many more.

What did he do? He said to his wife: "Rise and let us go to Damascus." And she took him by the hand and they went.

When they reached the villages near Damascus, people gathered around and said to him: "Here is Abba Golish!" And they said: "The idol treated you properly by blinding your eyes." But he told them: "I have come only to entreat him and make peace with him in the hope that he will open my eyes for me," (but he was laughing at them) until he entered Damascus.

The people of Damascus gathered around and said to him: "Master Abba Golish, what has befallen you?" "What you see," he answered them. Then they said: "Did you think that you could make mock of our idol? Now he has made mock of you as well!" But he laughed at them and said: "I have come to make terms with him in the hope that he will show me his mercy. So now go and gather all the people of the city together."

So they went and gathered by hosts, in and around the idolatrous temple and even on the roofs. When the spot was full, he told his wife to place him on a pillar he knew there. He went and stood thereon and said to them:

"Brothers, men of Damascus! When I was the priest who served this idol, people used to leave pledges with me, but I would betray them. For this idol had neither eyes to see nor ears to hear and demand settlement from me. But now I have gone to that One whose eyes move to and fro over the whole world and from whom no intention is concealed. There my hands wished to grope and take as they were accustomed. Yet scarcely had I done this than He exacted payment of me: for He blinded my eyes."

Now Rabbi Pinhas ha-Cohen bar Hama relates, as also does Rabbi Abbun, in the name of our masters: Even before he came down from the pillar the Holy and Blessed One restored to him the sight of his eyes so that he saw better than ever before, in order to hallow His Name in the world.

And thousands and myriads of the Gentiles were converted through him.

Talmudic Tales

36
THE EARLY DAYS OF HILLEL

Together with Shammai, Hillel the Elder, or Hillel the Babylonian (late first century B.C.E.–early first century C.E.), made up the last of the rabbinical pairs, zugot, that formulated civil and religious regulations. Shemaiah and Avtalyon, his teachers in the story, were the fourth of these pairs (late first century B.C.E.). According to tradition both were descendants of proselytes. There are comparable stories about the childhood or early days of scholars in both Jewish and classical traditions. Source: Rabbi Nissim ben Jacob ben Nissim ibn Shahin, Ḥibbur Yafeh me-ha-Yeshu'ah, p. 17.

Hillel the Elder was poor and needy. From his work he used to earn half a zuz. He sustained himself with half, and the other half he used to pay to the doorkeeper at the entrance to the house of study, so that he would admit him to hear words of Torah and the words of the living God from Shemaiah and Avtalyon.

Now it came to pass one wintry day that he had nothing to give the doorkeeper, who would not admit him to the house of study. So he went up on the roof and placed his head next to the skylight in order to hear words of Torah. Heavy snow fell upon him all night long and covered him over. But he did not sense it because of his great desire to hear Torah. When evening came he could not move because of the cold, so he lay there all night long.

In the morning Shemaiah and Avtalyon came to the house of study and looked aloft at the skylight through which light always entered, and found that this day was dark and no light reached them at all. So they searched and found Hillel lying as though he was dead. They took off his clothes and clad him in other garments and made a great fire beside him until his spirit returned. From that day forward they gave him permission to enter the house of study without charge. (Another version adds: Because of this incident they dismissed that doorkeeper.)

That is why the sages of blessed memory said: "Why should a man complain that he cannot permit himself to study Torah on account of poverty? If he says: 'I was poor and was too busy because of my poverty and need,' he is told: 'Were you more poverty-stricken than Hillel the Elder?' And to that he will find no answer. And likewise if a wealthy man should say: 'Because of my riches and wealth I had to cease and could not study Torah,' he is told: 'Are you wealthier than Rabbi Eleazar ben Harsom? For his father left him villages and orchards and gardens and ships on the sea, yet he never went to see them. Instead he left everything in the hands of his servants and engaged in Torah all the days of his life!' To that he will find no answer."

37
ELIEZER BEN HYRCANUS

This biographical legend opens the pseudoepigraphical work that is attributed to its hero. Eliezer ben Hyrcanus was a tanna of the second generation (80–110 C.E.). His teacher, Rabbi Johanan ben Zakkai, was a tanna at the end of the Second Temple period and in the years following the destruction of the Temple. The tale dates back to early talmudic-midrashic literature. Source: Pirkei de Rabbi Eliezer, chapters 1 and 2.

I

The tale is told of Rabbi Eliezer ben Hyrcanus. Men were plowing for his father and they plowed on good flat land while he used to plow in hard and stony soil. So he sat and wept. Then his father asked him: "Why are you weeping? Do you grieve because you are plowing the hard soil? Now you will be plowing in the good and easy soil." He sat by the level land and wept. His father asked him again: "Why are you weeping? Do you grieve because you are plowing on level land?" "No," said he. "Then why are you weeping?" Said he, "Because I wish to study Torah." "But," said his father, "you are twenty-eight years old—yet you desire to study Torah? Better take yourself a wife who will bear you children, and you lead them to school!"

Then Rabbi Eliezer spent two Sabbaths in which he ate nothing. At length Elijah, whom it is good to remember, revealed himself to him and said: "Why are you weeping, son of Hyrcanus?" "Because," said he, "I wish to study Torah." "If you wish to study Torah," said Elijah, "go up to Rabban Johanan ben Zakkai in Jerusalem."

So he rose and went to Rabban Johanan ben Zakkai. There he sat to one side and wept. "Why are you weeping?" asked Rabban Johanan. "Because," he answered, "I wish to study Torah." "Whose son are you?" asked Rabban Johanan. But he would not tell him. Then Rabban Johanan asked: "Have you never in all your life learned to recite the *Shema* ('Hear, O Israel') nor the eighteen benedictions nor the blessing after meals?" "No," he answered. Then Rabban Johanan said: "Rise and I shall teach you all three of them."

But he sat and went on weeping. And Rabban Johanan asked him again: "My son, why are you weeping?" And he answered: "Because I wish to study Torah." Then he began to teach him two laws each day of the week; and he would repeat them and recite them together. He spent eight days without eating anything. At length Rabban Johanan ben Zakkai could not bear the smell from his mouth and removed him.

He sat weeping. Once again he asked him: "Why are you weeping, my son?" And he answered: "Because you have moved me away from you as a man moves away a person who is smitten with boils." "My son," answered he, "just as the smell from your mouth came up to me so may the scent of the Laws of the Torah mount from your mouth to heaven!" And he asked him again: "My son, whose son are you?" Then he answered: "I am the son of Hyrcanus." "Why," said he, "you are the son of a great man, yet you have never told me!" And he went on: "By your life, you will eat with me today." But he answered: "I have already eaten where I lodge." "And where do you lodge?" asked he. "With Rabbi Joshua ben Hananiah and Rabbi Jose the Priest," he answered. Then he sent to his hosts and asked them: "Has Eliezer eaten with you today?" "No," they answered. "Yet eight days must have passed since he has eaten anything!" Then Rabbi Joshua ben Hananiah and Rabbi Jose the Priest went and told Rabban Johanan ben Zakkai: "During the past eight days he has eaten nothing."

II

The sons of Hyrcanus said to their father: "Go up to Jerusalem and disinherit your son Eliezer." He went up to Jerusalem to disinherit him, but found that it was a festive day for Rabban Johanan ben Zakkai. All the great men of the land were dining with him: Ben Tzitzit Hakesset and

Nakdimon ben Gurion and Ben Kalba Sabua. They told Rabban Johanan:
"The father of Rabbi Eliezer has come." And he told them: "Make place
for him!" So they made place for him and seated him beside Rabban Johanan.

Then Rabban Johanan turned his eyes on Rabbi Eliezer and said to
him: "Say some single thing to us from the Torah." And he answered:
"Rabbi, permit me to tell you a parable to which the thing can be compared:
It is like a cistern from which you cannot take out more water than you
put in. Precisely so I cannot say more words of Torah than I have received
from you." Then Rabban Johanan answered: "I shall tell you a parable
to which this thing can be compared: To a fountain which flows and from
which water comes and which can give out more water than it receives.
Precisely in that way you can utter more words of Torah than were received
on Mount Sinai." And he said further: "Do you feel ashamed because of
my presence? Well, I shall move away." And he rose and went out of the
room.

So Rabbi Eliezer sat expounding Torah with his face shining like sun-
light, and rays shooting out like the rays of Moses so that no man could
know whether it was day or night. Rabban Johanan went behind him and
kissed him on his head and said: "Abraham, Isaac, and Jacob, you may
be proud and happy that this one came from your loins!"

"To whom did he say that?" asked Hyrcanus. "To your son Eliezer,"
they told them. Then he said: "That is not what he should have said, but
happy am I that this one came forth from *my* loins!" So Rabbi Eliezer sat
expounding, and his father rose to his feet. When he saw his father, he
rose to his feet, startled, and said to him: "Sit down, father, for I cannot
discourse Torah while you are on your feet."

"My son," he answered, "that was not what I came for, but to disinherit
you. Yet now I am here and have seen you and the high esteem of which
you are worthy—it is your brothers whom I disinherit and all my property
I present to you as a gift." "Yet, father," said he, "I am not worth as much
as any one of them. If I had desired land of the Holy and Blessed One,
it was within His power to give it to me, as the Psalms say: 'The earth
is the Lord's and all that it holds, the world and its inhabitants' (24:1).
And if it were silver and gold that I had desired, He would have given
me, as Haggai the Prophet said: 'Mine is the silver and Mine is the gold,
says the Lord of Hosts' (2:8). Yet I desired nothing of the Holy and Blessed
One save Torah alone, as it is written in the Book of Psalms: 'Therefore
all charges regarding all matters I have performed uprightly; and I hate
every false way' (119:128)."

38
THE WIFE OF RABBI AKIBA

Rabbi Akiba (Akiva, Aqiba) was the most outstanding tanna *of the third generation (110–135 C.E.) who influenced and shaped traditional Judaism during its formative years. Much of the* Mishnah *reflects his teaching and interpretive methods. He was the archetypical scholar, and consequently his wife has become the ideal scholar's wife, who motivates, encourages, and supports her husband in his studies and later reaps the rewards of his fame. Source: Anon.,* Likkutei ha-Ma'asim *(Verona, 1648).*

Now let me tell you a story about what was done by one good woman of wealthy stock. The sages of blessed memory say that there was a man in the Land of Israel whose name was Kalba Sabua (sated dog). And he was given that name because if even a hungry dog were to come to his home, he would sate his hunger. Now Rabbi Akiba was his shepherd. And Kalba Sabua had only one daughter, and she was beautiful and gracious. She loved Rabbi Akiba and said to him: "Take me to wife!" And he said: "I shall do what you say."

This was told to Kalba Sabua, and he grew furious to death. Indeed, he vowed a vow before the Lord that he would not give her any part at all of his money because she had chosen an ignorant man.

But his daughter was not concerned at all this, and Rabbi Akiba married her. He spoke to her heart and said: "Consider our poverty and distress, yet restrain yourself and put your trust in God. For when I have money I shall make you a golden crown." As they were conversing together, somebody called out to them: "I have a pregnant wife who is about to give birth and I have no cover or material in which she can give birth. Maybe you can deal graciously with me and give me something."

Then Rabbi Akiba said to his wife: "See how well the Holy and Blessed One has treated us!"

In due course she said to him: "Listen to me, my master, take my counsel and study Torah." So he went and studied Torah from Rabbi Eliezer and Rabbi Joshua for twelve years. Then he returned to his city and there were twelve thousand disciples with him.

But he heard a man berating his wife and saying to her: "I heard what your father did to you because you married his ignorant shepherd who was not fitting for you; then after he married you he went his way for these twelve years and left you to live in widowhood!" But his wife answered: "I would have him to return to study for yet another twelve years as long as he is not ignorant when he comes back!"

As soon as Rabbi Akiba heard this, he returned to his school where he studied Torah for twelve years more. After that he returned home with twenty-four thousand disciples. And the elders of the city came to meet him in awe. He arrived amid great honor, but they did not know who he had been in the past. Then he sent to speak to his wife. She wished to go yet had nothing to wear except tattered garments. So she quoted Proverbs, saying: "The righteous man knows the state of the needy" (29:7). And she went out to meet him and prostrated herself before him. The disciples came to take her away, but he told them: "Let her be. She is bitter at heart, yet she was the one who caused me to study all this Torah that I have learned and that you too have learned."

Now Kalba Sabua heard that a sage had come to town, and he also came to meet him and asked him whether he would be prepared to annul his vow. For he grieved because his daughter was lacking in all things. And the man asked him and he informed him of the nature of his vow.

And Rabbi Akiba asked him: "Why did you make such a vow?" "Because," he explained, "she married a man who was not worthy of her and who had neither knowledge of Torah nor money." "And if," Rabbi Akiba asked him, "he had been a sage like me, would you have vowed such a vow?" "Heaven forbid," said old Kalba Sabua. "If he had been able to read or recite even one chapter I would have given him half my wealth." Then Rabbi Akiba declared: "I am your son-in-law and your daughter's husband." At this he rose and kissed him on the head and they embraced and kissed. And he gave him half his wealth.

So Rabbi Akiba became exceedingly wealthy and made his wife a golden crown as he had promised her. And the Holy and Blessed One delivered them from their distress and increased their wealth and riches.

See how much great honor this man achieved because of the abundant wisdom he learned during his exceeding poverty.

39
RABBI HANINA BEN DOSA AND HIS WIFE

Rabbi Ḥanina ben Dosa, a tanna of the first generation (40–80 C.E.), was known for his extreme piety and poverty. Source: Rabbi Nissim, Ḥibbur Yafeh, pp. 11–12.

Our sages of blessed memory said about Rabbi Hanina ben Dosa: "Day after day a heavenly echo comes from Mount Horeb and declares: 'The whole world is sustained for the sake of Hanina My son, yet My son Hanina finds enough in a pint of carobs from one Sabbath eve to the next.'"

When the wife of this godly man used to see the women cooking and baking in honor of the Sabbath on Sabbath eve, while she had nothing whatsoever to bake or boil, she used to feel ashamed in their presence. She would stoke up the oven and place pots of water in it simply in order to show her neighbors that she was cooking and baking like them. One Sabbath eve when she was heating up her oven, one of her neighbors came to her and said: "You have been heating the oven, yet I know very well that you have nothing to cook in it." And the woman went to inspect the oven and see what was in it; and she found that it was full of bread, while her kneading trough was full of dough. Then she called Rabbi Hanina's wife and said to her: "Go and take the bread out, for it is properly baked while the dough has risen in the trough." So she went out and took the bread and then baked the dough.

So things went with her, and the Holy and Blessed One performed signs and wonders of this kind on account of their merits and piety. On another Sabbath she took the cruse of vinegar instead of the cruse of oil and poured it into the lamp and kindled it without knowing what she did. When she saw what she had done, she moaned bitterly. Her husband Rabbi Hanina noticed this and asked her: "What has happened?" And she told him. "Do not grieve!" said he, "He who ordered the oil to burn can order the vinegar to burn too!" And the lamp burned all night long and all day long, and from it they kindled the light to separate the Sabbath from the weekdays.

Yet the time came when they found the yoke of hunger and poverty very hard to bear. Then Rabbi Hanina's wife said to him: "Beseech your God to give you some little part of all the bounty which He will be giving you in the World to Come." He did so; and a golden leg from his heavenly table was given to him.

That night he dreamed that the golden tables of his companions were all complete, while his table was one leg short. When he woke up, he told the dream to his wife, and she said to him: "In that case, indeed, request your God to take the leg back." He did so, and the leg was returned to its proper place. And our sages of blessed memory commented: "The second miracle was greater than the first, for we have learned the principle that heaven sometimes gives but it does not take back."

There are more tales about this godly man than could ever be told. It was said that his prayer never returned empty from the Holy and Blessed One at any time whatever. Thus our sages of blessed memory said that during a drought the rain fell as he was on the road. He could not abide this vast rainfall and said: "Everybody is at ease, but Hanina has to suffer!" At this the rain ended in the sky. When he arrived home at night, he said: "Can the whole world be suffering and Hanina be at ease?" and the rains came again.

Now consider how great this godly man was and how pious and righteous he was before the Holy and Blessed One. For all this time he was suffering and hungry and naked and lacked everything.

40
MATTIAH BEN HERESH

Mattiah ben Heresh was a tanna of the third and fourth generations (135–170 C.E.) who established a great academy in Rome. The tale belongs to a narrative cycle advocating repression of sexual desires for the sake of learning. Source: M. Gaster, The Exempla of the Rabbis, *No. 136, pp. 84, 93–94.*

The tale is told that once Rabbi Mattiah ben Heresh was sitting studying Torah. His face was bright as the sun and the moon and his features were like to the ministering angels in his fear of God. For he had never raised his eyes to look at the wife of any of his companions, and indeed, had never looked at any woman in the world.

Once he was sitting studying Torah in the house of study. Satan passed and saw him and felt envious. Said he: "Can there possibly be such a man as this who has never sinned?" And what did he do? He went up to heaven at once and appeared before the Holy and Blessed One and said to him: "Lord of the Universe, how does Mattiah ben Heresh appear to you?" "A perfect saint," said He. Then Satan said: "Lord of the Universe, give me the permission, and I shall entice him." "You will not succeed," said He. "Nevertheless," said Satan, "give me permission." "Go then!" said the Holy and Blessed One.

Thereupon he went and found Rabbi Mattiah seated studying Torah. And what did he do? He assumed the form of a woman more beautiful than any in the world, like unto Naamah the sister of Tubal-Cain, who misled the ministering angels, as it is written: "And the sons of God saw the daughters of men that they were fair" (Gen. 6:2). He went and stood before him. When the rabbi saw the woman, he turned himself about. Then Satan came and stood before him on the other side.

When the rabbi saw that the woman was following him around on every side, he said to himself: "I fear that my lust may overpower me and lead me to sin." And what did the saint do then? He summoned the disciple who served him and said: "Go and fetch me fire and long nails." He went and fetched them. And the rabbi thrust the nails in the flame until they grew hot as the fire, and then thrust them into his eyes.

When Satan saw this, he grew alarmed and trembled and fell back. And he ascended on high and appeared before the Holy and Blessed One and said: "Lord of the Universe, thus and thus it came about." And He answered: "Did I not tell you that you could not prevail against him!"

Then the Holy and Blessed One summoned Raphael and said to him: "Go and heal the eyes of Mattiah ben Heresh." He went and appeared before him. "Who are you?" said the rabbi. And the angel answered: "I am Raphael and have been sent by the Holy and Blessed One to heal your eyes." "Let me be," said the rabbi, "what has been has been."

Then Raphael returned to the Holy and Blessed One and reported: "Lord of the Universe! This and this is what he said to me." And the Holy and Blessed One instructed him: "Go and tell him: I can assure you that you will not be ruled by lust!" And then and there he healed him.

From this the sages said: "If a man does not wish to look upon a married woman, lust and the evil inclination will not rule over him." That is why we find written in Jacob's Blessing: "Joseph is a fruitful vine, a fruitful vine by a fountain" (Gen. 49:22). This should not be read "by a fountain" but "up and out with you, O eye!"* The eye that does not wish to enjoy what is not its own, will not to be ruled by lust or the evil inclination. May the Holy and Blessed One take away from us both the evil inclination and unjustified hate, and rebuke Satan so that he may never set out to mislead and denounce us.

---

*In Hebrew, these sentences involve two puns., 'Fountain' and 'eye' are homonyms, 'ayin, and the preposition 'by' and the phrase 'up and out with you,' 'alei and 'ali, are phonetically similar: 'alei 'ayin, "by a fountain," and 'ali, 'ayin, "up and out with you, O eye."

41
NATHAN OF THE RADIANCE

In talmudic tradition there are attempts to identify the hero of this tale as a historical figure; however, these suggestions point to two different exilarches who shared the epithet Nathan "de Zuzita." The phrase has often been translated as suggesting radiance or glow, but recent interpretations propose that the term metaphorically refers to sexual desire. Source: Rabbi Nissim, Ḥibbur Yafeh, pp. 29–30.

There was a certain wealthy Jew named Nathan de Tsutsitha who loved a wedded woman named Hannah. Her husband was exceedingly poor but she was beautiful beyond compare.

This Nathan grew ill on account of Hannah. The physicians who visited him told him: "You cannot be healed until you lie with her." The sages of Israel declared: "Let him perish rather than commit this transgression!" The physicians insisted: "Let her come and talk to him!" "Impossible!" declared the sages. And his malady lasted a very long time.

Now Hannah's husband owed many debts and was put in prison because he had nothing to give his creditors. His wife used to spin by day and night and bought food with the money she earned and brought it to the prison. He spent a long time in the prison and felt fit to die. So one day he said to his wife: "Anybody who redeems a single soul from death is as though he had delivered many souls. I am sick and tired of my life in prison. Take pity on me and go to Nathan and ask him to lend you the money and deliver my soul from death." Then she told him: "Surely you know and must have heard that he is sick and about to die on my account. Messengers from him come to me day after day with large sums of money. But I refuse to accept it and tell them that he will never see me! Now how can I go to borrow money from him? If you were in your right mind, you could not say such a thing to me, so the length of your imprisonment must have put you out of your mind." She was very angry with him and went home in a fury and never went to see him for three days.

On the fourth day she felt sorry for him and said: "Let me go and see him before he perishes." So she went and found him on the verge of death, and he said to her: "May the Holy and Blessed One demand from you an accounting for the injustice done to me and seize you for this sin against me. For I can see that you wish me to perish here and then you will wed Nathan." "Divorce me and let me be," said she, "and then I shall go to him." "Why," he answered, "that is what I said—that you wish to marry him." Then she cried out aloud and flung herself down to the ground and said: "Who has heard the like of this? Who has seen such a thing? This man tells me: Go and commit adultery and pollute yourself in order to get me out of prison!" And her husband answered: "Go away and let me be until the Holy and Blessed One has mercy on me!"

Then she went home and thought about her distress and her husband's too, and she took pity on him. She purified her heart and prayed and said: "I entreat You, O Lord, deliver me and aid me in order that I may not engage in a transgression!" And then she went to the house of Nathan. His attendants saw her and hastened to tell Nathan: "Hannah is at the gate!" "If it is true," said he, "you will all be freed!" Then she entered the courtyard, and his maidservant said to him: "See, Hannah is in the courtyard!" "Then you too will be set free!" he said to her.

So Hannah came to him. He lifted up his eyes and said: "Madam, tell me what you desire and what you wish, and it will be given to you. Whatever you request will be done." "My only request," said she, "is that you should lend my husband such and such a sum for he is imprisoned, and you will be righteous in the eyes of the Lord." Then he ordered his servants to bring out the money and gave her what she desired. And he said to her: "See now, I have done what you wish, and you know how ill I am because I love you. Now do my wish and make me whole again!"

Then Hannah answered him: "I am in your hands and under your wings and here I cannot refuse you. But let me tell you that this is the time when you can gain the life of the World to Come. Take care not to lose your reward and all that is good in that world for so small a thing, and do not make me prohibited to my husband. Assume that you have achieved your desire but do not lose so much that is good on my account, so that you will be left only with something that must finish in bitter remorse! And think of the anguish imposed by the Holy and Blessed One and do not do something that must finally avenge itself on you. Here you have but a little while, yet you will prevent yourself from gaining long life and a good reward in this world and the World to Come, something that a man can achieve only by dint of much toil and exhaustion. Yet you can fulfill the will of your Creator in a brief hour, if you merely hearken to my counsel and reject your lust and evil inclination. And all will be well with you!"

When the man heard her words, he rebuked his evil will. He rose from his bed and flung himself to the ground and prayed before the Lord to conquer his lust and break his desire and conduct him along the good and proper path and forgive his iniquities and enable him to repent entirely. And the Lord responded and consented. Then Nathan said to Hannah: "Blessed are you before the Lord and blessed is your sound sense which has now prevented me from performing this transgression and has indeed been a salvation to me. Go to your home in peace!"

So the woman went and redeemed her husband from prison. She told him what she had done but he would not believe her, suspecting that Nathan had been with her but she was hiding it from him.

Now in due course Rabbi Akiba looked out of his window and saw a man riding a horse with a radiance and brightness around his head that shone like the sun. He summoned one of his disciples and said to him: "Who is that man riding on horseback?" And the disciple said: "This is Nathan the Whoremaster." Then he said to his disciples: "Do you see anything around his head?" "No," said they. Then he told them: "Bring him to me quickly!" And he said to him: "My son, there is a great light over your head as you pass, and I know that you are going to inherit the World to Come. Now tell me what you have done." So he told him about Hannah.

Rabbi Akiba was astonished that he could have restrained and subdued his lust and become so completely penitent. And he said to him: "Indeed, you have done a great deed, and therefore the Holy and Blessed One has caused the light to shine around your head, this great radiance I have seen. If it is here in this world, how much more so in the World to Come! And you, my son, hearken unto me and take your seat before me so that I can teach you Torah."

He did so and took his place before Rabbi Akiba. And He who opens and does not close opened the portals of his heart to His Torah. And within a short while he achieved a high degree of wisdom and reached Rabbi Akiba's rank.

In due course Hannah's husband passed by the schools of Rabbi Akiba. There he saw Nathan de Tsutsitha seated at the same level as Rabbi Akiba. He asked one of the disciples how Nathan could have achieved this, and he was told the whole tale.

Then the man believed his wife. The jealousy that had possessed him passed away. He returned home and kissed his wife on the brow and said to her: "Forgive me and pardon me for having suspected you about Nathan. Today I saw him seated beside Rabbi Akiba, and I asked, and they told me all that happened. May the Holy and Blessed One reward you twofold and fourfold. I was in great distress and anguish in my soul until the Holy and Blessed One aided me by revealing this matter to me today."

42
NAHUM OF GAMZO

*Naḥum of Gamzo was a tanna of the second generation (80–110 C.E.),
known traditionally as Rabbi Akiba's teacher. His epithet involves a pun
on a city name, possibly his home town, and an idiom, gam zo le-tova,
"also this [is] for the better." Being the perennial optimist, according
to tradition, he used to utter this phrase in the face of personal or commu-
nal difficulties. Source: Rabbi Nissim, Ḥibbur Yafeh, p. 28.*

N ahum of Gamzo was a saintly man who was ailing in his body.
Besides his great wisdom and knowledge of Torah he suffered
from great and evil pains and illnesses. Yet he chose it all for himself and
entreated the Holy and Blessed One that he should suffer all this because
of a transgression on his part. Therefore he besought Him to impose the
punishment of his transgression in this world in order that neither sin nor
blame should be left with him but he would remain pure and clean for
the World to Come.

Now it is told of this man that he was blind in both eyes and paralyzed
in his hands and crippled in his feet while the rest of his body was covered
with boils and itched. His bed was constructed over vessels and troughs
that were full of water in order that he should feel the chill.

Now one day when the man was in his home the walls began to slant,
ready to collapse, and the whole building was clearly about to fall apart.
His disciples wished to take him out of the house, so that it should not
collapse over him. But Nahum said to them: "Take all the household utensils
out, both small and large, and do not leave anything, and then take my
bed out; for as long as I am in the house it will neither fall nor be destroyed."
His disciples did all that he ordered, removing everything from within till
nothing whatever was left there. Afterwards they removed him, and the
house collapsed at once. And when the disciples saw this, they gazed at
one another in astonishment. "Rabbi," they then said to him, "since your
ways are so acceptable to the Holy and Blessed One and you are so amply
righteous and pious and of so high a rank in Torah and wisdom—why
did these outlandish and harsh sufferings come upon you?" And he answered them: "My sons, I asked for all this anguish, and it has come to
me." "Yet, rabbi," his disciples then asked: "How could it have been? Please
tell us."

Then he told them: "One ordinary day I was going to the house of the sages. And I was leading with me three asses bearing corn and bread and food and different kinds of fruit and delicacies. As I was on the way, a man came to me and said: 'Good sir, give me something to eat for I hunger.' 'Wait,' said I to him, 'while I go and take something to give you from the asses.' When I came back to him, I found him lying on his face, dead. I was exceedingly disturbed and in great pain and sadness and sorrow and grief. So I fell on my face and placed my eyes on his eyes and my hands on his hands and my feet on his feet, and I said: 'May these eyes that took no pity on you be blind, and the hands that did not hasten to give you food be hacked off, and my feet likewise.' And I also said: 'May my body itch and be full of boils!' And when Rabbi Akiba saw me like this he said: 'Woe and alas that I should see you in such a state!' But I told him: 'Happy am I that you should have seen me thus, since it is a great reward for me and by this I have won my life in the World to Come!'"

43
ONKELOS THE PROSELYTE

Onkelos the Proselyte is a mythical figure to whom tradition attributes the Aramaic translation of the Pentateuch that was formulated in Palestine and Babylonia, and which was known in Jewish communities by the third century C.E. In talmudic sources there is an apparent confusion between Onkelos and Aquila, to whom tradition attributes respectively the translations of the Pentateuch to Aramaic and to Greek. Current scholarly consensus is that Onkelos is a Babylonian form of the name Aquila. In talmudic-midrashic literature both names refer to personalities of proselytes who were related to Roman rulers who oppressed the Jewish community in Palestine and destroyed Jerusalem. Source: Rabbi Nissim, Ḥibbur Yafeh, pp. 17–18.

I t is told of Onkelos, who prepared the Aramaic translation of the Torah, that he was a proselyte or *ger*. King Caesar heard that he had converted to Judaism, and sent messengers to fetch him. When he saw them, he sat expounding and reciting interpretations of the Torah and its reward to them until they, too, became Jews.

Then King Caesar sent messengers again and ordered them not to enter into debate with Onkelos in order that he should not do to them what he had done to the first ones. And he said to them: "Listen to one thing from me." "What is that thing?" they asked; and he answered: "It is the practice of the world that the slave proceeds before the master with light and torch in order to show him the way." "True," said they. Then he went on: "Now consider what the Holy and Blessed One did for the people of Israel. For it is written in the Book of Exodus (13:21): 'And the Lord went before them by day in a pillar of cloud, to show them the way, and by night in a pillar of fire, to give them light.'" And he went on interpreting and explaining to them until they, too, became Jews.

Then King Caesar sent a third set of messengers and ordered them not to speak to him or listen to anything that he said. So he went with them, but he raised his eyes and saw the *mezuzah* at the entry, and placed his hand on the *mezuzah*. "What is this?" they asked; and he said to them: "It is the general practice that a human king enters inner chambers while his ministers and servants guard him and take their seats at the gate. But the Holy and Blessed One does not do this. Instead He conducts them into their homes while He stays at the entry to guard them, as it is written in Psalms (121:8): 'The Lord will guard your going and coming!'" So they also became Jews, when they saw this. And when Caesar saw what was happening, he refrained from sending any more messengers.

Consider the greatness of this pious man and his deeds, who was a proselyte that loved wisdom and Torah.

44
MARTYRED BY THE ROMANS

Together with the story of Hannah and her seven sons ("The Mother") this legend serves as the archetypical martyrological myth in Jewish tradition. While rooted in the Hadrian persecutions of the second century C.E., the story is more mystical than historical in nature. Some of the sages were subjects of individual martyrdom legends, others appear only in this story of collective martyrology. Lists of the ten martyrs vary somewhat. Most of the names that appear in the present version are tannaim of the third generation (110–135 C.E.), contemporaries of Rabbi Akiba; the identity of others is not clear. For example, there are two known sages named Rabban Simeon ben Gamliel, but neither lived in the period of Hadrianic persecutions. Also the known Rabbi Eleazar ben Shammua lived a generation later, and the name of Rabbi Judah ben Dama occurs as a martyr only in the present version. The legend of the "Ten Martyrs" has become the subject of several piyyutim; *the best known of them, "Elleh Ezkerah," has been incorporated into the liturgy for the Day of Atonement. Source: A. Jellinek, ed.,* Bet ha-Midrasch *2:64–72; 6:19–30.*

I

W hen the Holy and Blessed One created the trees, they boasted of their height and made themselves taller and taller. When the Holy and Blessed One created iron, they humbled themselves and said: "Woe unto us, for the Holy and Blessed One has already created the thing that shall cut us down!"

So it was after the destruction of the Temple. The vicious ones of that age said proudly: "What loss is it to us that the Temple has been destroyed? Why, among us there are sages who instruct the world regarding God's Torah and His commandments!"

Thereupon the Holy and Blessed One set it in the heart of the Roman emperor to learn the Torah of Moses from sages and elders. He began with the Book of Genesis and studied until he reached "These are the judgments" (Exod. 21:1). When he reached the verse: "And he who steals a man and sells him . . . shall be put to death" (Exod. 21:16), he immediately ordered that his palace should be filled with boots, and he sent to summon ten sages of Israel.

When the sages came before him, he set them on golden seats and said to them: "I have a difficult point of law to ask you, and tell me only the law as it is and the truth and the proper judgment." "Speak!" said they to him, and he said: "If anyone steals a man from the brothers of the Children of Israel and then sets out and sells him, what law applies to him?" "The Torah," said they, "declares: 'He shall be put to death.'"

Then he answered them: "In that case you deserve death." "Tell us why," said they, and he answered: "Because of Joseph who was sold by his brothers. If they had been alive, I would have sentenced them, but since they are not alive, you will bear the sin of your forefathers."

"Give us three days' time," said they to him. "If we can find any extenuating circumstances for ourselves, it is good, and if not, then do what you desire." And to this he agreed.

They departed from him and entreated Rabbi Ishmael the High Priest to pronounce the Great Name and ascend to heaven and ascertain whether the decree had come from His Blessed Name. Rabbi Ishmael purified himself by immersion and rituals, then swathed himself in his prayer shawl and put on his phylacteries and pronounced the Expressed Name in its full detail. Thereupon the spirit raised him and brought him on high to the Sixth Firmament. There the Angel Gabriel met him and said: "Are you Ishmael whose Maker praises Himself with you every day, declaring that He has a servant on earth who resembles His very features?" "I am he," said the rabbi. "Why have you come up hither?" asked he. "Because," answered Rabbi Ishmael, "the malicious rulers have made a decree against us in order to make an end of ten sages in Israel. Now I have come up to know whether this decree comes from the Holy and Blessed One."

"Ishmael, my son!" then said Gabriel to him, "by your very soul, I have heard from behind the Curtain that ten sages of Israel have been handed over to be slain by the malicious rulers."

As soon as Rabbi Ishmael heard this, he was satisfied at once. He traversed the Firmament this way and that and saw an altar near the Glory Seat. "What is this?" he asked Gabriel, who said: "It is an altar." "And what," asked he, "do you sacrifice upon it every day? Are there sheep and cattle on high?"

"On it," said the angel to him, "we sacrifice the souls of the righteous every day." Thereupon Rabbi Ishmael descended and reached the earth and told his companions that the decree had already been passed and written and sealed.

II

They were seated pair by pair: Rabbi Ishmael and Rabban Simeon ben Gamaliel; Rabbi Akiba and Rabbi Hanania ben Teradion; Rabbi Eleazar ben Shammua and Rabbi Yeshebab the Scribe; Rabbi Hanina ben Hachinai and Rabbi Judah ben Baba; Rabbi Huzpit the Interpreter and Rabbi Judah ben Dama.

The emperor entered and all the great Romans behind him. "Who is to be slain first?" said he to them. And Rabban Simeon ben Gamaliel responded: "I am a patriarch and son of a patriarch and the offspring of David, king of Israel, may he rest in peace. I shall be slain first." Then Rabbi Ishmael the High Priest also responded: "I am a high priest and the son of a high priest and the offspring of Aaron the Priest. I shall be slain first and let me not see the death of my companion."

"One says," said the emperor, "let me be slain first and the other also says let me be slain first. In that case, cast lots between you."

The lot fell on Rabban Simeon ben Gamaliel, and the emperor ordered that his head be cut off first, and they cut it off. Then Rabbi Ishmael the High Priest held it between his thighs and wailed in his bitterness over it, saying: "Alas for Torah and alas for its reward! O tongue that explained the Torah in seventy tongues, how do you now lick the dust!" And he wailed and mourned for Rabban Simeon ben Gamaliel.

"Old man," the emperor said to him, "wherefore and why do you weep for your companion? You ought to be weeping for yourself." "I do not weep for myself," answered Rabbi Ishmael, "because my companion was greater than me in Torah and wisdom, and I also weep because he has preceded me to the Upper Assembly."

While he was speaking and lamenting and weeping and keening, the emperor's daughter looked out of the window and saw how beautiful was Rabbi Ishmael the High Priest. She felt so much pity for him that she sent to ask her father to grant her a single request.

"Daughter," the emperor sent to inform her, "I shall do anything you ask me except with regard to Rabbi Ishmael and his companions." "I beseech you," she sent to him, "keep him alive." "I have already taken oath," he sent to inform her. "In that case," she sent to him, "I beg you to have his face skinned in order that I may be able to gaze upon it instead of a mirror."

At once he gave the order to have the skin removed from his face. When they reached the place where the phylacteries rest, he cried so loud and bitterly that heaven and earth trembled. He cried afresh, and the Glory Seat shook. Then the Ministering Angels said to the Holy and Blessed One: "Is this saint to whom You showed all the secret treasures of the world on high and the things concealed below, to be slain so cruelly by that wicked man? Is this the Torah and is this its reward?" "Let Me be," said He to them, "for his merits will sustain the generations that follow him." And a divine voice went forth and declared: "If I should hear one more sound from him, I shall restore the whole universe to void and chaos." When Rabbi Ishmael heard this, he grew silent. "You still put trust in your God!" said the emperor to him, and he answered: "Though He slay me, I keep my hope in Him" (Job 13:15). And with those words the soul of Rabbi Ishmael departed.

III

And after him they brought forth Rabbi Akiba ben Joseph, who expounds the tittles of every letter in the Torah, revealing all aspects therein as they were made known to Moses at Sinai. When they brought him forth to be slain, the emperor received a letter that the king of Arabia was invading his land, and it was necessary to go. So he ordered that Rabbi Akiba should be kept in prison until he returned from the war.

When he returned from the war, he ordered that he should be brought forth. They combed his flesh with iron combs. At every stroke of these combs Rabbi Akiba repeated: "Righteous is the Lord, 'perfect is the work of the Rock, for all His ways are judgment, a God of faith without any evil, righteous and upright is He'" (Deut. 32:4). And a divine voice was heard saying: "Happy are you, Rabbi Akiba, because you were righteous and upright, and your soul has departed in uprightness and righteousness."

After he passed away, Elijah the Prophet, whom it is good to mention, came and put him on his shoulder and bore him five leagues. Rabbi Joshua of Gerasa met him and said: "Are you not a priest?" "The body of a saint," answered he, "does not pollute." So Rabbi Joshua of Gerasa went with him until they reached a certain very handsome cave. When they entered, they found a fine bier and a candle burning. Elijah, whom it is good to mention, took him by the head and Rabbi Joshua by the feet and set him out on that bier. The Ministering Angels wept for him for three days and three nights. Afterwards, they buried him in that cave. Next day Elijah, whom it is good to mention, took him and brought him to the Assembly on high in order that he should discourse there on the tittles of the letters. And all the souls of the saints and the God-fearing ones came to listen to his expositions.

IV

And after him they brought forth Rabbi Hanania ben Teradion. They said of him that he was pleasing to the Holy and Blessed One and to man alike, and he had never cursed his fellowman even in the privacy of his own bed. When the emperor in Rome commanded that Torah was not to be studied, what did Rabbi Hanania ben Teradion do? He went and gathered congregations together in public and sat himself down in the markets of Rome where he used to teach Torah and engage in it and expound it. So the emperor ordered that he was to be wrapped up in a Torah Scroll and burned. The executioner took him, wrapped him up in a Torah Scroll and kindled the pyre. Then he took fleeces of wool and soaked them in water and placed them over his heart in order that he should not perish swiftly. His daughter stood there, crying: "Alas, father, that I should see you like this!" But he answered her: "I deem it good, daughter, that you see me thus!" His disciples stood by saying: "Rabbi, what do you see?" And he told them: "I see parchment sheets being burned and the letters flying in the air." Then he began to weep, and his disciples asked him: "Why are you weeping?" "If I alone was being burned," he told them, "it would not be difficult for me, but now I am being burned and a Torah Scroll together with me!"

Then the executioner said to him: "Rabbi, if I remove the wet wool from your heart in order that you should pass away speedily, will you ensure me life in the World to Come?" "Yes," said he. "Swear to me," said the executioner, and he swore it to him. As soon as he had taken oath, the executioner increased the flame and removed the wool, and he passed away. Then the executioner flung himself into the flames and was burned. And a divine voice was heard declaring: "Rabbi Hanania ben Teradion and the executioner are assured of life in the World to Come."

V

And after him they brought forth Rabbi Judah ben Baba, who had not slept longer than the fitful sleep of a horse from his eighteenth year to the age of eighty. Now the day on which they led him forth to execution was Sabbath eve, and it was after the ninth hour (in the middle of the afternoon). He began to entreat them: "By your lives, wait a little longer for me so that I can fulfill a certain commandment which the Holy and Blessed One has commanded me." "Do you still trust in your God?" they asked; and he told them: "Yes."

Then they said to him: "Is there still any power left to this God in whom you trust?" And he answered: "Great is the Lord and exceedingly worthy of praise, and to His greatness there are no bounds" (Ps. 145:3). Then they said to him: "If He has any strength, why has He not delivered you and your companions from this reign?" "We owe death," said he, "to a great and awesome King, and He has handed us over to this king in order to demand our blood from him in due course."

They went and told the king what he said. The king sent to him and asked: "Have they told me the truth about you or not?" "It is true," said he. Then the emperor said: "How obstinate you are, when at the very gates of death you still continue to maintain your obstinacy." And Rabbi Judah answered him: "Woe to you, Caesar, you wicked son of the wicked. The Holy and Blessed One has seen the destruction of His House and the slaying of His pious men and saints, and will He not avenge Himself at once in His zeal?"

"By your life, Caesar," said he then, "wait for me until I have fulfilled a certain commandment named Sabbath, which is after the fashion of the World to Come." "I am prepared to agree to your request," said he. Thereupon he began to hallow the day, reciting: "And the heavens and the earth were finished" (Gen. 2:1). This he chanted with beauty and strength, and all who were standing nearby stood wondering. When he reached the words "And God completed," they would not permit him to finish, but the emperor ordered him to be slain. They slew him and his soul departed at the word "God" and a divine voice was heard saying: "Happy are you Rabbi Judah who was like to an angel, for your soul departed at the word 'God.'"

But the emperor ordered that his body should be cut up into little pieces and flung to the dogs. So he was neither mourned nor buried.

VI

And after him they brought forth Rabbi Judah ben Dama. It was the eve of the Feast of Weeks and Rabbi Judah said to the emperor: "By your life, wait a little while so that I can fulfill the commandment of this holy convocation and say the hallowing prayer in order to praise the Holy and Blessed One who gave us the Torah." "And you still put your trust," said the emperor, "in the Torah and God who gave it?" "Yes," said he. "What is the reward for the Torah?" asked the emperor. "Of that," said he, "David, may he rest in peace, declared: 'How manifold is Your goodness which You have in store for those who fear You' (Ps. 31:20)." "There are no fools in the world," then said the emperor, "who can compare with you for supposing that there is another world!" "There are no fools in the world," answered he, "like those of you who deny the living God. Woe unto you and woe for your shame and woe for your reproach, when you see us with the Lord in the light of life while you shall remain in *Sheol* below at the lowermost level!"

This infuriated the emperor. He ordered that he was to be tied by the hair of his head to the tail of a horse and dragged through every street in Rome. After that he ordered that he was to be cut into little pieces. But Elijah, whom it is good to mention, came and took the pieces and buried them in a certain cave which was near the river that runs down by Rome. All the Romans heard the sound of lamentation and weeping coming from that cave for thirty full days. They came and told the emperor, and he said to them: "Even if the whole world returns to chaos I shall not cease until I have had my will with those ten elders as I have taken oath."

VII

And after him they brought forth Rabbi Huzpit the Interpreter. It is said that he was a hundred and thirty years old when they took him to execution and was handsome and comely and like to an angel of the Lord of Hosts. They came and told the king of his beauty and extreme age and said to him: "By your very life, our lord, take pity on this old man!" Then the emperor said to Rabbi Huzpit: "How old are you?" And he answered:

"A hundred and thirty years less one single day, and I would request you to wait with me until that day is over."

"What difference is it to you," wondered the emperor, "whether you perish today or tomorrow?" "I wish," he answered, "to fulfill another two commandments." "And what commandments do you wish to fulfill?" he asked. Then the rabbi answered: "To read the portion 'Hear, O Israel' in the evening and the morning in order to accept over myself the royal power of the great and awesome and especial Name."

Then the emperor said to him: "Impudence and audacity! How long will you go on believing in your God who is powerless to deliver you from my hands? Why, my fathers destroyed His House, and left those who served Him as carrion around Jerusalem, unburied! And now your God is old and no longer has the strength to save. For if He had strength He would have avenged Himself and His people and His Temple as He did to Pharaoh and Sisera and all the kings of Canaan!"

Now when Rabbi Huzpit heard this, he wept exceedingly and took hold of his garments and rent them because of this insult to His Blessed Name and the shaming of Him and he said to the emperor: "Alas for you, emperor, what will you do in the latter day when His Blessed Name will make a visitation upon Rome and your gods?" "How long am I going to stand arguing with this fellow?" said the king, and he ordered him to be slain; and they stoned him and hung him.

Then came his officials and sages and entreated him to bury him, for they had pity on his old age. So the king ordered that he should be buried. And his disciples came and buried him and made a great and very grievous lament for him.

VIII

And after him they brought forth Rabbi Hanina ben Hachinai; and that day was Sabbath eve. Now all his life from the age of twelve till ninety-five years Rabbi Hanina had fasted. And his disciples said to him: "Rabbi, do you wish to taste something before you are slain?" "Hitherto," said he, "I have fasted and neither eaten nor drunk, and now that I do not know whither I shall go, you come and ask me to eat and drink!"

He began to recite the hallowing of the day, from "And the heavens were finished" to "And He hallowed it." But they would not permit him to finish, slaying him first. Then a divine voice was heard saying: "Happy are you, Rabbi Hanina ben Hachinai, for you were saintly and your soul has departed in sanctity."

IX

And after him they brought forth Rabbi Yeshebab the Scribe. They say that he was ninety years old when he was taken to execution. When they brought him forth, his disciples came and said to him: "Rabbi, what is going to happen with the Torah?" And he told them: "My sons, the Torah is going to be forgotten in Israel in the future, because this wicked nation has had the impudence to conspire to take our pearls from us and to destroy them; if only I could serve as an atonement for the age! Yet I can see that there is not a street in Rome without its corpse slain by the sword, because this wicked nation is going to shed the innocent blood of Israel."

"Rabbi," they then said to him, "and what will happen to us?" "Support one another and stand firm," said he, "love peace and justice, for maybe there is hope!"

Then the emperor said to him: "How old are you, old man?" "I am ninety years old today," said he, "and even before my mother gave birth to me the Holy and Blessed One had decreed that my companions and I were to be placed in your hands, but the time will come when the Holy and Blessed One will demand the ransom of our blood from you." "And is there another world then?" said he. "Yes," answered the rabbi, "and as for you, woe to you and woe for your shame when He demands the blood of his righteous ones at your hand!"

"Hurry and kill this one, too," said the emperor, "and let me see the strength and might of his God and what He will do to me in some other world!"

And he commanded that he should be burned.

X

And after him they brought Rabbi Eleazar ben Shammua. It is said that he was a hundred and five years old that day, and from his childhood to the end of his life no man ever heard him utter anything unworthy, and he never disputed with his companions either in word or deed but was humble and abased of spirit. Furthermore, he had been fasting for eighty years.

The day he was slain was the Day of Atonement. His disciples came and asked him: "Rabbi, what do you see?" And he told them: "I see Rabbi Judah ben Baba whose litter is being borne, and the litter of Rabbi Akiba ben Joseph nearby, and they are discussing a matter of law together." "And who decides between them?" asked they; and he told them: "Rabbi Ishmael the High Priest." Then they asked him: "Who is winning?" "Rabbi Akiba,"

said he to them, "because he toiled with all his strength in the Torah."
Then he told them: "My sons, I see further that the soul of each and every
saint purifies itself in the waters of Shiloah (Siloam) in order to enter in
purity this day into the upper assembly and to hear the exposition of Rabbi
Akiba ben Joseph who will expound the subject matter of the day to them.
And all the angels are bringing golden thrones for each and every saint
to sit thereon in purity."

The emperor ordered that he should be slain. And a divine voice was
heard saying: "Happy are you, Rabbi Eleazar ben Shammua, for you were
pure and your soul has departed in purity!"

45
THE BOOK OF GENESIS

*This story belongs to the "clever child" narrative cycle, emphasizing, how-
ever, the value of learning rather than wit. Source: Anon., Ḥibbur
Ma'asiyyot, pp. 58–60.*

A certain pious man was seventy years old and had no son. He
was very wealthy. Every day he used to go to the synagogue.
When the children came out, he would embrace them and kiss them and
say to them: "Children, tell me what verses you have learned!" And each
and every one of them would recite the verse he had studied. Then he
would bless them and say to them: "Happy are you and happy your fathers
who have merited sons who engage in Torah." But in his heart he said:
"Alas for the one who has no son! What pleasure do I have of all my property?" So he went and dispersed his properties among the disciples of the
sages, saying: "Maybe I may yet have a share of the next world together
with them!" And the mercies of the Holy and Blessed One revolved so
that He gave him a son when the man was seventy years old.

When the child was five years old, he put him riding on his shoulders
and brought him to the house of study, where he said to the teacher: "With
which book will you begin to teach my son?" "With Leviticus," said the
teacher. But the boy's father said to him: "Start my son with the Book
of Genesis, which declares the praises and worth of the Holy and Blessed
One."

So day by day he rode him on his shoulders to the house of study.

"How long are you going to tire yourself riding me on your shoulders?" asked the boy. "Let me be, for I know the way and I can go alone." "Go, my son, as you desire," said his father.

Now it came about one day that the king's messenger met him when he was alone and saw that he was very good-looking and dressed in fine clothes; so he stole him and took him away to his city. In the evening his father saw that his son had not returned, so he went to his teacher and asked: "Where is my son whom I sent to you?" "I do not know," said the teacher, "for he did not come to study today." When the father heard this he wailed and wept and cried to all: "Have you seen a handsome boy, looking thus and thus?" "We have not seen him," said they; and when his father and mother heard this, they wailed and wept and groveled in the ashes until their weeping mounted up on high.

Now the mercies of the Holy and Blessed One revolved again, and He sent a heavy sickness upon the king by whose servant the boy was caught. And the king ordered that a book of remedies should be brought to him. As they brought it, Gabriel came and replaced it by the Book of Genesis. The king's sages opened it but could not read the book at all; and his attendants said to him: "We believe that it must be a Jewish book." They sought for a Jew to read it, but did not find any. Then the king's messenger said: "My lord king, when I went to the Jewish village I stole a Jewish child from there. Maybe he can read this book." "Go and fetch him to me," said the king. So he went and brought him before the king.

"My son," said the king to him, "if you know how to read this book, then happy are you and happy are we!" When the boy saw the book, he cried out and wept and flung himself to the ground. "Have no fear of me," said the king. And the boy answered: "I do not fear you but I was the only child of my father and mother, and the Holy and Blessed One gave me to them in their old age, when he was seventy years old. And this is the book that my father taught me, so that is why I wept." "Can you read it?" asked the king. So he began reciting the whole of the first chapter. "And can you explain it?" asked the king. Then the Holy and Blessed One gave him understanding and knowledge to interpret the whole passage. When the king heard the wisdom and comprehension, and how the Holy and Blessed One created His world, he confessed and gave thanks to the said Creator. Thereupon he was healed and sat up on his bed. And he said: "Blessed is the Lord who sent me healing by this lad!"

Then the king said to him: "My son, ask what you want me to give you." And the boy answered: "My lord king, I ask of you only to restore me to my father and mother." So the king immediately ordered that the boy should be taken to his treasury and given silver and gold and jewels beyond measure, and that he should then be restored to his parents. This they did, and when his father and mother saw him they uttered praises and thanksgiving to the Holy and Blessed One.

At that time our sages of blessed memory declared: "Consider. This child had learned nothing more than the Book of Genesis, yet the Holy and Blessed One gave him so much. Then now much more will be received by the one who studies Torah and Mishnah! And furthermore, to this child who honored his father only by saying on one occasion: 'Do not ride me on your shoulders and do not tire yourself for I can walk by myself,' the Holy and Blessed One gave all this money. So, how much greater the reward which will be received by the one who honors his father and his mother!"

46
THE WEASEL AND THE PIT

A cryptic allusion to this romantic tale is found in the Babylonian Talmud, but its full narrative articulation became available only in the Middle Ages. In the nineteenth century the basic theme of the tale became very popular in Hebrew and Yiddish literatures. Source: M. Gaster, The Exempla of the Rabbis, *No. 89, pp. 74, 59–60.*

Rabbi Hanina said: "Consider how great are witnesses who are sureties!" And whence do we know? From the weasel and the pit. And if this could befall with one who takes weasel and pit as witness and surety, how much more so with one who takes the Holy and Blessed One as witness.

Once upon a time a certain girl was going home. She was bedecked with gold and silver. But she lost her way and walked in uninhabited places. The noon hour came, she was thirsty and had no companions. Then she saw a well with a rope and bucket hanging from it. She took the rope of the bucket and climbed down and drank. But when she wished to climb up she could not do so; and she wept and wailed and shouted aloud.

A man passed by and heard her voice. He stood over the well, gazed down but could not distinguish anything. "Who are you?" he asked. "Of humankind or of the imps?" "I am of humankind." "Maybe you are an evil spirit and are deceiving me," said he. "No," she answered. "Swear to me," said he then, "that you are a human being." So she took oath.

"What has happened?" he asked; and she told him the whole story. "If I bring you up," said he, "will you mate with me?" "Yes," said she; and he brought her up.

Once he brought her up he wished to mate with her. But she said to him: "Of which people are you?" "I am of Israel," said he, "I come from such and such a place and I am a *cohen* (priest)." Then she said to him: "I also belong to this and that family, well-known and distinguished people." And she went on: "A person like you, who belongs to the holy stock which the Holy and Blessed One selected and hallowed out of all Israel—do you wish to act like a brute beast without a marriage document and proper hallowing? Come for me to my father and mother, and I shall plight my troth with you." So they made a covenant with one another. And she asked: "Who will be witness between you and me?" Now a weasel was just passing in front of them. Said he: "By heaven! Let the weasel and the well be witnesses that we shall not play one another false." Then he went his way and she went hers.

Now the girl remained true to her promise. If anybody came to seek her hand, she would reject him. When her family began to put pressure on her, she began to behave as though she were demented and began tearing her own garments and the garments of anybody who touched her. At last people left her alone, and she remained true to that man.

As for him, once he had gone away from her his instinct possessed him, he forgot her, went to his city, engaged in his craft, and wedded a wife. She became pregnant and bore him a son. But when he was three months old, a weasel choked him. She became pregnant again and bore a son who fell into a pit. Then the man's wife said to him: "If your children had died in the ordinary way I would have accepted the judgment and held it just. But now that they have perished in these strange fashions I feel there must be a reason. Tell me all you have done!" Then he told her the whole story, and she said: "Go to the portion that was given you by the Holy and Blessed One."

He went away and sought her in her town. "She is demented," they said to him, "and anybody who wishes to wed her is treated in this and this way." Then he went to her father and told him the whole tale. And he went on: "I accept her with any blemishes there may be in her." The father called witnesses. Then he went to her, and she began to act after her fashion, but he merely said: "Weasel and pit." Then she answered him: "I, too, have kept my word."

And she returned to herself at once. They increased and multiplied both in children and possessions; and to them may be applied the verse in the

Psalm (101:6): "My eyes are on those who are faithful in the land, to dwell with Me."

47
JOSEPH THE SABBATH-LOVER

The theme of "treasure found in the fish belly" is known internationally and is found in classical and talmudic-midrashic literature. In the present tale it serves to underscore the significance of Sabbath observance in Jewish society. Source: Rabbi Nissim, Ḥibbur Yafeh, p. 10.

Our sages, may they be well remembered, related that a certain wealthy Gentile was the neighbor of Joseph the Sabbath-lover. And this Joseph was so called because he used to spend far more than he had in honor of the Sabbath, reducing his sustenance and livelihood all the week round in order that he should have plenty for the Sabbath day. And he had no treasures and no money.

Now the magicians and the stargazers said to his neighbor the Gentile: "Know that this Jew your neighbor will consume all your wealth and property and enjoy them." At this, the man grew very apprehensive and fearful. He collected all that belonged to him and sold it and purchased one single fine jewel. This he knotted in the turban round his head, for he feared that if he left it at home his neighbor Joseph would take it.

In due course the Gentile went to walk along the bank of the River Euphrates when a mighty mountain-breaking and rock-smashing hurricane came and blew his turban off his head and flung it into the River Euphrates. And the Lord appointed a great fish to swallow the turban.

In due course a fisherman caught the fish and asked his companions: "Who will buy this fish from me?" "The best purchaser you can find for it," said they, "is Joseph the Sabbath-lover." So he brought it to him, and he purchased it from him at a very high price.

When Joseph the Sabbath-lover slit the belly open in order to prepare it for the Sabbath, he found the jewel within. He sold it for a vast amount of money and was delivered from his distress and troubles. In this way God delivered him from his poverty and need. And his affairs spread far and wide, and he remained a wealthy man all the days of his life.

48
DAMA BEN NETINAH

The red heifer, para adummah, *was essential for the purification ritual, cleansing people who were contaminated by contact with the dead. Source: A. Jellinek, ed.,* Bet ha-Midrasch *1:76.*

Consider what was done by a certain Gentile in Ashkelon named Dama ben Netinah. On one occasion the sages came to purchase precious stones from him for the high priest's *ephod,* to a value of sixty myriad dinars. Now the key was under his father's head, and he did not wish to disturb him. Some years later the Holy and Blessed One repaid him fully for his behavior. In his herd he had a red cow. The sages of Israel came to him, and he told them: "I know that even if I were to ask all the money in the world of you, you would give it to me; but all I ask of you is the money I lost on that occasion because I honored my father." So they paid him that sum.

On one occasion he was seated with the great men of Rome wearing silk. His mother came and tore it off him and spat in his face. And he made no reply.

49
RABBI JOSHUA BEN ULAM AND NINUS THE BUTCHER

The theme of paradise as a reward for a single good deed is extremely popular in Jewish folk narratives. The tale often takes the pattern of the present story: a pious man learns that his neighbor in paradise will be an apparently impious, low-class person and he seeks him out inquiring what charitable acts has he performed to merit such a reward. Source: Ch. Albeck, ed., Midraš Berešit Rabbati: ex libro R. Mosis Haddaršan, *pp. 146–147.*

It is told that Elijah appeared in a dream to Rabbi Joshua ben Ulam and said to him: "Rejoice, for you and Ninus the Butcher of Kfar Kitor have equal seats and equal shares in Eden!" When he woke up Rabbi Joshua thought to himself: "Woe is me! Since my birth I have shown my full awe of my Maker and have toiled only in Torah and have never even walked four ells without *tzitzit* (fringes) and *tefillin* (phylacteries), and have had eighty disciples; and yet all my deeds and Torah are counterbalanced by some butcher! I take oath that I shall not enter the house of study or sit there until I go and find that butcher who is to be my companion in Eden."

So what did he do? He went from town to town and land to land and asked about the city and the man. When he came to the city, he asked after him, saying: "Where does Ninus live?" And all the townsfolk said: "Good sir, what do you desire of that man? You are a saintly diadem of Israel, yet you ask after him." "What does he do?" asked he; and they said to him: "Be seated and refresh yourself, you and your disciples, for you are weary from the way. As for that Ninus, he is a butcher, and why do you need him?" "By the Temple service," declared the rabbi, "neither I nor my disciples will eat anything until you show him to me." They sent for him at once, saying: "Rabbi Joshua has asked after you." "Who am I," said he to them, "and who are my fathers that Rabbi Joshua the Light of Israel should send for me?" "Get up," said they, "and come with us." But thinking to himself that they were mocking him, he said to himself: "I will not go."

So they returned to Rabbi Joshua and said to him: "Alas, light of our eyes, we have gone to him but he sent us packing." At this, Rabbi Joshua and his disciples rose and went to him. He promptly came and prostrated himself before Rabbi Joshua, saying: "My lord, what do you desire of me? How does this day differ from any other that you should seek me?" "I have something to say to you," said the rabbi. "Say it, my lord," said he, and Rabbi Joshua asked: "What is your calling?" "I am a butcher," said he, "and I have an aged father and mother who can neither stand nor sit; and I clothe them and feed them and wash them with my own hands."

At this, Rabbi Joshua rose and kissed him on the forehad, saying: "My son, happy are you and pleasant your fate; and happy is my portion, for I am privileged to be your companion in Eden; and happy is the father from whom you have come!"

50
The Drunkard and His Sons

This story, which is part of the Aesopic tradition, occurs in both the midrashic and the medieval fable literatures, and has been recorded also as a modern Jewish oral folktale. It reflects Jewish burial methods in the Graeco-Roman period. At that time the dead was put into a sarcophagus that was placed in a burial cave carved into a limestone mountain, or in a hollowed rock in the cave wall. Source: I. Lévi, "Un recueil de contes juifs inédits," pp. 60–62.

There was an old man who had two sons. He himself was very attracted to wine and loved to drink. Whatever his sons earned during the day, he would drink at night. Said one to the other: "What shall we do with our father who drinks everything so that we cannot even buy ourselves shoes for our feet? If you listen to my advice, we shall hold back our wages for two or three days and then let him drink the whole value together so that he becomes thoroughly drunk (and will die of too much drink)." What did they do? They gave their father so much wine to drink that he fell fast asleep. Then they summoned the neighbors and said: "Come to our father who has passed away!" They made him shrouds and bore him away to the graveyard. Now in those parts and those days the dead were buried in hollowed rocks which were like a house and were placed on the ground. And the old man was so fast asleep in his intoxication that he lay as still as a corpse. So they put him in the grave and went back home.

Next day Ishmaelites came bringing wine and roast meat and bread and all kinds of food to that city which was under siege. The enemy came upon them, and when the merchants saw that they were being pursued, they hid all the food and drink in the cave and fled away on their camels. On the third day the old man woke up and was confused and did not know where he was. He groped around and called and could find nobody moving in the rock. But he groped with his hands and found wine kegs and meat and bread and cheese. "My sons have abandoned me here," said he, "but Blessed be my Creator who has aided me!" And what did he do? He sat and ate and drank until he was drunk and played games with his hand as though it were some musical instrument.

After three days had passed his sons went to see whether he was dead or not. They came to the rock and heard their father making music. "He is still alive," said they; and they went to him and asked: "How are you, father?" "You wicked creatures," said he to them, "you thought to do me evil but the Holy and Blessed One thought to make something good of it and has kept me alive today. Go away, my Creator will aid me all my life long!"

So they went looking and found the wine in kegs and meat and bread and cheese aplenty. Then they said to their father: "Come home, and we swear that we shall supply you with your needs all our life long!" And they loaded up the food and the wine and fetched it home and provided for him all their lives long.

51
THE COMMANDMENT OF TZITZIT

This tale belongs to a cycle of exempla advocating control of sexual desire. This was a Stoic value that became part of the rabbinical teachings, as it is found in Pirkei Avot, *the "Chapters of the Fathers": "Who is strong (or: a hero)? Whoever conquers his impulse" (4:1). Source: Anon., Midrashot u-Ma'asiyyot, pp. 46–47.*

We find that he who devotes himself to the performance of one single commandment may have it serve him as a reason to be saved from transgression and it may bring him ample reward and be fully effective for the World to Come.

Our rabbis, may they be remembered for good, tell of a certain man who was particularly careful and nimble in respect of the commandment of the tzitzit (fringes). One day he was told that there was a certain Roman woman in the seaport who took four hundred zuz for a day spent with her. He went to her city and came to her house and called for them to open. The maidservant came out to him and he gave her the money which she took to her mistress, who told the servant: "Go and tell him to go away now and come back later." And the maidservant told him so, and he went away and waited until the time she had said. Then he went back to her gateway, and the maidservant told her lady, who ordered him to come.

So he entered the house where he found that there were twelve couches, six of silver and six of gold, all draped with fine covers; and she was seated naked on one of them. Now when the youth divested himself of his prayer shawl, the four fringes at each corner bunched themselves each one on its own and appeared to him like four witnesses. So he descended from the couch and fell to earth on his face, fully ashamed, and beat his head against the ground.

When the woman saw this, she went down to him and took oath, saying: "I shall not let you be until you tell me what blemish or defect you have seen on my body." Then he swore to her: "Never have I seen so beautiful a woman as you, and there is no blemish in you; but the Holy and Blessed One has commanded us to fulfill a certain commandment which is the wearing of the *tzitzit* (Num. 15:37-41), concerning which we find the word "I" written twice in the Torah, as much as to say, first: I shall hold anyone who transgresses My Torah guilty, and second: I shall bring My bounty to those who observe it. When I saw the *tzitzit* now, they seemed to me like four witnesses giving evidence against me; so I feared for my soul and now I pray to the Lord for atonement."

Then she adjured him again, saying: "I shall not let you be until you tell me your name and your city and the name of the rabbi with whom you study, and the place of his school where he teaches the young." And he told her for she was very insistent; and he departed from her happy and cheerful since he had subdued his evil intention and brought his desires low and had been delivered from transgression.

Now after this the woman went and divided up all her possessions. A third she gave to the king and a third to the poor and a third she brought with her to the school. Then she went and came before Rabbi Hiyya, the teacher of the student, and requested him to immerse her and make a Jewess of her since she wished to accept the faith of Israel. "Go away from me," said Rabbi Hiyya to her, "for you must desire or love one of my students and wish to wed him." Then she brought forth an account of all that had happened to her with the student and gave it to the rabbi. When Rabbi Hiyya had read it through he said: "Rise, my son, and wed her, for the Holy and Blessed One prevented you from coming to her sinfully, since you feared for your soul and did not transgress the commandment." So Rabbi Hiyya gave orders and the woman went and was immersed. And the student took her as his wife and came to her; and disciples of the sages were born of her.

Come and consider the greatness of this student who first desired to come to her when it was prohibited and a transgression but conquered his evil inclination and defeated his desire and his heart and did not approach her when it was prohibited. For the Holy and Blessed One gave him his recompense and prepared her for him, so that he took her by permission and remained with the boundless rewards of the World to Come.

52

RABBI JOSHUA BEN LEVI AND ELIJAH THE PROPHET

Rabbi Joshua ben Levi, a Palestinian amora of the first generation (220–250 C.E.), was known for his great piety and humility, and merited a vision appearance of Elijah the Prophet. The present tale occurs only in medieval literature and may reflect Islamic influence. However, the image of Joshua ben Levi in talmudic-midrashic tradition would certainly qualify him for his role in the present theodicy legend. Source: Rabbi Nissim, Ḥibbur Yafeh, pp. 4–6.

Rabbi Joshua ben Levi fasted for many a day and prayed to his Blessed Creator that he might be allowed to see Elijah, whom it is so good to remember. And at length Elijah appeared to him and said: "What do you desire of me? I shall fulfill it." Then Rabbi Joshua said: "I long to accompany you and see what you do in the world in order that I may benefit from it and learn much wisdom." "You will be unable," Elijah told him, "to bear all that you see me doing, and it will trouble you if I should tell you the reasons for my deeds and works." At this, Rabbi Joshua told him: "My lord, I shall not ask and I shall not be a trial to you nor shall I bother you with questions, for all my wish is to see your deeds and nothing more." So Elijah made a condition with him that if Rabbi Joshua should ask him to explain the reason for his deeds and signs and wonders, he would tell him; but also if he did so ask, Elijah would leave him at once.

So they set out together until they reached the home of a poor and needy man who had nothing more than a cow in his courtyard. The man and his wife were sitting at the entry. They saw the wayfarers coming and went to meet them and wished them peace and rejoiced with them and offered them the best in their home. They brought before them whatever they had to eat and drink. So they ate and drank and spent the night there. When morning came, they rose to depart. Elijah said a prayer over the cow, and it died at once. Then they both went their way.

Rabbi Joshua saw what had happened and was astonished and confused, saying to himself: "What this poor man received did not befit the honor he showed us. Surely something else could be done instead of slaying his cow when he had no other," and he said to Elijah: "Good sir, Why did you slay the man's cow after he had honored us so much?" But Elijah answered: "Remember the condition which we agreed to, that you would remain silent and say nothing; but if you wish us to part from one another, I shall explain." At this, Rabbi Joshua stopped asking questions.

They both went on all day long. At evening they came to the home of a wealthy man who disregarded them and did not set out to honor them in any way. There they stayed without food or drink. Now in his house this wealthy man had a fallen wall which he should have rebuilt. In the morning Elijah prayed, and the wall was restored of itself. They both went away from there. Rabbi Joshua continued to be puzzled and grieved by Elijah's deeds. But he controlled his impulse to ask him questions.

They went on all daylong. In the evening they reached a synagogue where there were benches of gold and silver, and each person was seated in his place according to his proper worth and esteem. "Who will feed these poor men tonight?" asked one; and another answered: "The bread and water and salt which will be brought here for them will be enough." So they waited but they were not treated with due and proper courtesy; and they stayed there until daylight. In the morning they rose and went their way, but first Elijah said to the people in the synagogue: "May God make you all leaders!" Then they continued all day long. Rabbi Joshua became even more puzzled and grieved, but he said nothing.

They reached a certain city as the sun was declining. There the townsfolk saw them and came to welcome them with great delight. They received them gladly and rejoiced with them and took them to the best of their homes, a large house of theirs, and there they ate and drank and lodged with much honor. In the morning, Elijah prayed and then said to the townsfolk: "May the Holy and Blessed One set only one leader among you!"

Now when Rabbi Joshua heard this, he could no longer control himself or remain silent after all he had seen Elijah do and he said to him: "Now let me know the secret of all this." And Elijah answered: "Since you wish to part from me, I shall explain it all to you and inform you of the reasons behind all you saw. As for the man whose cow I slew, it had been decreed that his wife should perish that day; but I prayed to God that the cow might serve in her place. I also saw that the woman would bring much benefit and great advantage to their home. Then there was the man whose wall I set up for him. If I had left this to him, he would have gone down to the foundation and would have found a vast hidden treasure of gold and silver, which was why I built it for him. In any case the wall will soon collapse, never to be rebuilt.

"Then there were the men for whom I prayed that there should be many lords and leaders among them; for that will harm them greatly and lead to great disputes in their counsels and thoughts. For wherever there are many leaders, the place is ruined and destroyed and blameworthy. Then there were the men for whom I prayed that they should have a single head. That will be to their benefit and advantage because they will bring their thoughts and deeds to a common purpose and will rejoice, and there will be no disputes among them, and their counsel will not chop and change, nor will their thoughts be reversed. For as the proverb says, Too many captains sink the ship. And people also say: The city is settled under a single head."

And Elijah also told him: "Before I leave you I wish to tell you how you can prosper. If you see a wicked man prospering, do not envy him or be surprised, for it will prove to be to his disadvantage. If you see a righteous man grieving and suffering all his life and toiling to weariness and hungering and thirsting and naked and lacking for all things, or suddenly suffering, do not let it enrage you and do not permit your impulse to mislead you or to doubt your Creator. Bear in mind that He is righteous and His judgment is righteous and He observes all the ways of a man. And who can upbraid Him, saying: 'What are You doing?'"

After that, they bade one another farewell, and Elijah went his way.

53
EXTENUATING CIRCUMSTANCES

The hired hand in this story follows the dictate "Judge all men in the scale of merit," in Avot 1:6. Source: Joseph Sh. Farḥi, Oseh Pele, *3:319–320.*

I t happened in the holy city of Safed, may it be builded up and established, that a certain man went to another city and hired himself out to a householder for a period of three years to practice his craft for him. And it so came about that the end of the three years fell on the eve of the Day of Atonement. Then the hired man said to the householder: "Pay me my wages, for I wish to go home to provide for my household and spend the holiday with them."

"I have no money," said the householder. And the hired man answered: "If you have no ready money, give me fruits from your fields according to the price at which they are sold in the market." "I have none," said he. "Then give me a piece of land," said the craftsman, "and I shall try to sell it." "I have none," said he. "Then give me animals to an equal value," said the craftsman. "I have none," said he.

He tried again and said: "Give me pillows and cushions and movables from your household." And still he answered: "I have none." Finally the hired man gave up asking, when he saw that whatever he said the other answered that he did not have it; although he knew that the householder did not lack for anything. So he made his way to his city, fuming and distressed, without a single farthing.

After the festival the householder took all the money which he owed to the said hired man together with three beasts, one carrying foodstuff, the other wine, and the third fruits of all kinds. And he set out for the holy city of Safed, may it be builded up and established, and there he lodged in the home of the said hired man. After they had eaten and drunk, he paid him his hire to the full.

Then he asked his hireling: "By your life, I wish you to tell me: When you asked me to pay you your hire and I told you that I had no ready money—of what did you suspect me at heart?" And the other answered: "I judged you favorably, thinking to myself: Maybe he found some goods to buy cheaply and spent all his money on it, so that he really has no ready money now; and since it was the eve of the Day of Atonement, he is not in a position to sell part of his goods in order to pay me."

Then he went on: "And when you asked me to give you beasts in payment and I told you I had none, what did you think?" "I thought," answered he, "that you may have hired them out to others and cannot take them back until the time of their hire is over." "And when you asked me," pursued the householder, "to give you a piece of land and I told you I had none—what did you think of me then?" "I supposed," answered he, "that you must have leased your land to tenants on an agreement that they would give you such and such a share of the crops per year, so the fields are not in your possession." Then he asked again: "And when I told you that I did not even have any fruit or crops, what did you think?" "I assumed," said the hireling, "that you had not yet deducted the tithe, and that was why you could not give them to me; and since it was the eve of the Day of Atonement, there was no time left for separating it." Then he asked once more: "And when I told you that I did not even have pillows and cushions, what did you think then?" "I thought," said he, "that you must have dedicated all your property."

Then the householder swore to him: "In all truth, that is how it was. I dedicated all my property because of my son Hyrcanus who did not study Torah, in order that he should not enjoy it; and when I went to my friends the sages of the south, they relieved me of my vow. Now just as you have judged me favorably, so may the Holy and Blessed One judge you favorably. For whatever you considered extenuating circumstances in respect of all the things which you asked of me, so it was in actual fact. You did not miss anything."

That is as far as the story goes.

54
GENEROSITY

This story belongs to the "neighbor in paradise" narrative cycle. The professions of the apparently "unworthy" neighbors in the world to come reflect the social stratification of Jewish society from the scholars' perspectives. In addition to butchers, barbers, tax collectors, and prison wardens function in this role. Source: Rabbi Nissim, Ḥibbur Yafeh, pp. 20–21.

There was a certain God-fearing and humble scholar who asked his God to let him know who his companion would be in the World to Come. He fasted for many days and offered many prayers and entreaties until he was informed in a dream by night: "Your companion will be So-and-So the butcher." When he awoke from his sleep, he was disturbed and upset and sighed and grieved. Once again he fasted and prayed to the Lord until he was informed in a dream: "You have already been told that So-and-So is to be your companion in the World to Come." When he heard this again, he was stupefied and moaned and wept greatly. But then he heard a voice from heaven: "Had you not been a pious man with many good deeds in your favor, you would have perished. Why are you vexed when you are told that So-and-So the butcher is to be your companion? Do you know what good deeds that butcher has done, which are far more than most men could do, and can you comprehend how high his rank is in the World to Come?"

At this the scholar rose in the morning and went to the butcher's shop. He greeted him and sat down beside him and said to him: "I would like you to tell me what you do and what kind deeds you perform." At this the butcher said to him: "Sir, you see my work. But of all I earn I give half for charity, while from the other half my family and I support ourselves." "Many people," said the scholar, "give even more for charity. But now tell me whether you have ever done anything which is more than most men could do."

The butcher remained silent for quite a long while. Then he said: "Good sir, I have just remembered something I did several years ago." "And what was it?" asked the sage. And he answered:

At that time too I was busy at my work when a caravan of Gentiles came to the city, bringing many captives with them. Among them was a little girl, weeping bitterly. I went to her and said: "Child, why are you weeping and wailing like this?" Then she said to me: "Sir, I am a Jewess and I fear that these non-believers may take me far away from Jewry. I wish I could go to some Jewish place where Jews would redeem me."

As soon as I heard this my heart felt soft and I pitied her and told her: "Be quiet and have faith, for I shall redeem you." Then I went to her owner at once and purchased the girl at a high price, more indeed than I could afford.

Now the girl was twelve years old, and I brought her home and clad her till she grew. I had an only son who was twenty-one years old and one day I spoke to him in secret and entreated him saying: "My son, take my advice and do my behest and satisfy my wish in order that things should be well with you in this world and the World to Come." "Tell me what you desire," said he, "for I shall not depart from your command either to the right or the left." "My wish," said I to him, "is that you should take this maiden for wife, and I shall prepare you most worthy and fitting garments and jewelry." "I am in your hands," said he, "do what you think fit."

I was very happy and prepared all they would require from thread to shoelace. Nothing was missing. Then I made a great feast for the wedding, and there was not a single townsman who did not come. And I summoned all the poor and seated them beside the townsmen so that they should not feel ashamed. Then I set food and dainties before them all, and they ate and drank and were happy and of good cheer. All except the men who were seated at a certain table and ate nothing. "Brothers," said I to them, "why do you behave like this? Is there anything the matter with the food?"

"Heaven forbid," said they to me, "we have never seen better. But this poor man who is seated with us is weeping and shedding tears and sighing ever since he has taken his place here. And because of his moaning and weeping we are unable to eat."

At this, I took him by the hand and brought him out of the room by himself and said to him: "Brother, why do you treat me so badly and grieve the guests? Tell me what ails you and why you feel so bad, and do not conceal anything from me. If you are in debt, I shall give you what you need; and if you need a loan, I shall lend it to you." "I am not in debt," said he, "and I do not need a loan, but I weep because of this maiden whom you are marrying to your son. She is from such-and-such a city, and I was betrothed to her several years ago on this very day. And she is betrothed to me, but she was taken captive and I have come after her, and this is the writ of our betrothal." And he brought forth the writ, and I saw that it was as he said. Then I asked him: "What sign have you that this is the maiden?" And he answered me: "Once I saw her in her father's house, and on her body was this and that sign at this and that spot." Then I believed his words and said to him: "Be strong and control yourself, for I shall satisfy your longings."

Then I called my son and said to him: "My son, you have done my will regarding this maiden. Now do what I wish in whatever I tell you, and it will be good for you." "As I did to begin with for your sake," said he, "so I shall do now. I shall not disobey." Then I told him: "This maiden has been betrothed to someone else and I have already seen the writ of her betrothal, and the man who was betrothed to her is here, so she is forbidden to you. Now it is my desire that you should give him all I prepared for you in the way of garments and jewels, and restore her to her husband; and you will merit a worthy reward, and I shall find you a better wife than this and give you twice as much." "Do so," said he, "and I shall do what you have asked."

So I took the newly arrived man and the maiden and placed them beneath the bridal canopy. The groomsmen and bridesmen were present and said the wedding blessings. I gave them all I had in my house, and all that was prepared for my son. They stayed with me for a long time, happy and of good cheer, not lacking for anything, so that they forgot their trouble and distress. At length they wished to return to their own city. I gave them fine gifts and provision for the way and sent them off in peace. And I have always asked wayfarers regarding their well-being.

Then the scholar said to him: "May you be blessed before the Lord. You have set my heart at rest and I rejoice that you will be my companion in the World to Come."

55
Rabbi Beroka and Elijah the Prophet

The talmudic-midrashic references to Rabbi Beroka are scanty and there is very little biographical tradition about him. This tale belongs to the theodicy narrative cycle. Source: Rabbi Nissim, Ḥibbur Yafeh, pp. 2–3.

Our rabbis of blessed memory related that once when Rabbi Beroka was walking in the market, Elijah, whom it is good to remember, came toward him and revealed himself to him and spoke to him. Then Rabbi Beroka asked him: "Is there any man in this market who merits to live in the World to Come?" "No," answered the prophet. While they were still talking to one another, a man without fringes and wearing black boots on his legs passed them by. Then Elijah said: "This man who has just passed us is an heir of Eden!"

At this, Rabbi Beroka called him, but he made no answer. He asked permission of Elijah, ran after him and caught up with him. Then the man said to him: "I am the prison warden, and it is my practice to imprison the men separately and the women separately. At night I set my bed between the men and the women and I guard them all night long; for I fear that the prisoners might otherwise rape the women. When a Jewess is imprisoned with me, I try to keep watch over her and to save her. On one occasion a Jewess was brought to prison who was a married woman. I saw that some of the prisoners thought to act improperly with her. So I took a measure of yeast and gave it to her and told her: 'Daughter, rub this yeast over your flesh and say that you are in your courses!' She did so and she was saved, for no man approached her."

Then Rabbi Beroka said to him: "Why do you wear black boots on your feet and why are there no fringes in your prayer shawl?" —And from the account of our sages we can understand that it was not the practice of Jews to wear black boots in that land and in those times.—And the prison warden told him: "So that they should not recognize that I am a Jew, for it is my practice to go to the royal palace. There I hear the decrees they plan to pass against Israel, and I hurry away and inform the sages so that they may fast and pray to the Lord to bring their decrees to naught and confuse their counsel and turn their thoughts away from us." Then Rabbi Beroka asked him: "Why did you not respond when I called you?" And the prison warden answered: "Because I have been informed that all the ministers had gathered at the royal palace to introduce a decree against

Israel. So I hastened in order to inform the sages to appear before our King the Lord of Hosts and entreat Him and beg for the surviving remnant."

(The rabbi returned to Elijah.) While he was still talking with him, two men passed, and Elijah said: "These two are heirs of Eden." So Rabbi Beroka called them and asked: "What do you do?" And they told him: "It is our regular practice when we hear that a man is distressed and feels bitter and moans and aches and is confused that we go to his home to condole with him and console him and speak to his heart in order to make him rejoice and be done with his sighing and his distress and grief and sadness at all that has befallen him and the troubles which compass him about. This we continue to do until he feels consoled and his heart grows strong and his spirit courageous, and he begins to rejoice and be glad."

56
THE STORY OF JOSEPH THE GARDENER
OF ASHKELON AND HIS WIFE

The two sages are Rabbi Eliezer ben Hyrcanus and Rabbi Joshua ben Ḥanania, two tannaim of the second generation (80–110 C.E.), who were disciples of Rabbi Johanan ben Zakkai. The tale appears in Jewish folk literature only since the Middle Ages, reflecting influence of Islamic tradition. Source: Rabbi Nissim, Ḥibbur Yafeh, pp. 12–13.

Now I shall mention something that was very small to begin with but finally grew very great.

Our sages of blessed memory relate that Rabbi Eliezer and Rabbi Joshua made the pilgrimage to the Temple. On the eve of the Day of Atonement they were at the Temple Mount when an angel came toward them bearing a white robe that shone like the sun, and it had no seam to it. One of them said to the other: "This robe must be for one of us!" Then they approached the angel and asked him: "For whom is the robe?" And he answered: "There are many far better robes for both of you; but this robe is for a certain man from Ashkelon named Joseph the Gardener." Then they parted and went their ways.

When the festival days were over they went together to the man of

Ashkelon. The people of Ashkelon rejoiced to see them. They came forth to meet them and requested them to be their guests. But they did not agree, saying: "We shall stay only in the home of Joseph the Gardener!" So they sent people with them to the home of Joseph.

When they reached the entry to his garden, they saw him at a distance picking vegetables. They greeted him with peace, and he responded. Then they said: "We wish to stay with you"; and he answered: "My masters, have you forsaken wealthy and honorable men in order to come to me? The Holy and Blessed One knows that I have no more than two loaves of bread in my home." "What you have," said they, "will suffice, and we shall not require any more." So he set it before them, and they ate bread and drank water and said the blessing.

Then they said to him: "You see that we came to you and did not wish to go to your townsmen. So tell us now what your deeds are." And he answered: "My masters, you see my poverty, and you see that I have no other work but this gardening which you have seen." "In spite of that," said they, "tell us whether you have always engaged in this work since your youth." And he answered: "If you so wish I shall tell you about myself and my affairs, I shall reveal it all to you. Know in truth that my father of blessed memory was one of the leading and wealthiest men of this city. But when he departed this life, I lost that wealth, and the townsfolk saw me and they expelled me and hated me. So I left the city weeping and built my home here and planted this garden and sowed vegetables in it. Whatever grows here I sell, and give half to the poor as charity while I support myself and my household with the other half."

Then they told him: "Know that the Holy and Blessed One will give you a very great reward. For in the hands of an angel we saw a white and smooth robe, and the angel told us it is yours. But the hem did not have a train. Therefore we came to bring you the tidings that the Holy and Blessed One will be very good indeed to you, and maybe you can still increase your merit." And the man blessed them and praised them; and they went their way.

Then his wife said to him: "I heard the sages of Israel telling you that the train of your robe was missing. Now listen to me and take my advice and try to complete the robe." "You speak most generously," said her husband to her, "but you know my poverty. I have nothing with which to achieve any merit whatsoever." "Listen to me, my lord," said she, "and take my counsel in order that things may go well with thee. Take me and sell me in the market and give my price as charity to the poor. Then maybe your robe will be complete." And he answered her: "I fear to do so, for maybe the purchaser will seduce you or rape you, and I shall lose the whole robe." "I swear to you," his wife assured him, "by my faith in heaven, that no such shame will come about through me!" So he hearkened to her words and went and sold her and gave the money as charity to the poor.

Now her master saw that she was beautiful and wished to win her over, but could not succeed. He set her in charge of his treasury and gave her his keys. But she said to him: "My lord, I am not worthy to be your housekeeper." Then he became very angry with her and gave her to his shepherd. He ordered him to master her, but he could not seduce her. The shepherd took her and beat her until he wounded her, but could not prevail. He embittered her life with hard labor and every kind of trouble. But she controlled herself and waited for the mercies of heaven.

A long time passed. Then her husband disguised himself and came to see her, pretending to be a stranger. He found her bitter of spirit and unhappy. All her beauty was gone, and she wore "a garb of belted sackcloth instead of her robe; a burn instead of beauty" (Isa. 3:24). And he said to her: "Would you have me purchase you and wed you and deliver you from your distress?" "Good sir," said she to him, "that is impossible for I have a husband." And he went on trying to entice her and seduce her with many smooth words, but she would not listen.

When her husband saw this, he understood that she had not broken her vow, and he removed his disguise; and she recognized him. They kissed one another and embraced and wept bitterly so that their outcry went up to God. Then they heard a voice that cried: "Be informed that your robe is complete and your wife's robe is better than yours! Go to such-and-such a place where you will find a vast treasure that your father hid."

So they went there, and they found silver and gold and precious stones. And he took them and redeemed his wife, and he continued to engage in charity and acts of kindness all the days of his life.

57
THE RESTLESS DEAD

This legend functions to sanction the mourner's Kaddish prayer, which became part of the religious service in the Middle Ages. While in most of its versions Rabbi Akiba, the leading second-century tanna, is the main character, in isolated versions Rabbi Johanan ben Zakkai, the first-century tanna, or Rabbi Israel Baal Shem, the legendary founder of the Hasidic movement, serve in this role. Source: M. Gaster, The Exempla of the Rabbis, *No. 134, pp. 84, 92–93.*

They say that Rabbi Akiba was once passing through a graveyard when he met a man who was black as charcoal and was carrying wood on his shoulder and running along under the load like a horse. Rabbi Akiba ordered him to stop and said to him: "My son, why are you engaged in this hard labor? If you are a slave and your master gives you this heavy burden, I shall redeem you from him and set you free; and if you are a poor man, come and I shall enrich you." "Let me pass, good sir," said the other, "for I may not tarry."

"Tell me," said Rabbi Akiba, "are you of humankind or an imp?" "He to whom you speak," said the other, "is dead and is sent every day to hew the wood with which he is burned."

"My son," said Rabbi Akiba, "what did you do in the world you have left behind?" "I was a tax collector," said he, "and I was forbearing to the wealthy but slew the poor. And furthermore I had intercourse with a betrothed maiden on the Day of Atonement." "My son," said the rabbi, "have you ever heard that you have any way of escape from those appointed over you?" "Good sir," said he, "do not delay me or those set over me will slay me, for they are masters of torment and perform it. And there is no hope for this man. But I have heard of something that I cannot do. I have heard them tell that if such a one as I had a son who could stand amid the congregation and say: 'Bless you the Lord who is ever blessed,' and the congregation were to answer, 'Amen,' then he who was once a man will be freed of his torments. Now I have no son, but I left my wife pregnant and do not know whether she gave birth to a son or a daughter. Yet even if I have a son, who would teach him Torah? For I had no friend in the world I have left behind."

At this Rabbi Akiba undertook to go to the city of the dead man and ask whether he had left a son. If so, he would teach him Torah. And he asked him: "What was your name?" "Akiba," said he. "And what was your wife's name?" asked the rabbi. "Shishna," said the dead man. "And what was your city?" he asked. And the other said: "Laodicea."

So Rabbi Akiba went and asked after him. "Rabbi," said the townsfolk, "may the very bones of that wicked creature be pounded to dust!" "In spite of it," said he to them, "tell me about him." "He has a son," said they, "who is uncircumcised." Then Rabbi Akiba sent for him and circumcised him and taught him Torah and the blessing after food. He would not learn until Rabbi Akiba had spent forty days fasting. And a voice echoed from heaven and asked: "Rabbi Akiba, are you fasting for such a one?"

And the rabbi answered: "Lord of the Universe, was it not before you that I gave a pledge!"

Thereupon the Holy and Blessed One opened the boy's heart, and the rabbi taught him the "Hear, O Israel" and the Eighteen Benedictions and placed him among the congregation. He said: "Bless you the Lord who is ever blessed," and they responded, "Amen."

At that selfsame moment his father was released from the sentence imposed on him. And he came to Rabbi Akiba in a dream by night and said to him: "May your mind be at ease as you have set my mind at ease!" Thereupon Rabbi Akiba exclaimed: "Blessed is the Ever Present, who performs the will of those who fear Him!"

58
THE TALE OF BEN SEVER AND SHEFIFON BEN LAYISH

The biblical verse righteousness delivereth from death *(Proverbs 10:2, 11:4) is implicit in this tale about these two fictional rabbis. Source: M. Gaster,* The Exempla of the Rabbis, *No. 137, pp. 84–85, 94–96.*

There was a pious man, the rabbis tell, whose name was Ben Sever (the Explainer), and he was so called because he used to explain the Torah. And he was a great and saintly man. Once he heard about a Jewish orphan who was betrothed to a woman, yet was not able to wed her though many years had passed. Now as soon as this saint heard of this, he took gold and silver vessels and all kinds of food and drink, enough to load five donkeys, and he went to that city. He came to the orphan and prepared him a house and spread him a bed and arranged the bridal canopy for him and gave him all he required. Then he went back home.

On the way back he came to a great mountain that was twelve miles long where there was a great dragon that was twelve miles long; and it used to bite and burn up all who passed that way. But when it saw Ben Sever, it made a bridge of itself and he passed over it.

When he came down from it, he was met by an exceedingly ugly man who greeted him with peace, and he returned the greeting. "Do you not recognize me?" said the man. "No," said he. Then the man said: "I, the Angel of Death, have come to take your soul, for your name has already been given by heaven."

What did the saint do? He raised his eyes aloft and said: "Lord of the Universe! It is written: 'He who keeps the commandment will meet no evil' (Eccles. 8:5). I went to perform a commandment. Am I to die now on the road without going to declare my will to my wife and children?" At this a divine voice was heard, declaring: "Wait five days and a half for him, five days for him to return home, and half a day to declare his will to his household."

So he went weeping. On the way a certain man met him and greeted him, and he returned the greeting. Then he asked: "Is there a disciple of the sages here?" And the man answered: "There is a great sage here named Shefifon ben Layish." "Lead me to him," said Ben Sever, "for maybe we shall discuss Torah and rejoice, as the Psalm says (19:9) 'the ordinances of the Lord are proper and rejoice the heart.'"

So they led Ben Sever to him. As soon as Shefifon ben Layish saw Ben Sever, the latter's face became as bright as the sun, and Shefifon recognized that the other was a great sage and a saint. After he had enterERD and sat a little while, his face grew greenish. Then Shefifon ben Layish said to him: "When you entered, your face was bright but now it is greenish. Maybe you need to eat and drink, having come from the road?" "No," said he and told his tale. "Stay with me," said Shefifon ben Layish, "and have no fear. I guarantee that you are not going to die now." "The Psalm," answered Ben Sever, "says (49:8): 'A brother cannot redeem a brother.'" "In spite of that," said the other to him, "stay with me!"

And thereupon Shefifon ben Layish and all his disciples rose and imposed a three-day fast in that city and its environs. The whole countryside grew dark at once, and the disciples came and said: "Rabbi and light of our eyes, the whole world is growing dark." "Go out and look carefully," said he to them. "If the whole world is dark, then what has been has been. But if it is only the city and its environs, we may rest assured that the Holy and Blessed One will look upon our entreaties and do our will."

At this, the Angel of Death came down from that cloud, crouched down beside Shefifon, and said to him: "Give me the pledge I left with you." "You left no pledge with me," answered he. "Restore Ben Sever to me," said he, "for death." Then Shefifon said: "I adjure you by the Holy Name that you should return to the Holy and Blessed One and tell him: 'Ben Layish has refused to give me Ben Sever for death.'" And he added: "Go and say this to the Holy and Blessed One: 'His soul is not more precious to the Holy and Blessed One than mine, nor mine than his!'"

So the Angel of Death went and said to Him: "Shefifon ben Layish told me: 'My soul is not more precious to Him than his soul, nor his soul than mine; so if He must slay him, let Him slay both of us together; but if there is to be light, let it be for both of us!'" Thereupon a divine echo was heard, saying: "What am I to do with those two saints? I issue a decree, but they bring it to nothing by their prayer." And the divine echo went on: "I add to them two hundred years apiece."

They say that during those two hundred years no woman miscarried, and the sword was not used in the world, and no wild beast held sway in the world, and no son died before his father, and no man was less than seventy years old when he died, nor was there any famine. It was of them that the Psalmist said (145:19): "He fulfills the wishes of those who fear Him."

59
RABBI JOSHUA BEN LEVI AND THE ANGEL OF DEATH

Rabbi Joshua ben Levi was a Palestinian amora of the first generation (220–250 C.E.) and was known for his great piety and humility. According to talmudic-midrashic tradition, Elijah the Prophet revealed himself to Joshua ben Levi because of his meritorious qualities. He was known for his love and knowledge of the haggadah, *the metaphoric, narrative, and fictive part of traditional literature. Although the present tale has a talmudic source, Rabbi Joshua ben Levi developed into an apocalyptic figure only in medieval folk literature, joining other figures who "entered paradise alive." Source: M. Gaster,* The Exempla of the Rabbis, *No. 138, pp. 85, 96–97.*

It is told that once when Rabbi Joshua ben Levi was sitting and expounding the Torah, the Angel of Death came and stood in his doorway and said to him: "Peace be with you, rabbi!" But he made no answer until he finished his exposition. Then he responded: "Peace be with you, rabbi!" "Why," asked the angel, "are you so proud that you do not respond to a greeting?" "Heaven forbid," said the rabbi, "it was only in order that I should complete the law which I was studying." Then the angel said: "Rabbi, do you not recognize me?" "No," said he. "I am the Angel of Death," said the other, "and the Holy and Blessed One has sent me to take your soul." "By my life," said the rabbi, "even if you stand here a thousand years I shall not entrust my soul to you. Go away."

At this, the angel went up aloft and appeared before the Holy and Blessed One and said: "Lord of the Universe! He would not permit me to stand before him." "Go," said the Holy and Blessed One, "and bedeck yourself with the symbols of death."

They used to say that the length of the Angel of Death was as from one end of the world to the other. From the sole of his foot to the crown of his head he is full of eyes. He is clothed with fire and covered with fire. He is all fire, and the knife is in his hand. Hanging thereon is a drop of gall from which men die and through which they become fetid and by which their faces turn green.

Now he went and bedecked himself and stood at Rabbi Joshua ben Levi's door and said to him: "The Holy and Blessed One has sent me to take your soul." "Heaven forbid," answered the rabbi, "I shall not entrust my soul to you. But if you wish to take my soul, lead me to the Garden of Eden and show me the spot where I am going to rest."

At once the Angel of Death ascended to heaven and said to the Holy and Blessed One: "Lord of the Universe, he would not allow me to take his soul, but this and this is what he told me." Then the Holy and Blessed One answered: "Go and lead him to the Garden of Eden and take out Hiram, king of Tyre, and send him in." Thereupon the angel took the rabbi on his wings and brought him to the Garden of Eden. "Raise me high," said Rabbi Joshua to him, "so that I can see the whole garden and then go down with me and show me where my resting place is going to be." So he raised him high till he could see the entire garden, then he brought him low and said: "This is the spot where you will rest in future."

"Show me the sword with which you take the souls," said Rabbi Joshua. And he gave him the sword. "Is this the sword," asked Rabbi Joshua, "with which you take all the souls?" "Yes," answered the angel. After he had inspected the sword from all sides, he flung himself down into the garden. Then the Angel of Death said to him: "You have not given me your soul, but give me the sword." "By my life," answered Rabbi Joshua, "I shall give you nothing."

Back the angel went to the Holy and Blessed One and complained: "Lord of the Universe! He has taken the sword away from me and flung himself into the Garden of Eden." "Go," said the Holy and Blessed One, "wherever Rabbi Joshua was accustomed to go. If you find that he swore by My Name, ask whether he ever broke his oath. If he did, drive him out of the garden and take his soul. But if not, take the sword and let him be."

Off went the Angel of Death and found Rabbi Joshua's friend, Rabban Gamaliel. "Your friend Rabbi Joshua has behaved very nicely, entering Eden and taking my sword away from me." "By my life," said Rabban Gamaliel, "he has treated you properly. But now take these jottings and give them to Rabbi Joshua. If he sees any Gentiles at all in the entire Garden of Eden, let him write of it to me." When Rabbi Joshua read the note, he went to the gates of Eden where he found three halls, one of silver, one of gold, and one of glass. When he went to survey the hall of glass, he found all those who had converted and joined Israel in it. In the hall of silver he found all the kings of Israel who had followed the right way. In the hall of gold he found Abraham, Isaac, Jacob, Moses, Aaron, and David. And there he saw a great couch on which lay a youth weeping, tears running down from his eyes; and beside him stood an elder with a kerchief in his hands, saying: "How long must you weep? The Holy and Blessed One will satisfy your request!"

When he saw this, Rabbi Joshua asked the Fathers of the World: "Who is the man with the kerchief in his hand?" "That," said they, "is Elijah, whom it is good to mention and who will bring good tidings to Israel, as it is written in Isaiah (52:7): 'How beautiful on the mountains are the feet of the herald, declaring peace, bringing good tidings.'" "And who is the man lying on the couch?" he asked; and they told him: "That is Messiah ben David who will yet comfort Israel, as it is written there (Isa. 40:1): 'Comfort, oh comfort My people, says your God.'"

Rabbinical Tales

60
THE SONS OF MOSES

These tales are attributed to Eldad ha-Dani, a traveler and raconteur with an alliterative name, who mysteriously appeared at the end of the ninth century in the Jewish community of Kairouan in Tunisia. His stories about the Sons of Moses and the Ten Lost Tribes have fired the imagination of world Jewry. On many occasions subsequent Jewish travelers, explorers, and emissaries set out to discover the utopian Jewish communities about which Eldad ha-Dani told. Whether he was a historical or a fictional character, the stories about him and the tales that are attributed to him have developed in oral and written traditions and have attained literary renown. These tales are woven out of traditional Jewish themes and historical accounts. The legendary river Sambatyon is mentioned already in the post-biblical literature, and the belief in the continuous national existence of the "Ten Tribes" that were exiled after the fall of the Kingdom of Israel in 722 B.C.E. is apparent in several biblical texts. The stories of Eldad ha-Dani, however, offer the fullest narrative articulation of these themes. Source: A. Epstein, ed., Sefer Eldad ha-Dani, *pp. 64–65, 54, 65–66, 53, 38–39, 71–72 (abridged and rearranged).*

Our sages relate:
When Israel was exiled to Babylon and came to the River Euphrates (as it is written: "By the rivers of Babylon, there we sat down and wept" Ps. 137:1), the peoples said to the Levites: "Stand in the presence of idols and utter your song as you used to sing in the Temple!" The Levites answered them: "Fools that you are! If only we had uttered song for each and every wonder that the Holy and Blessed One performed for us, we would not have been exiled from our land, but He would have added more honor to our honor and more greatness to our greatness. Should we then

sing in the presence of idols?" They promptly arose and slew them, heaps upon heaps. Yet although they slew so many of them, they rejoiced greatly because they did not engage in idolatry. That is why we find written: "And they that laid us in heaps demanded joy!" (Ps. 137:3). As for the surviving Levites, what did they do? They cut off their fingers so that they would be unable to pluck their harp strings, and when the others said: "Make music," they would show their cut fingers and tell them: "'How shall we sing the song of the Lord in a strange land' (Ps. 137:4), when our fingers are cut off?"

When night came, a cloud descended and covered them and their wives and daughters and sons, but the Holy and Blessed One gave them light by a pillar of fire and led them all night until the morning broke, and He left them on the seashore. When the sun rose, the cloud and pillar of fire departed, and the Holy and Blessed One stretched out before them a certain river whose name is Sambatyon, and thus closed the way before them so that no man would be able to pass over to them. The sea was round about them for a distance of three months' march in all directions and on the other side no wind blew, but the Holy and Blessed One extended that river and closed the way before them. The breadth of that river was two hundred ells. And the river was full of sand and stones that were moving and made a great noise at night that could be heard for half a day's journey, and the sand and stones moved on and on all the six days of the week, but they would rest on the Sabbath. And soon, from Sabbath eve until Sabbath end, fire would go up by the streambed, and the fire would flash and glow. No man could approach within a mile of the stream, and the fire would burn up all that might grow around the river until the earth would be swept clean and bare.

Now those Levites are the B'nai Moshe, the descendents of Moses, and they stayed this side of the stream, and among them there is no impure beast nor impure animal nor any kind of vermin that crawls on the earth; but they have flocks and herds with them. Near them there are another six springs, but they all gather to a single lake from which they water their land. Now in that lake swarm all kinds of fish, and by the springs and around the lake fly all kinds of pure fowl, and they have every kind of fruit among them. When they sow and reap, they sow one measure and reap a hundredfold. And they are men of faith, knowing Torah, Mishnah, and Haggadah. And they are wise, piously God-fearing and holy, and never take oath in vain. They live to a hundred and twenty years, and among them no son will die during the lifetime of his father, but they live to see three and four generations. They themselves build houses and plow and sow because they have neither menservants nor maidservants; and they do not close their houses by night. A little boy can go with his beast for several days' journey without reason to fear either robbers or wild beasts or vermin of the earth or demons or any evil thing, because they are holy. Indeed, they still maintain the sanctity of Moses our Master, may he rest in peace, which is why the Holy and Blessed One gave them all this and made them His choice. They see no man and no man sees them save four tribes alone, these being Dan and Naphtali, Gad and Asher who dwelt beyond the rivers of Kush.

* * *

There is another tribe of the children of Moses our Master, may he rest in peace, the saintly servant of the Lord, and it is known as the tribe of Yanus (meaning "he shall flee"), because they fled from idolatry and remained firm in their fear of the Name; and they encamped near the stream whose name is Sambatyon. The stream surrounds them for a journey of three months by three months. They dwell in magnificent houses and splendid buildings and in towers which they prepare for themselves in times of their joy upon elephants. Among them there is nothing impure and no impure bird or impure beast or impure animal, nor flies nor fleas nor lice, no foxes or scorpions or serpents or dogs—nothing save flocks and herds and fowl. Their flocks yean twice a year, and they sow and reap two times a year. And they have gardens and orchards and olives and pomegranates and figs and all kinds of pulses and melons and cucumbers and onions and garlic and barley and wheat, and from any one measure come a hundred. And all of them are pure, immersing themselves when required, and they take no oath at all. If anybody utters the Name to no purpose they cry out upon him and say: "Because of this sin of taking oath your children will die young." And they live long. And all of them are Levites, and they have neither priests nor Israelites among them.

61
DAN AND HIS BROTHER TRIBES

See above note.

Our rabbis tell:

When Jeroboam, the son of Nebat, rose and fashioned two gold calves and caused Israel to sin and the kingdom of the House of David was divided, he gathered ten tribes of Israel together and said to them: "Go forth and do battle with Rehoboam and with the inhabitants of Jerusalem!" "Shall we wage war," said they to him, "with our brothers, the offspring of our lord David, king of Israel and Judah?" And the elders of Israel came up to him and said: "In the whole of Israel we have no warriors and men of war to compare with the tribe of Dan. Command them to wage war against Judah."

Thereupon Jeroboam said to them: "Sons of Dan, go forth and wage war against Judah and Benjamin." "By the life of our father Dan," said they to him, "we shall not wage war against our brothers, and we shall not shed their blood when there is no reason!" And thereupon the sons of Dan took swords and bows and arrows and spears and dedicated themselves to wage war against Jeroboam until the Lord saved them from shedding the blood of their brothers.

Then they sent a proclamation through the whole tribe of Dan saying: "Sons of Dan, flee and depart from the land of Israel and let us go to Egypt!" For they planned to destroy the land of Egypt and slay all its inhabitants. But their princes said to them: "Where will you go? Why, it is already written in the Torah: 'You shall not see them again forever'" (Ex. 14:13). Then they considered going to Moab and Ammon, but when they found written in the Torah that the Holy and Blessed One had restrained Israel from inheriting their border, the Holy and Blessed One gave them a good inspiration. And the sons of Dan went up toward the River Kishon, riding their camels until they reached the river of Kush. There they found a fat, good, and spacious land, fields and vineyards, gardens and orchards. Nor did the inhabitants of the land prevent the Children of Israel from dwelling together with them but made an alliance with them. So the men of Kush used to pay them a tax and dwelt together with them for many years, until they increased and multiplied exceedingly.

Then after the death of Sennacherib three tribes of Israel journeyed to join them, these being Naphtali, Gad, and Asher. They journeyed and encamped until they reached the borders of the men of Dan, where each of the tribes slew men of Kush for three months of the year and took the spoils for his own tribe.

* * *

The four tribes, which are Dan, Naphtali, Gad, and Asher, have set up their camps in Havilah the Ancient, where the gold is. These are fine places that are to be found in the kingdom of Parvaim, under the rule of Horinus. They trust in their Maker first, and God is their aid. And these tribes have set their hands on the necks of their foes. Year after year they make war with seven kingdoms and seven lands, and these lie beyond the river of Kush. And these four tribes have gold and silver and precious stones and flocks and herds and camels and asses in exceedingly vast number, and they sow and reap though they dwell in tents. When they desire, they set out and encamp in their tents from border to border for two days' journey on two different seas. And where they encamp you will not find room to place even a single human foot.

The name of their king is Uzziel, while the name of their great prince is Elizaphan of the children of Elizaphan of the sons of Oholiab of the tribe of Dan. His flag is white on which is written in black: "Hear, O Israel! The Lord our God, the Lord is One!" (Deut. 6:4). And when he wishes to go forth to war, the herald sounds the ram's horn and the captain of the army comes, and the forces set out with one hundred and twenty thousand little white flags. Every three months another tribe sets out to war and the tribe remains without, and whatever spoils they take from their foes they divide with their own tribe.

This they do until the completion of the three months when they come back and bring all the spoils to King Uzziel, who shares it with all Israel, for this is their law from King David to this day. And King Uzziel takes his own portion and gives it to all the sages who are versed in the Torah and are tent-dwellers.

As for the sons of Samson, who are of the tribe of Dan, they surpass them all. They do not flee in any circumstances (in war), for this would be a great shame for them; and they are now like the sand of the sea for multitude and have no occupation other than war. And when they go a-warring, they say: "It is not good for a man to flee, let the young man perish rather than flee, let him be strong at heart with the Lord." Then they repeat several times and all of them cry together: "Hear, O Israel! The Lord our God, the Lord is One!"

* * *

And Eldad the Danite relates:

There are four tribes in one place, Dan and Naphtali, Gad and Asher. The name of this place is Havilah the Ancient, where the gold is. They have a judge named Abdon, and they impose the (traditional) four death penalties of the courts, and they dwell in tents and encamp and strike camp and travel from place to place. They wage war with the seven kings of Kush. To travel through their land takes seven months, but five of those kings surround them from the rear and either side and wage war with them at all times. If anybody is tenderhearted, they give him to the inheritance of the Lord. They have the whole of Scripture but do not recite the Scroll of the story of Esther because they were not affected by that miracle. Nor do they recite the Scroll of Lamentations so that they should not break their hearts. And in all their Talmud they make no mention of any sage by name but say Joshua declared according to the word of Moses who spoke according to the Power.

And every violent man among them is devoted to war, and they never cease from their craft, these engaging in Torah and these in warfare, among all the four tribes. When they set out for battle they do not set out in mixed companies. For their given three months the warriors of Dan follow their war on their horses from which they do not descend all week long. But on the Sabbath eve they descend wherever they may be, while their horses remain fully caparisoned bearing their arms; and if no foe comes against them, they celebrate the Sabbath according to the law. But if their foes swoop down on them, they set out with all their weapons and slay a-many among them in accordance with the power of the Name that is over them. And among them are warriors of the sons of Samson, who are the children of Delilah, and they run ahead to war, and the least of them can pursue a vast number of the foe; and when one of them raises his voice, it sounds like a mighty shouting, like the lion roaring; for he cries in a loud voice: "Victory is the Lord's, and Your valor rests on Your people of the tribes of Jeshurun! Selah!"

After the destruction of the First Temple, Naphtali, Gad, and Asher came to Dan; for in the beginning they used to live with Issachar in their cities and they used to quarrel with them, since they said to them: "You are the sons of the maidservants!" Now since they feared that war might break out between them, they set out and traveled till they reached Dan and became four tribes in a single place.

× × ×

And those four tribes—Dan, Naphtali, Gad, and Asher—remain with their cattle on the bank of the River Sambatyon to shear their flocks, for it is a flat level land and clean, where neither thorn nor greenstuff grows. And when they see the tribe of Moses they gather and stand on the bank of the river and they shout: "Brothers of the tribes of Jeshurun!"—and they greet one another in peace.

62

BUSTANAI

This is a dynasty-founding legend that legitimizes the political authority of secular leadership of the Jewish community in the Babylonian exile by linking it to the Davidic dynasty. Bustanai was confirmed as exilarch by Calif ʿAli (656–661) or by the governor of Iraq, Saʿid ibn-abu-Waqqās. The story about Bustanai occurs first in a ninth-century chronicle. Source: E. Arakie, Sefer ha-Maʿasiyyot, *No. 111.*

I

It is told that in the days of the kingdom of Persia a certain foolish king arose, and it occurred to him to destroy the royal offspring. So he seized all the offspring of the House of David throughout his realm and slew them. He arrested their kinfolk and sons-in-law and all who were closely acquainted with them and put them in prison, and he gave orders that the swill of unclean food be poured over them in order to pollute them and make them filthy with carrion cooking. He decreed that their children be dashed to the ground and their pregnant women cleft apart. Yet God took pity on the seed of the House of David; and the bride of one of their youths, who was slain during the days of her espousal, was left alive after she had conceived.

Now this king dreamed that he was standing in a garden by a pavilion which contained every kind of tree that was pleasant to see and gave good fruit. Knowing that this orchard was not his, he flung the fruit to the earth in furious jealousy. After splitting and cutting down the trees, he went searching further to see whether there were any roots left so that he could uproot them and make sure that not a single root capable of giving rise to fruit and branches should be left. After some time he found one root from which something like a branch was growing out of the earth. He lifted up the axe in his hand to destroy it when, lo and behold, an old man stood before him. Reddish he was with fine eyes and good to look at. This old man upbraided him and cried a loud and bitter cry and snatched the axe from his hand and smote him on his brow so that his blood ran down his face and beard, and he was about to perish. He fell with his face to the ground and wept and entreated the old man, saying: "I pray you, my lord, let me entreat you not to destroy me, for what have I done to you? What has my sin and transgression been for you to come against me?"

Then the old man answered him: "This is far from enough to repay the evil you have done me. You have come to my garden to lay it waste. If you found good fruit, why have you not eaten from it and placed some in your basket? And if you desire fruit trees, why have you not planted your own? Not only have you ripped off branches and leaves and flowers and plants and fruits but you wished to wreak your worst and to uproot everything without even leaving a growing root! I moaned for the garden which I planted and watered and tended so many years, and all that was left to me of the entire garden was this one root. 'Maybe there is hope in it,' said I, 'and this will be my consolation when I water it and tend it until its branches grow and from it I can renew my whole garden.' Yet you have raised your axe to destroy it as well and leave not a single sprouting root in my garden, and in your arrogance you thought that you are righteous in your own eyes. Why, this is a criminal transgression and the little I have done is a recompense for your abominations, for I ought to remove you from the land of the living and blot your memory out from under the heavens!"

Then the king went on weeping before him and lay prostrate at his feet and entreated: "I pray you, my lord, I have done foolishly, but now I repent my deeds and after I have learned of this I smite myself on the thigh. Let my soul be precious in your sight and do not slay me, for in all truth I give you an assurance that I shall water this plant at the proper times and shall visit it on occasion and preserve it day and night until it spreads branches like a mighty cedar. From its offshoots I shall plant every bed in your garden until it once again becomes what it was. And as for what I have done—forgive me, for I erred!"

When the king woke up from his dream he found his blood running over his couch. And he was distressed and his mind was upset until daylight. In the morning he rose early and summoned all his sages and wizards and told them his distress. They were silent for they could not find any answer to give to him. But one of his attendants spoke up saying: "My lord king, surely you know that the sages of the Jews and their royal offspring were counselors to kings in their Exile, and all the requirements of the realm were entrusted to them. The monarchs who preceded you used to give them their regular requirements and gifts day after day, in order that they might interpret and tell them various enigmas and all wisdom and the fleeting thoughts and dreams of night. Now you have taken counsel to slay them in wrath and make an end of them. They are imprisoned and shackled under guard. Yet now, if it seems proper in your eyes to seek out of those wise men of theirs who are subject to detention one who has the understanding to stand before you, you tell him your dream and hear what he has to say. Maybe you will find a satisfactory answer from them." This found favor in the king's sight and he ordered that one of their wise men be brought, and his prison garb changed so that he should stand before him, since he had an urgent question which his own sages could not answer, though they were the wisest of the wise and nothing was hidden from them.

So the royal attendant came and brought the king's words to the imprisoned Jewish nobles. Thereupon one of the most ancient and wise among them, into whose family one of the youngest of the House of David had wedded only to be slain during his espousals, responded and said: "I shall stand before the king and tell him whatever he has in his heart." "Why should you hurry to do this?" his imprisoned friends and kin asked him. "You do not know the question that you will be asked." But he told them: "The king has dreamed a dream, and just as he saw it, so did I see it. Furthermore, I know its meaning." Thereupon his friends and kin blessed him, saying: "May the Lord your God aid you and give your grace and kindness so as to speak in the presence of the king and not be shamed." Then the royal attendant said to him: "Wash and anoint yourself. Here are garments. Take them and put them on and leave your prison garb behind, for such is the royal behest!"

But the old man took oath that he would not bathe himself and would not change his prison garb until he had appeared in the royal presence. So he went and spoke in the presence of the king, and the signs of his mourning could be clearly seen, and the odor of the filthy slops poured over him could be smelled, and every eye that looked upon him wept.

Then the king said to him: "I have dreamed a dream, but there is no one who can interpret it. Do you know how to explain a dream when you hear it?" "Why," said the old man, "solutions are God's! Tell me, my lord king, or if you prefer, I shall tell it to you."

"If you know it," said the king, "tell it." So he told it to him, reminding him of all the details he had forgotten. The astonished king said: "There is no turning right or left from all you have said. But now explain the meaning, for that will be the test." Then he began to interpret it, tears running from his eyes. And he said: "My lord king, the garden you saw is the family of the House of David. The trees therein, both large and small, were his offspring, elders and young men and children. The fruits which were so pleasant to see and good to eat were the sages who were versed in every wisdom and knew all knowledge, who did righteousness and performed justice. That you stood in your wisdom over against the garden and wished to cut down every tree with its branches and leaves together—that is the decree you made to slay them and cleave apart the pregnant women and dash the children to the ground and smite them with the sword and massacre them all. When you went searching through the garden to see if there was any root or shoot or seedling so that you could uproot it and you found one root with a shoot sprouting from the ground— it is the truth. It will soon become known that one pregnant woman of the House of David has remained alive. The root you saw in your dream and against which you raised your axe was your intention to seek them all out and destroy the royal offspring. As for the old man who appeared and upbraided you and cried out aloud—that is David, king of Israel, may he rest in peace. As for your entreaty to him to water all the beds until the shoot grows into a mighty cedar—that means that you will restore and make a covenant from this day forth to guard the pregnant woman with all her kin."

Then the king answered: "Indeed I know that your interpretation is true. Now seek and find whether any woman is left who is pregnant from the offspring of the House of David, and I shall treat her graciously and favorably view the child that will come forth from her. I shall fulfill all I have promised and bring him up as long as I live on earth!"

When the old man heard these words, he could not restrain himself but burst into tears and wept aloud, saying: "My lord king, I am the one that has drunk the goblet of venom to the very dregs. I had married my daughter to one of the choicest of the youths of that family. And while he was rejoicing with her you made the decree to destroy the whole House of David, and an end was made of him among them. I was imprisoned together with their kinfolk and acquaintances, while my daughter has remained a widow for several months, but I do not know whether she is pregnant or not."

"Go home," said the king, "and tell your daughter that I have set you free today, together with all your companions who were imprisoned with you. I have given command that none of you is to be tormented any more, and I shall keep my eye upon you." And the king took his ring off his finger and gave it to him in regard to all these matters; and they released all the prisoners.

So the old man returned home where they told him that the Lord had made his daughter fruitful. He rejoiced and thanked the Lord, and all Israel rejoiced together with him. Then the old man returned to the king and informed him. He too rejoiced and summoned a certain eunuch and ordered him to prepare a pavilion in the royal court and have it ready for the expectant woman with all she required, and to bring the young woman before him. Together with her father and kinsfolk they prepared everything for her with the utmost honor as the king commanded. And the king urged his attendants to provide her with her couch and dainties in summer and winter so that nothing might be missing, and all things should be in full royal style.

When her time was finished, she gave birth to a son and called his name Bustanai, for the word *bustan* means garden in Persian, and it was a garden that the king of Persia had seen in his dream. So there was great joy in Israel, and good tidings went to those near and far that the Lord had left a survivor for David and had remembered His mercies and His loving-kindness and had not permitted his offspring to be cut off entirely. And they all praised the Lord their God.

II

The child Bustanai grew and was weaned and studied Torah and Mishnah, Talmud and Law, and wisdom and understanding. The king was informed and wished to see him. He ordered him to be brought before him, and God had given the child of the glorious loving-kindness that had marked David. So he stood before the king in the beauty of his wisdom, and the king and all his sages were astonished at the lad.

So Bustanai stood before the king from the time he entered until evening, without moving his head or shifting his foot. A fly came and stood on his temple which was like a pomegranate clove, and it bit him and stung him, but he did not drive it away, and his blood dripped in the royal presence. "What has happened to you?" asked the king; and he answered: "It is what you see, my lord king." He looked and saw that the insect was biting at his temple. "Why don't you drive it away?" said the king to him, and the youngster answered: "We have inherited the tradition from our ancestors that ever since we lost our royal crown and have been required to take up station in any royal palace, we do not speak or laugh or raise our hands before the kings in whose presence we stand."

The king approved of this, for he knew that a wise person was speaking. He ordered that he should be given the second chariot to ride in and gave him gifts in right royal fashion, and they cried as he went: "This is the way to treat the knightly prince of the Exiles of Israel!" For the king knew his wisdom and intelligence. Israel rejoiced exceedingly that God had left a remnant to David and had fulfilled the promise of Isaiah (37:31): "And the remnant of the House of Judah that is left shall prosper." And the king ordered him to appoint judges under him and engage in all the requirements of the realm and lead the sages who headed the academies, one on his right hand and one on his left; the right-hand sage being the Gaon of Sura and the left-hand one the Gaon of Nehardea and Pumbeditha, their function being to serve as supreme judges with his permission throughout the borders of Israel. This practice continued throughout Israel for a long time until the king of Ishmael arose and set judges and assessors to act as judges for all the nations and did not require the judges of Israel. But the princes of the Exiles have not ceased until now.

And therefore there is a fly on every seal of the princes of the Exiles with which they seal on account of this incident which occurred to Prince Bustanai before the king when the insect descended on his temple, and he did not raise his hand because of the awe of the royal presence.

III

As for other facts about the greatness of Bustanai, who was elevated by the king over all the captains and the viceroys, they will be found written in the records of the House of David. But we see fit to mention and show a little of his greatness.

Once the king of Ishmael, namely, Ali ben Abu Taleb, passed nearby with many high officers and captains. Bustanai came forth to meet him with the Torah Scroll and Holy Scriptures and Holy Names in his hand. With him was a vast assembly of Israel and he went to receive Ali, the king of Ishmael, who rejoiced greatly to meet him and requested him to bless him and pray for him. Ali gave him fine garments from the spoils he had taken and asked whether he had any sons. He answered that he was not yet wedded because he had not found a suitable spouse of his own age. At this the Khalif Ali was very much astonished, because Bustanai was then thirty-five years old. He therefore gave him the daughter of the king of Dara to wife. The maiden was a beautiful virgin, but he did not wish to take her. Ali adjured him until he received her from him, and Ali said to him: "She is fit and proper for a man like you, and after all David your father took for himself beautiful concubines without a marriage writ and without nuptial rites." But Bustanai answered him: "His Blessed Name permits Israel to take beautiful women only in time of war. Other than in time of war it is necessary to have a marriage writ and nuptial rites and immersion." Then Ali said: "You have authority to do all these with her." So Bustanai took her to wife after her immersion and gave her a marriage writ and nuptial rites. She found favor in his eyes, and sons were born to him of her.

After his death his sons from another wife objected to them and said: "You have no portion in the heritage of our father with us, for you are the sons of a maidservant." So a quarrel began among them. They were supported by partisans, and the matter was brought to the courts where it was decided that they could not be separated from the heritage of their father and there was no blemish in their pedigree, even if their mother had not a marriage writ. For it is a point of our law and practice that a man does not regard his regular cohabitation with a woman as fornication, and certainly not a prince and sage like Bustanai.

All this is written in the Books of the House of David. They have enigmas and hints marked and pointed which proclaim their royal worth in every generation. May the Lord in His mercies restore the crown as of old, to fulfill the verse: "And I will restore your judges as in the beginning" (Isa. 1:26). Amen!

63
THE STORY OF BULAN, KING OF THE KHAZARS:
THE REVELATION

Writing in Arabic, Judah Halevi (before 1075–1141) completed Sefer ha-Kuzari, *his philosophical and theological defense of Judaism, in 1140, a year before his emigration to Eretz-Israel. As a narrative frame Judah Halevi employs a tradition about a historical event that took place, according to Judah ben Saul ibn Tibbon (c.1120–c.1190), the Hebrew translator of the work, four hundred years earlier. The Khazars, a people of Turkic stock, originally nomadic, established a powerful kingdom that extended between and along the north shores of the Black and the Caspian seas, from the seventh and up to the tenth, or according to another opinion the thirteenth, century. The ruler of the Khazars, their Khaqan, converted to Islam in 737 and three years later accepted the Jewish faith. According to historical analysis, for the Khazars the conversion to Judaism was an act of political defiance against the Arabs who fought them, giving them a measure of independence. In Jewish society there were apparently at least two traditions about the conversion of the Khazars: the first explained the event in the framework of medieval religious disputation, while the second considered it as a slow process that resulted from Jewish migration and intermarriage with the Khazars. Source: Judah Halevi,* Sefer ha-Kuzari *(Warsaw, 1911), pp. 35–38 (abridged).*

Togarmah, one of the sons of Japheth, had ten sons and these were their names: The first-born was Avivar, the second Thuris, the third Avar, the fourth Ogoz, the fifth Bizel, the sixth Tharna, the seventh Khazar, the eighth Janur, the ninth Bolgar, the tenth Savir. The Khazar people are the offspring of Khazar, the seventh.

When their forefathers were few in number, the Holy and Blessed One gave them strength and bearing and bravery and they waged war after war against many peoples that were greater and more mighty than they. The Almighty aiding, they expelled them and inherited their lands, while they subjected others to taxation unto this day. The land in which they dwell was formerly dwelt in by the Vanenthar (Volga Bulgars), but the ancestors of the Khazars came and waged war against them. The Vanenthar were as numerous as the sand upon the seashore yet they could not withstand Khazar but abandoned their land and fled. Khazar pursued them until they overtook them on the river called the Don. Unto this day they are encamped by the River Don, and are near Constantinople, and the Khazars possess their land unto this day.

After this, ages passed until there arose a certain king named Bulan who was a wise man that feared the Lord, trusting Him with all his heart. He did away with the wizards and idolators, driving them out of the land, and took refuge in the shadow of His wings. Now an angel of the Lord appeared to him in a dream and said to him: "O Bulan, the Lord has sent me to you to say: O My son, I have heard your entreaty and indeed I have blessed you and made you fruitful and multiplied you exceedingly, and I shall establish your dominion until the end of ages, and further I have placed all your enemies in your hand."

In the morning Bulan the King arose and thanked the Lord and feared and served Him even more. In due course the angel appeared to him a second time and said to him: "O My son, I have seen your ways and approve of your deeds. I know that you will follow Me with all your soul and all your might, and I wish to give you laws and judgment. Then if you observe My commandments and laws, I shall bless and increase you." Then the king replied to the angel that was speaking to him: "O my Lord, You know the thoughts of my heart and have inspected my reins, for I place my faith only in the Lord. But the people over whom I reign are unbelievers and I do not know if they will have faith in me. If now I find favor in Your eyes and if Your mercies can revolve upon me, I pray You to appear to So-and-So, their great prince, and he will aid me in this."

The Holy and Blessed One did what he desired, and the angel appeared to that man in a dream. Early in the morning the prince arose and came and told the king. Then the king gathered together all his nobles and servants and all his people and set those things out before them. The matter seemed good in their eyes and they accepted the judgment and came under the wings of the Shekinah.

Then the angel of the Lord appeared to the king once again, saying: "O My son, heaven and earth cannot contain Me. Yet in spite of this, fashion

Me a house in My Name and I shall dwell therein." Then the king answered him: "Lord of the Universe! You know that I have no silver or gold. What shall I build with?" But the Lord said to him: "Be strong and courageous and take all your forces and rise and go toward Deralan and the land of Ardevil. I have caused them to fear and dread you and shall place them in your hand. And, behold, I have prepared two treasuries for you, one full of silver and one full of gold, so take them. I shall be with you and shall preserve you and aid you and you shall bring all the money in peace and build a house in My Name."

So the king believed in the Lord and acted in accordance with His word and went and waged many wars and was victorious in them by the aid of the Almighty. He destroyed that country and took the money and returned in peace. Then he dedicated the money and with it he fashioned a tent and an Ark and a candelabrum and a table and altars and holy vessels by the Lord's mercy and the power of the Almighty. And they exist to this day and are safeguarded by the king.

64
THE STORY OF BULAN, KING OF THE KHAZARS: THE DEBATE

See above note.

Now after this, the name of King Bulan spread throughout the lands. The king of Edom and the king of Ishmael sent their messengers with much money and many gifts together with their wise men to the king, in order to incline him toward their laws. Now the king was wise, may his soul be preserved in the bundle of life with the Lord his God! He ordered that a sage of Israel be brought. Then he inquired and examined and questioned well and set them together to dispute concerning their laws. And each one broke down the words of his companion, and they could not agree on any one code. When the king saw this, he said to them: "Go to your tents now and come to me on the third day." So they went to their tents.

Next day the king sent to the priest of the king of Edom (Byzantium) and said to him: "I know that the king of Edom is greater than all the kings and his code and belief is fine and honorable, and I desire your belief. Yet I wish to ask you a certain question. Tell me in all truth, and I shall show my friendship toward you and honor you. What do you say—which is better, the faith of Israel or the faith of Ishmael?" And the priest answered and said to him: "O king, live forever! If you ask about belief, there is none to compare with the faith and belief of Israel. The Holy and Blessed One chose Israel from all peoples and tongues and called them 'My first-born son,' and performed great signs and wonders with them, and He brought them forth from the land of Egypt and delivered them from the hands of Pharaoh and Egypt. He caused them to pass through the divided sea on the dry land while He drowned their pursuers in the deeps of the sea. Then He brought down the manna for them when they were hungry, and fetched forth water from the rock for them when they thirsted. Then He gave them the Torah from out of the fire and the flames and brought them to the land of Canaan where He built them the Temple. Yet after all this they rebelled and sinned and disobeyed the law so that He grew angry with them and exiled them and sent them away from before Him and dispersed them to all the four winds of heaven. Had it not been thus there would have been no law to compare with the law of Israel in the world. For what is the law of Ishmael? Neither Sabbath nor festival, neither commandments nor statutes. They eat any impurity, camel flesh and horse flesh and dog's meat, any abomination and vermin! The faith of Ishmael is no true faith but rather like the faiths of the heathen."

Then the king responded to him: "Indeed you have spoken to me truthfully, and I shall show my friendship to you and shall send you back with honor to the king of Edom."

On the second day the king sent and summoned the kadi of the king of Ishmael and said to him: "There is only one question I wish to ask you. Tell me in truth and do not withhold it from me. When it comes to the faith of the Christian and the faith of the Jew, which of them is better in your eyes?" Then the kadi answered the king: "The faith of the Jew is a true faith, and they have commandments and laws, but when they erred the Holy and Blessed One grew angry with them and let them fall into the hands of their foes; yet redemption and salvation are theirs. The faith of the Christian is no faith. They eat swine and every abomination and bow down to the works of their own hands and they have no hope."

Then the king answered and said to him: "You have spoken to me in all truth, and I shall be your friend."

On the third day he summoned them all together and said to them:

"Speak each one in turn and explain to me which faith is best." They began and disputed together yet they could not sustain their words. At length the king asked the priest: "What do you say? Which is more worthy, the faith of the Jews or the faith of Ishmael?" And the priest answered: "The faith of Israel is more worthy than the faith of Ishmael." The king asked the kadi: "What do you say? Which is more worthy, the Christian faith or the faith of Israel?" And the kadi replied: "The faith of Israel is more worthy."

Then the king answered: "You have already admitted with your own mouths that the faith of Israel is the best and most proper. I personally have already chosen the faith of Israel which is the faith of Abraham, and may God Almighty be my aid. As for the silver and gold which you propose to give me, my God in whom I trust and under the shadow of whose wings I take refuge will bring it to me painlessly. And now you yourselves go to your own lands in peace!"

From that day forward the Almighty helped the king and increased his power and strengthened his arm. He circumcised the flesh of his foreskin, he and his attendants and servants and all his people. Then he sent and brought sages of Israel to his land who interpreted the Torah and set out all the commandments for him in due order. Until this day the people of the Khazars maintain the honored faith—may the Name of the Holy and Blessed One be praised and the mention of Him be exalted forever. From that day forward, when our forefathers entered beneath the wings of the Shekinah, the God of Israel subdued all their foes before them and laid low all the peoples and tongues that were around about them, so that no man withstood them to this day. They have all become their tributaries, whether they are rulers of Edom or Ishmael.

After these things there rose a king of his offspring named Obadiah, who was righteous and upright. He renewed the kingdom and set the faith in accordance with all the legal requirements. Also, he built synagogues and houses of study and brought together many of the sages of Israel and gave them ample silver and gold, and they interpreted for him the twenty-four Books of the Bible, the Mishnah, the Talmud, and the prayer books of the cantors; and he was God-fearing and loved the Torah and the commandments, a true servant of the Lord, with the spirit of the Lord leading him. After him came Hezekiah his son, and after him Manasseh his son, and after him rose Hanina the brother of Obadiah, and Isaac his son, Zebulun his son, Moses his son, Nissim his son, Menahem his son, Benjamin his son, Aaron his son, and Joseph, the son of Aaron (who relates all the above facts in his letter to the learned Hisdai [ibn Shaprut] son of Isaac, son of Ezra). All the above were kings and the sons of kings. No stranger may be seated on the throne of their fathers, but the son is seated on the throne of his father. That is their practice and the practice of their forefathers ever since they have existed on earth.

65
IN THE DEPTHS OF THE SEA

This story originally appears as the first segment of a narrative about the transference of rabbinic authority from Babylonia to Southern Europe, North Africa, and Egypt. Initially scholars sought to uncover the historical core in this story, but further research and the discovery of new historical documents clearly demonstrated the ahistorical nature of the story. Often it employs recurrent themes in Jewish historical narrative tradition. Despite its fictive quality, this legendary narrative is about historical figures. ʿAbd ar-Raḥmān an-Nāṣar ruled over Spain from 912 to 961, and he had a naval officer by the name of ibn Rumāḥis (d. 980). Ḥushiel ben Elḥanan and father of Ḥananel was the head of the Jewish community in Kairouan, Tunisia (end of tenth, beginning of eleventh centuries); Rabbi Moses ben Ḥanokh (d. 965) and father of Rabbi Ḥanokh was a leading rabbi in Cordoba, Spain; and Rabbi Shemariah ben Elḥanan (d. 1011) was in Alexandria, Egypt. Source: Abraham ibn Daud, Sefer ha-Kabbalah (written, 1160–1161; Oxford, 1887), pp. 67–68.

A high officer appointed over the ships set out from the city of Cordova. His name was Ibn Rumahiz, and he was sent by the king of Ishmael in Spain whose name was ʿAbd ar-Rahman an-Nazzar. This officer with mighty fleets went out to conquer cities and hamlets close to the border, but they went as far as the seashore of the Land of Israel and then turned to the Greek Sea and islands therein.

Now he found a ship and on it four great sages who were proceeding from the city of Bari to a city called Sefsathin. These sages were going to gather funds for bridal dowries, but Ibn Rumahiz captured the ship and arrested the sages. One of these was Hushi'el, the father of our Rabbi Hananel; and one was our Rabbi Moses, the father of Rabbi Hanokh. They imprisoned him with his wife and with Rabbi Hanokh his son, who was still a little boy. The third was Rabbi Shemariah son of Rabbi Elhanan. And as for the fourth, I do not know his name.

Now the officer wished to compel the wife of Rabbi Moses and violate her, because she was exceedingly beautiful. But she cried to Rabbi Moses her husband in the holy tongue and asked him whether those who drown in the sea will come to life at the revival of the dead or not. And he answered in the words of the Psalm (68:23): "The Lord hath said, from the Bashan I bring back, I shall bring them back from the depths of the sea!"

When she heard this, she flung herself into the sea and drowned and died.

66
THE DEATH OF POETS: JUDAH HALEVI

Judah Halevi (before 1075–1141) was a major poet and philosopher who traveled extensively throughout Spain. At an advanced age he decided to emigrate to the Land of Israel, but stopped in Egypt and died there before reaching his destination. Source: Gedalyah ibn Yaḥya, Shalshelet ha-Kabbalah, *p. 44.*

Our Rabbi Judah Halevi bar Samuel the Spaniard was a great sage of that age, and a grammarian and a poet and versed in all that the intelligence can comprehend. And he wrote the *Book of the Kuzari.*

Now I have been told by a certain elder that when Rabbi Judah Halevi reached the gates of Jerusalem he rent his garments and walked barefoot on the ground to fulfill the words of the Psalm (102:15): "For Your servants desire her stones and entreat her dust!" And he recited the lament which he wrote, and which begins:

Zion, wilt thou not ask if peace be with thy captives . . .

And a certain Ishmaelite grew envious of him because of his great devotion, and rode him down with his horse and trampled him and slew him.

Rabbi Judah Halevi was fifty years old when he went up to the Land of Israel.

67
THE SAGE AND THE PRINCE

Rabbi Solomon ben Isaac (1040–1105), known by the Hebrew initials of his name as Rashi, was the leading medieval commentator on the Old Testament and the Babylonian Talmud. He was born in Troyes, the capital city of the Champagne province of northeastern France, and, except for his years of study, he lived there all his life. Godfrey of Bouillon (c. 1058–1100) was the duke of Lower Lotharingia who lead the nobility of northern France and western Germany in the First Crusade. After the conquest of Jerusalem he was elected to be its governor, and was later titled "Defender of the Holy Sepulchre." He ruled over Jerusalem for only one year and died in Jaffa in 1100. The present tale is an example of a recurrent theme in Jewish tradition: a king, or his military commander, seeks advice from a Jewish rabbi. Source: Ibn Yaḥya, Shalshelet ha-Kabbalah, p. 38.

I have seen it written that there was a certain prince in France named Gottfriedo Bulion (Godfrey of Bouillon) who was a brave warrior, but a cruel and viciously destructive man. Now the wisdom of Rashi was widely known even among the peoples, for all nations would make enquiry of him. And the prince sent for him to come from the city to his land. But Rashi refused to go because he knew this man, and that he would distress him. The prince grew angry and came riding with all his host to the home of Rashi. There he went up to his house of study where he found all the doors open as well as all the books, but he saw no man. Then he cried in a loud voice: "Solomon! Solomon!" And Rashi replied: "What does my lord desire?" "Where are you?" said the prince; and Rashi replied: "Here I am!" This happened a number of times. Then the prince was confused and left the house of study and asked: "Is there a Jew here?" One of the disciples came before him, and the prince said: "Tell the Rabbi to come to me, and I promise him by my head that no harm will befall him." Then Rashi came down to the prince and kneeled before him, but the prince raised him up, saying: "Now I have seen your wisdom. Indeed I wish you to advise me about a great matter which I must perform. I have prepared a hundred thousand horsemen and two hundred great ships and I wish to conquer Jerusalem. Likewise I have seven thousand more horsemen in the city of Ekron, and I trust in them to defeat the Ishmaelites who dwell there, because they lack knowledge of the art of war. Now tell me your opinion and have no fear!"

Then Rashi replied in few words: "You will go and conquer Jerusalem and reign there for three days. On the fourth day the Ishmaelites will drive you out, and you will flee and return to this city with three horses." The prince felt very bitter and said: "Maybe your words will prove true. But if I come back with four horses, I shall feed your flesh to the dogs and slay all the Jews in France."

So he departed and everything which Rashi had prophesied happened. But he returned with four horses. Then he proposed to do him harm, but the Lord overturned his intention. For when he entered at the city gate, a stone fell from a hole above the gateway and slew one of his companions with the horse on which he rode. Then the prince was very startled and admitted that the words of the Jew were correct. So he went to bow down before Rashi before he returned to his own home. And he found that he had departed this world and mourned for him exceedingly.

This I have found, and I have written it in brief.

68
THE STORY OF POPE ELHANAN

There are two distinct traditions of this story. The first relates the events to the medieval scholar and poet Rabbi Simeon bar Isaac (born c. 950), while the other associates Rabbi Solomon ben Abraham Adret of Barcelona (c. 1235–c. 1310) with this event. These two rabbis were major medieval Jewish scholars. It is possible that Elhanan was the name of Rabbi Simeon's son, as it appears in one of the prayers that he wrote. In searching for a historical core to this legend, some scholars have suggested the possibility that Elhanan was forcefully converted to Christianity during the 1008–1012 persecutions of the Jews in northern France and Germany, and that later his father tried to bring him back into the Jewish faith. Others have pointed to the Papal schism in 1130, in which one of the contestants, Cardinal Pierleoni, was a fourth-generation descendant of a converted Jew, and his Jewish origin played a role in the dispute that followed the election. Source: A. Jellinek, ed., Bet ha-Midrasch 5:148–152.

The story is told of Rabbi Simeon the Great, who dwelt in the city of Mayence, which lies on the River Rhine. He had three sheets of mirror glass hanging in his house, and in them he saw all that had been and all that would come about. After his death a flowing spring emerged from the head of his grave.

This Rabbi Simeon was a very great man indeed, and he had a little son named Elhanan. One Sabbath day a gentile woman came to stoke the oven as was her practice every Sabbath. She saw that Rabbi Simeon and his wife were not at home because they had already departed for prayers in the synagogue, and only the nurse was there together with the boy. So she picked him up in her arms and went out with him. The nurse saw what the gentile woman had done, but it never occurred to her to suppose that she had any evil intentions, for she said to herself: "She only wants to play with the little one and will soon come back and bring him home." But the treacherous woman did not return. Instead she carried the boy away and brought him under the new covenant, congratulating herself at heart that she had brought a good freewill offering to her God, as was the thought of all Christians in those days.

When Rabbi Simeon and his wife returned from the House of the Lord, they did not find the nurse at home either. For she had seen that the gentile woman tarried to bring the boy back and she had gone out to seek her and pursue her, but she could not find her. She returned to Rabbi Simeon's home very upset, and wailed and shrieked with all her might. "Why are you wailing like this?" said Rabbi Simeon to her. "Tell us what has happened." Then she answered: "Honored rabbi, the gentile woman who stokes the oven on the Sabbath day came and has stolen your son and fled, and I do not know where she can have hidden herself together with him." Thereupon Rabbi Simeon and his wife and the nurse hurried out to seek and inquire, but in vain, for the boy was not to be found and had vanished. Then the parents burst out weeping and lamenting bitterly and cried and shrieked with their very dreadful pain at heart. Thereafter Rabbi Simeon fasted to afflict his soul by day and night, and he prayed unto the Lord to restore his son to him. But his prayer returned empty, for the Lord refused to reveal unto him the place where the boy was.

Now the boy was brought to the priests, and they brought him up and taught him, and he grew into a great scholar, because his heart was as wide as the heart of his father Rabbi Simeon. And the boy went up from one school of wisdom to another, and in this way he ascended higher and higher until his wisdom grew exceedingly great and he came to Rome. There he continued to study many languages and made his name. From day to day he grew greater and greater until he was raised to be a cardinal. His fame spread throughout the land, and everybody spoke honorably of him and to him and praised him exceedingly for his studies, his beauty, and his priesthood. At that time the pope died, and no cardinal as wise and learned as this new cardinal was found to take the place of the deceased pope. So they chose him and seated him on the papal throne.

Now the new pope knew well, and had known long since, that he was of Jewish stock and that his father was Rabbi Simeon the Great of Mayence. Yet since he was so amply provided for and regarded as great among the Gentiles, his heart would not permit him to abandon all this honor and return to his father, his people, and his God. Now that he had been made the head of all the Christians he very much longed to see his father and considered how to bring him to Rome by cunning. So he wrote a letter to the bishop of Mayence, since all the bishops were under his command, and ordered that the Jews were not to be permitted to keep their Holy Sabbath, nor might they circumcise their sons, nor might their women immerse in running water to purify themselves from the pollution of their courses. The pope's reason for doing this was: "If the Jews hear such a thing, they will be filled with fear and dread and will swiftly send me their greatest men in order to entreat me to abolish this harsh decree. Then undoubtedly they will send me my father at their head."

So he thought in advance, and so indeed it came about. When the pope's letter reached the bishop, he summoned the Jews and on behalf of the pope commanded them in accordance with the decrees that had reached him and could not be withdrawn. The Jews became very alarmed and entreated the bishop to remove this evil from them, but all he could answer was: "Please do not make any entreaty to me, because I am not in a position to aid you. Here is the pope's letter. Read it and you will see that I have no power to help. But if you wish to seek mercy, then my counsel to you is that you should send some of your wise and respected men to the pope in Rome and bring your entreaties to him. Maybe he will accede to you and withdraw this decree."

Then the Jews of Mayence came before the Lord with penitence, prayer, and the practice of charity. Thereafter they selected two rabbis and Rabbi Simeon the Great as their head to go to Rome, saying: "Maybe the Lord will do us a wonder and turn the pope's heart to favor us." But in the meantime they did circumcise their sons and did not act in accordance with the decree, for in secret the bishop had agreed to permit this until the emissaries returned.

So the three chosen rabbis betook themselves to Rome. There they took counsel with the Jews of the city as to the steps to take with regard to this great evil. When the Jews of Rome heard these tidings, they were exceedingly astonished and said: "Who can believe this? No pope has ever been as good to the Jews as this one is. He always has Jews in his company, some of them are his confidants and counselors, and they always play chess together with him, and indeed he cannot live without them. How can he suddenly turn to enmity?" And they also said that they could not believe that this decree could have come from the pope but that the bishop had invented it on his own in order to do ill to the Jews of Mayence.

Then Rabbi Simeon showed them the letter which the pope had sent, with his seal upon it. So the Jews of Rome saw and knew that it was true, and they said: "It can only be that the wrath of the Lord has been kindled against you so that he incited the pope to make this decree against you!" And they proclaimed a fast and also prayed greatly and practiced charity.

The wardens of the Rome community then went to the cardinal who always appeared before the pope and entreated him on behalf of the Jews of Mayence. And the cardinal answered: "You know that this letter was sent by the pope himself to the bishop of Mayence, and who am I? What can I do for you if I cannot help?" However, he promised them to sustain their entreaties and intercede and speak in their favor. He further instructed them to prepare a letter of appeal, and he would present it to the pope. And so they did.

When the appeal and request reached the pope and he read it, he knew that these must be the emissaries from Mayence and ordered that they should appear before him. So Rabbi Simeon the Great came with the two rabbis who accompanied him to the chief cardinal. And he informed the pope that the Jews had come as commanded and were requesting to see him in person and speak directly to him. Then the pope replied: "Let the leader of the three come and appear alone before me!"

So Rabbi Simeon came, being the head and senior over his two companions, and he looked like an angel of the Lord of Hosts. When he saw the pope's face, Rabbi Simeon kneeled down before him and prostrated himself; and at that time the pope was sitting and playing chess with a certain cardinal who sat opposite him. As soon as he saw Rabbi Simeon the Great, he started and commanded him to rise from his knees and sit in a chair until he finished the game; for he recognized his father the moment he appeared, but his father did not recognize him.

After he finished the game he turned to Rabbi Simeon and said to him: "What is your request?" And Rabbi Simeon burst into bitter tears and told him his request and prepared to fling himself at his feet once again. But the pope would not permit him to do this and answered: "I have listened carefully to your request and your entreaty has entered my ears; but many charges about you Jews have reached me from Mayence, and that was why I made this decree."

In the course of this talk the pope began to debate with Rabbi Simeon with exceedingly great logic and casuistry, so that Rabbi Simeon barely found any answer to these shrewd and keen questions of his. Indeed, he was very astonished when he saw the wide range of this Gentile, which was virtually unbelievable. For half the day they sat and engaged in debate until at last the pope said: "My friend, I see that you are a great scholar, and your brothers who sent you to me will have no reason to regret the hopes they placed in you. Now every day Jews come to play chess with me, so now please sit with me here and let us play a game together, and you do not need to fear for your request."

Now Rabbi Simeon was a remarkably skilled chess player whose like was not to be found in the whole land, and yet the pope defeated him this time, to Rabbi Simeon's great astonishment. Then they began discussing religions again, and Rabbi Simeon heard such great and remarkable things from the pope that he had to wonder.

At the end of all this Rabbi Simeon repeated his appeal and wept bitterly. Then the pope said: "Let all those present depart!" So they went out. Then he fell on the neck of Rabbi Simeon and wept and said to him: "Father and friend, do you not recognize me?" But Rabbi Simeon did not understand what the pope's words could indicate, so he answered: "When have I ever had the honor to know your holy self?" Then the pope went on: "Father and friend, did you not lose your son when he was still a little boy?" At this Rabbi Simeon was exceedingly startled and shaken and answered: "It was as you say." At that the pope made himself known to him, crying out: "I, I am that son of yours and I was stolen by the gentile woman on the Sabbath day. Yet what sin can you have done to bring this distress upon you? That I have never been able to know. Yet what I do know and have proved is that the matter came from the Lord. Now that my very soul has gone out to see you face to face and tell you, I have made up my mind to abandon this new faith and return to the God of my fathers. That was why I cunningly sent that decree, knowing ahead that the Jews of the city would send you to appear, and entreat me to make an end of this evil. Now I therefore abolish it and all will be well with you. And yet, my father, surely you will tell me, is there any hope for my latter end, and can there be any atonement for me before God?" Thereupon Rabbi Simeon replied: "My dear son, remove that concern from your heart because you were compelled, and you were stolen from your fathers and your faith when you were still a little boy." "And yet, father," the son went on asking, "I have long known that I was born a Jew. In spite of which I have settled down among the Gentiles till this day, and the ample well-being I enjoyed prevented me from returning to the true God. Will God be prepared to forgive me?" And Rabbi Simeon answered: "Nothing can withstand repentance, and He who confesses his sin and abandons it will be shown mercy."

"Then now," said the son, "you return home in peace in the name of the God of Israel and present the letters that I shall give you to the bishop, and he will let you be. Yet do not permit any man to know what we have been saying. And before very long I shall come to you in Mayence. Yet ere I abandon my place and post, I shall do something as a memorial and leave it behind me in favor of the Jews."

So Rabbi Simeon returned to his friends and to the Jews of Rome and showed them the pope's letter abolishing the decree; and they rejoiced exceedingly. Then he returned to his city and presented the missive to the bishop, and there was gladness and joy for the Jews throughout the city. But to his wife he revealed the secret that their lost son was a pope. When she heard this she burst into a great outcry and wailing and refused to be comforted. But Rabbi Simeon told her: "Be quiet and do not grieve, for in a little while this son of ours will be home with us!" Meanwhile the pope wrote a book against the faith and left it as a memorial. He left a behest that all popes who followed him should read it, and then fled in secret. He came to Mayence and returned to the God of Israel in truth and full faith and became a very important Jew in the eyes of all the people. But in Rome nobody knew where he had gone or what had happened to him.

It was about this incident that Rabbi Simeon the Great wrote a Yotzer hymn in praise of the Creator for the Second Day of the New Year, containing the word Elhanan ("God-has-shown-grace") in the verse "God has shown grace to His heritage to improve it in sweetness." So there is no reason for the readers to believe that the words of this story are empty or false. They are true and correct and there is no falsehood in them.

Yet there are many who say that it was in the game of chess that Rabbi Simeon recognized that he must be of Jewish stock. And there were also many who say that indeed he recognized that this must be his son, because the pope played in the way his father taught him when he was still a boy, and he began to teach him the game.

May the Lord pardon us our sins because of the merits of Rabbi Simeon the Great. Amen, Selah!

69
THE STORY OF RABBI AMNON

Rabbi Amnon is a legendary figure; his name does not appear in any of the writings of the period. Yet, for all its fictive nature, the tale does portray certain aspects of the social relations between the upper classes of the Jewish and the German societies. The story first appeared in Or Zaru'a, *a thirteenth-century halakhic compilation by Rabbi Isaac ben*

Moses of Vienna (c.1180–c.1250). He claimed that he copied the story from a manuscript in the handwriting of the poet Rabbi Ephraim ben Jacob of Bonn (1132–c.1197). Rabbi Kalonymus ben Meshullam (early eleventh century), who, according to the story, wrote down Rabbi Amnon's prayer, belonged to one of the most prominent Jewish families that migrated from Italy to Mainz. The prayer itself, which has become one of the most moving parts of the liturgy for the Day of Atonement, antedates both the twelfth century, in which it was written down, and the eleventh century, in the milieu of which it is told. Quite likely it was composed by one of the Palestinian poets between the seventh and ninth centuries. Source: Ibn Yaḥya, Shalshelet ha-Kabbalah, p. 44.

This was copied down in an old prayer book, letter by letter, from the copy of the manuscript written by our Rabbi Isaac of Vienna who wrote the work *Or Zarua* (Light Is Sown), who testifies that he found this story in the very handwriting of Rabbi Ephraim, the son of Rabbi Jacob of Bonn.

Rabbi Amnon of Mayence was a leader in his age and wealthy and of high pedigree and handsome. And the lord and princes of Mayence began to demand conversion of him, but he refused to listen. But when they spoke to him day after day and he would pay no attention, the lord became very insistent with him. And when they bore down strongly on him, Rabbi Amnon said to them: "I want to consider and think the matter over for another three days." This he said in order to defer them. But no sooner had he left the lord than it came to his mind that he had said something in which there could be an element of doubt; and he was gravely concerned.

On the third day the lord sent for him, but he refused to go. So the king brought him against his will and spoke to him sternly. Then Rabbi Amnon gave answer: "I shall sentence my own self. Since my tongue spoke falsehood, let it be sentenced to be cut out!" For he wished to hallow the Lord, since he had uttered words that implied a doubt regarding the Deity. But the king answered: "I shall not cut out your tongue for it spoke truth. But I shall cut off the feet which did not come to me, and I shall torment the entire body." So he gave orders and they cut off his hands and his feet. At each joint they asked whether he was prepared to convert; and he responded: "No!" When they had finished, the king ordered that he should be set down in a certain place with all the joints of his fingers beside him, and they sent him home. That is why he was called Amnon, "man of faith," because he believed in the Living God.

After these things had happened, Rabbi Amnon ordered that on New

Year's day he should be taken to the synagogue beside the prayer leader. And during the *Kedushah*, the hallowing prayer, he said to the prayer leader: "Wait for me a little while, and I shall hallow the Name." Then he declared in a great voice: "Therefore let all sanctity go up to You as I have hallowed Your Name for the sake of Your kingdom and Your unity!"

And then he continued: "Let us declare this day's mighty sanctity, for it is of dread anxiety." And he continued with the whole prayer. When he completed it, he vanished from the eyes and was not to be seen, because God had taken him. But on the third day he came in a vision of the night to our Rabbi Kalonymus son of our Rabbi Meshullam and taught him the entire hymn. And he ordered him to send it throughout the Dispersion of Israel.

That is why the Jews of Germany have established the practice of reciting this prayer on the New Year's day.

70
RABBI MOSES BEN MAIMON AND THE PHYSICIANS: THE POISON

Maimonides (1135–1204), known as the Rambam, the acronym of his Hebrew name, Rabbi Moses ben Maimon, was a philosopher, codifier, and rabbinical authority, and a royal physician in the court of Saladin (1137–1193). After Saladin's death and the settlement of the succession disputes, Al-Afḍal Nur ad Din ʿAli, who ruled for two years (1198–1200), appointed Maimonides as his chief court physician. As a leading figure in medieval Jewry, whose reputation and importance has been maintained throughout history, Maimonides has become the subject of a cycle of folk legends, most of which revolve around real or imagined rivalry between him and other court physicians. Source: (a) E. Arakie, Sefer ha-Maʿasiyyot, No. 16.

It is told that the Rambam, Rabbi Moses ben Maimon, may he rest in peace, was a minister of a king of Spain who raised him up above all his other ministers on account of his wisdom. For he was versed in all knowledge, and particularly in the knowledge of remedies; so the king loved him very much. In due course and by reason of the great honor the king showed him, the other ministers began to envy him and denounce him to the king, so that he fled away to Egypt. And he knew the Arabic language perfectly, but did not know the Chaldean and Median languages.

While he was in Egypt, he took disciples from Alexandria and Damascus and established a great Yeshiva, and his fame spread afar. His wisdom was widely known among the Jews but concealed from the Gentiles, because he was not familiar with those languages. So he chose to study the languages of Chaldea and the Hagarenes, and within seven years he had mastered those tongues too, and his fame became known throughout the land. Then the king of Egypt took him to be a physician.

Now in Egypt it was the custom for the sultan to be seated on his royal throne on certain days, and he had seven levels of seats representing the seven sciences of those times; and the great sages and ministers used to be seated upon them. Now the king did not know on which of these levels to seat the Rambam, for he found that he was wiser than all the sages in all the sciences and fields of knowledge. And by reason of his great modesty the rabbi never wished to take his seat on any of these levels.

Now after the ministers and sages of the king who took their place on these levels saw the great honor and affection which the king bestowed upon him, they envied him exceedingly and spoke misleadingly to the king regarding him. In due course they began to discuss the science of medicine in his presence, after having arranged among themselves that whoever overcame the other would be the greatest and wisest of the physicians.

They agreed to accept a drug which the Rambam would prepare for them, while he accepted the drug that they would prepare for him, and they all would drink it off in the presence of the king. But they insisted that the Rambam should drink the potion that they prepared for him first, and only afterwards would they drink. And he agreed to this.

Now on the appointed day the Rambam told his pupils of this matter, and it seemed very wrong to them. But he laughed at them and instructed them as to all the remedies and treatments which he would need before and after drinking, and they prepared all these very carefully. Then the disciples proclaimed a fast and prayed to the Lord for their master, while he went to the king. There the physicians gave him a goblet of poison which he drank, returning home at once. His disciples did all that he had instructed them, and the Lord was with him, and he was healed.

Now on the third day he also appeared before the king, bearing poison with him. The men there were astonished and wondered how the Jew had been preserved; yet in their own despite they had to drink, and ten of them perished in the presence of the king. And the king was indeed astonished at him and honored him even more than he had done before. So the rabbi became most highly honored and glorified in the eyes of the king and the ministers, while the faces of his foes turned black as the sides of a cooking pot; and he lived henceforth in peace.

71
A SWIFT WAY BY SEA: THE RAMBAM

Maimonides lived in Fez, Morocco for five years, 1160–1165, and left the city under duress. The concept of a magically swift journey occurs already in the talmudic-midrashic literature, in which it is known as kefi-zat ha-derekh, *"the jumping of the road." Source: J. Sasportas et al.,* Me'ora'ot Zevi, *p. 33.*

When the Rambam of blessed memory was living in the holy congregation of Algiers, which is in the country of Barbary in the land of Africa, he was regarded as a great man, just as he was regarded always and everywhere. For wherever he came he was praised and exalted. He was likewise very powerful in the sight of the judges of that land, who had their seat in the said capital. But among them was a certain clever yet evildoing judge who had an old grudge against the Rambam and envied him and his wisdom.

It came to pass that certain Jews who resided in that capital brought a query before the Rambam. It involved a case in which a gentile resident of Algiers had touched open barrels of wine. The Rambam adjudged—in accordance with traditional Jewish law—that the said wine must be regarded as libation wine to idols, and therefore it was not to be drunk. A further ritual question was brought before him in respect of certain vermin which had fallen into a barrel of oil. But the Rambam adjudged that the oil was ritually pure and might be used for consumption.* Now certain evil Jews used these two judgments in order to denounce the Rambam to the said judge who was infuriated, and said: "In that case my people and I are worse in his sight than vermin, and now is the proper time and occasion to take vengeance on him!" And he laid plans to have him put to death.

This became known to the Rambam, either by some manifestation from

---

*In accordance with the legal principal that an impurity of one-sixtieth of the total mass does not have a serious effect.—Henry A. Fischel.

heaven or else because some acquaintance told him. So he swiftly took all his precious belongings of gold and jewels together with his money and placed them in his bag, and he went to a certain seaman and told him: "I feel in a sad mood, can you take me for a sail in a boat along the seashore in order to restore my good spirits? I shall pay you." And the seaman said: "I can do so." So the Rambam and the seaman entered the boat where the seaman promptly fell fast asleep. For the Rambam had in all secrecy taken the Divine Name by which it is possible to shorten the way—this he had prepared while he was still at his home—and had placed it in the prow of the boat. So the Rambam and his wife and children, who had gone sailing with him, arrived within a bare quarter of an hour at the shores of the land of Egypt, which is hundreds of leagues away from Algiers. There the boat stopped and at that very moment the seaman awakened.

When the seaman saw that he was in a strange land and heard a language he did not know being spoken around him, he grew very frightened and cried aloud most bitterly, supposing that this had been done by witchcraft. But the Rambam spoke gently to him and explained: "Have no fear; within another quarter of an hour I shall return you to Algiers from which you came. But take heed that when your boat arrives there and you wake up from your sleep, you should swiftly take this written sheet that I leave in the prow of the boat and fling it into the sea. And if you say anything of this to any man once you are there, you will perish at once." But the seaman assured him: "I shall do what you desire," and he took oath. After that the Rambam paid the seaman his wage and sent him back. And he returned to Algiers in a quarter of an hour and did all that the Rabbi had ordered him.

72
THE PARABLE OF THE TWO PRECIOUS STONES

Solomon ibn Verga (1460–1554), a historiographer and a community leader, wrote Shevet Jehuda *circa 1520, but it was published posthumously in Sabbioneta circa 1560–1567. This book includes reports of the sufferings the Jews of Spain experienced after their expulsion in 1492. The parable of the two stones was a popular religious allegory in Italian Renaissance literature. Source: Solomon ibn Verga,* Das Buch Schevet Jehuda, *ed. M. Wiener, pp. 53–54.*

There was a story of King Don Pedro (II) the Aged and the sage Nicolao de Valencia. Nicolao said: "Sire, I have heard that it is your lofty desire to go to war against your foes. Now why should my lord proceed against those foes who are abroad and leave those who are at home? For they are the Jews who hate us so much and in whose books it is written that they must not greet us peaceably." Then the king answered: "Have you actually heard this with your own ears?" And Nicolao answered: "I have heard this from one of them who has come to our faith." "He," said the king, "is not worthy of belief, for one who changes his faith will find it easy to change the facts. And furthermore, hate based on religion is only doubtful hate, for it aims only to show his love of his new faith." But Nicolao answered: "All I am concerned for is their arrogance, for to your very face, sire, they will say that your faith is false!"

"Let us summon one of the wise Jews and ask him," said the king. When he appeared before him, the king said to him: "What is your name?" And he answered: "Ephraim Sancho." "It would seem," laughed the king, "that you must be a graft, and the lower half of you which bears the sign of the covenant bears your name Ephraim, while from the upper half you are a Christian because you admit to the name of Sancho." To that the Jew replied: "Your majesty, Sancho is the name of my family, and it was actually Santzi, but it has been corrupted by the populace." "Do I seek to wed your daughter," asked the king, "that you are telling me of your family?" "Your majesty," replied the Jew, "I added Sancho for a mark of distinction, for there are many men named Ephraim in the streets, and if your majesty asked me my name, I had to assume that you wished to know who I am in particular."

"Let that be," said the king, "for what caused me to bring you here. It is in order to declare which of the two faiths is better, the faith of Jesus or yours." And the sage replied: "My faith is better for me, since I am what I am, for I was a slave to slaves in Egypt and God brought me forth from there with signs and wonders; but your faith is better for you because of its constant and prolonged authority and duration." "I ask you," said the king, "about the faiths in themselves and as such, not in respect of their followers." To this the wise man answered: "If it seems fit to you, your majesty, I shall answer you after three days of consideration." And the king said: "Be it so."

When the three days were over, the wise man came looking very grieved and disturbed. "Why do you look so downcast?" asked the king; and the sage answered: "Because I was cursed today and groundlessly so, and I beseech you, your majesty, to take up my suit. This is what happened: About a month ago my neighbor went on a long journey but left two precious stones for his two sons. Now the two brothers have come to me and requested me to tell them what the singular character of each stone is and the difference between them. 'Who knew that better than your father?' I said to them. 'There is no greater expert than he in all that concerns precious stones and the art of cutting them and not for nothing is he known to be a lapidary. Send for him and let him tell you the truth!' And because I gave them that reply, they cursed me and beat me." "Why," exclaimed the king, "they cursed you without cause, and they deserve to be punished!"

Then the wise man answered: "Your majesty, let your own ears hearken to the words you uttered! Consider, Esau and Jacob were brothers and each one of them was given a certain jewel, and now your majesty asks which of them is better? Let the king send a messenger to our Father in heaven, for He is the great lapidary, and He will tell you the difference between the stones!"

"Do you see, Nicolao," exclaimed the king, "the wisdom of the Jews? This sage is indeed worthy of honor and gifts. As for you, you deserve to be punished for uttering falsehood about the Jewish community."

73
THE GOLEM: THE FASHIONING OF THE GOLEM

Rabbi Judah Loew ben Bezalel (c.1525–1609) was known as Der Hohe Rabbi Loew, *or the* Maharal *mi-Prague. The latter is an acronym of the Hebrew epithet* Morenu Ha-Rav Rabbi Loew, *"our teacher and master Rabbi Loew." He was a talmudist, a moralist, and a mathematician. When Yodel Rosenberg (1860–1935) published the stories about the Maharal and the Golem he claimed he copied them from a manuscript written by the Maharal's son-in-law, Rabbi Yizhak Kohen, who participated in the narrated events. But errors in names and topography suggest that this claim was more a literary convention than testimony. Quite likely, Rosenberg drew upon oral tradition and literary sources from the eighteenth and nineteenth centuries. The Maharal began to be associated with magical activities at the beginning of the eighteenth century. The tradition about the creation of the golem flourished initially in Poland, centering around the figure of Elijah Baal Shem of Chelm (d. 1583); only in the middle of the nineteenth century is there evidence of the attri-*

bution of the creation of the golem to the Maharal. These stories have had a strong literary impact on modern literature. Source: Yodel Rosenberg, Nifla'ot Maharal, pp. 3, 4, 8, 11, 12, 23.

In the city of Worms there dwelt a certain great and saintly man named Rabbi Bezalel unto whom a son was born on Passover eve in the middle of the Seder ceremony. This befell in the year five thousand two hundred and seventy-three of the Creation (1513), when Israel was being grievously persecuted by the Christian peoples. For they charged them with requiring Christian blood for the Passover Festival in order to mix it in their unleavened bread. Now the very birth of Rabbi Bezalel's son brought about deliverance. For when his mother felt the birth pangs and the members of the household hurried into the street in order to fetch a midwife, they found people bearing a dead Christian child in a sack in order to bring a false charge against the Jews. And Rabbi Bezalel his father prophesied about his son: "He will console us and deliver us from the blood libel. His name in Israel will be called Judah Leon, in accordance with the verse in Genesis: 'Judah is a lion's whelp; on prey, my son, have you grown'" (49:9).

The child grew up into a great scholar and was also very wise, knowing all the sciences and all languages. He became a rabbi in the city of Posen and from there was appointed rabbi and head of the court in the holy congregation of Prague in the year five thousand three hundred and thirty-two of the Creation (1571/72). When he was welcomed as rabbi it was a time of distress for the Jews on account of the blood charge, from which they suffered a great deal. Much blood of Jewish souls—who were completely innocent—was groundlessly shed, like water, on account of that despicable charge.

So the rabbi asked a question of the heavens in a dream. He asked by what power he could withstand the priests who were opposed to the Jews. The answer that reached him followed the letters of the Hebrew alphabet: And Be Creating, Dedicate Earth Fittingly, Golem Handles Israel's Jew-hating Knife-bearers."*

Now the sage decided that these ten words contained various combinations of divine names by the power of which it would be possible to fashion a living golem from earthy matter. So he secretly summoned both his son-in-law and his great disciple, Rabbi Jacob Sasson, and showed them the re-

*The above version is merely intended to show the kind of message given. The actual translation is: You create a golem of adhesive material that shall cut off strangers, the horde who rends Israel.—Trans.

sponse from heaven which he had obtained as answer to his dream query. And he entrusted them both with the secret regarding the creation of the Golem from clay and earth of the ground. And he told them that he wished to take them to aid him in this work of creation, as such a creation requires four forces of the four elements which are: Fire, Air, Water, and Earth. And of his own self the sage said that he was born under the spell of the element of Air, while his son-in-law was born under the power of the element of Fire, and his disciple under that of the element of Water. Therefore, the three of them could complete the entire work of creation. But he commanded them not to reveal the secret to any human being, and urged them to engage in the suitable propitiatory prayers and actions for seven full days.

After the seven days were over, and this befell in the year five thousand three hundred and forty of the Creation, on the twentieth day of the month of Adar, at the fourth hour after midnight, the three of them left the city of Prague for the river. There they searched along the riverbank until they found a spot containing clay and mud, and from it they fashioned the shape of a man three ells long, and they drew a face in it and made him hands and feet, and when they had finished, this was like a man lying on his back. Then the three of them stood at the Golem's feet facing his face, and the rabbi ordered his son-in-law to make a circuit of the Golem seven times, proceeding from the right and going around as far as the Golem's head, and from the head to the feet on the left. And he entrusted him with combinations of letters to be uttered as he made the circuit. This he did seven times. When the circuits were completed, the body of the Golem had grown as red as glowing coals.

Then the rabbi instructed his disciple to make seven such circuits likewise, and entrusted him with other permutations and combinations of letters. The disciple did what his master required and when he completed his circuits, the fire died down, for water reached the body and vapor began to rise from it, nails sprouted at the fingertips, and he likewise became as hairy as a thirty-year-old man. Then the rabbi likewise made seven circuits around the Golem and after he had completed them, the three of them together recited the verse that is in the Book of Genesis: "And He breathed the spirit of life into his nostrils, and man became a living creature" (2:7). For in the air one breathes there must also be Fire and Water and Spirit, those being the three (maternal) elements, as it is written in *Sefer Yetzirah*, the Book of Creation.

When they had finished reciting this verse, the Golem opened his eyes and stared at the rabbi and his disciples like a man in confusion. Then the rabbi called him in a commanding voice: "Rise to your feet!" And the Golem rose to his feet. They clad him in garments which they had taken with them, such garments as were suited to a court attendant. And they also put boots on his feet.

Then the rabbi said to the Golem: "Know that we have created you of earth from the ground in order that you should guard the Jews from all evil and distress which they suffer at the hands of their foes and traducers. Your name will be Joseph. You will live with me and dwell in the courtyard of my court. You will work as a bailiff, and you will obey my orders in all that I command you, even if it is to enter the fire or drown in the great waters, or leap from the tower, until you have performed my command in its entirety and done whatever I have sent you to do!"

The Golem nodded his head at the rabbi's words like a man agreeing with his companion. In brief, the Golem became a man like all others. He saw and heard and understood, but he had no power of speech in his mouth. Three men left the city by night, and at six o'clock in the morning, ere it was day, four men came back home.

What the rabbi told his household about the Golem was that as he went before dawn to the ritual bath, he met the poor dumb man in the street and saw that he was very much an innocent and simpleton. So he had taken pity on him and fetched him to assist the bailiffs. To be sure, he gave them an order that he was not to be employed for any household duties. And he told those who had aided him in fashioning the Golem that he had given him the name of Joseph because he had drawn down into him the spirit of Joseph Sheda, "the Demon," who is referred to in the tractate *Pesachim* of the Babylonian Talmud, and who was half-man and half-demon. He had served the sages of the Talmud and delivered them from great trouble many a time.

The Golem always sat in a corner of the courtroom beside the table, leaning his head on his two hands like a true golem that has no wisdom or understanding. He neither thought nor was concerned with any matter in the world. The rabbi said about him that if he were to walk through fire he would not be scorched, and river currents would not sweep him away, nor would the sword slay him.

Rabbi Maharal made use of the Golem only to deliver Israel from trouble and distress. Most of all he used him in order to combat the blood charge which, as already remarked, was exceedingly widespread, so that the Jewish residents of the city of Prague and the vicinity suffered greatly from it. When the rabbi had to send the Golem to some place where it was not advisable for any man to see him, he used to invest him with a charm written on vellum by which he became invisible, while he himself could see.

During the whole month before the Passover he used to patrol the streets of the Jewish quarter at night by order of the rabbi. If he saw any man carrying a burden on his shoulder or dragging some burden in a cart, he would run to him and inspect what he was carrying or dragging. If he saw that this was a dead child that they wished to fling into the street of the Jews, he would seize the man and the corpse and bind them together with a rope he wore corded around him, and would drag them by force to the council house, where the chief constable and city watch were to be found; and there the man would be imprisoned and judged as a criminal.

The might of the Golem was above the natural, and he did a great deal as long as he existed.

74
THE GOLEM: THE DEATH OF THE GOLEM

See above note.

After the law that no trials on the blood charge would be heard any more was published and the land grew quiet, the rabbi made an end of the Golem. He commanded his disciples to make a circuit around him seven times by night and to repeat the permutations and combinations of letters which they had uttered when he was fashioned, but in the opposite order. When the seventh circuit was completed, the Golem remained lying like a piece of hardened clay without any spirit of life.

They removed his garments, wrapped him up in two old prayer shawls, and concealed him under a pile of tattered books in the rabbi's attic.

In the Land of Israel

75
A STORY OF THE TEMPLE

The present legend was recorded from oral tradition during the nineteenth century from different sources independent of each other. Through travel accounts and literary renditions it has become part of the legendary stock of ethical and pedagogical narrative collections; at the same time, it has continued to enjoy oral circulation. Source: S. B. Ḥuẓin, Ma'aseh Nissim, p. 35.

The place where our glorious Temple was built had long been a field owned by two brothers. One of them had a wife and children while the other had no wife and children. Yet they dwelt together in a single house, wholehearted, at ease and rejoicing in the portion of land they had inherited from their father; and they tilled the field by the sweat of their brows.

During one wheat harvest they bound up shocks in the field and beat out the ears and made two equal piles of the grain they had reaped, one pile for each of them; and they left them there in the field. That night the brother who had neither wife nor children lay on his bed and thought to himself: "I am all by myself and have nobody who is dependent on me for his daily bread. But my brother has a wife and children, so why should my portion be like his?" So he rose in the middle of the night and stole like a thief and took sheaves from his own pile and placed them on his brother's pile.

And his brother said to his wife: "It is not fair to divide the corn in the field into two portions, half to me and half to my brother. My lot and fate is so much better than his, since God has given me a wife and children while he goes alone and has no pleasure or song or delight in anything but the grain he gathers in the field. Come with me, wife, and we shall secretly add to his portion from our own." And they did so.

Next morning both men were astonished to see that their piles were equal as they had been at first. But they said nothing that day. Instead they went and did the same thing on the second night and the third and the fourth; and every morning they found that the heaps were equal.

Then each of them made up his mind to investigate. When each went to do his deed at night, one brother met the other carrying the sheaves. Then they understood what they had been doing, and they embraced and kissed one another. And they gave thanks to God who had given each of them a brother who engaged in good deeds and went his just and upright way.

That was the place that the Lord desired, the spot where the two brothers had thought the good thought and done the good deed. That was why it was blessed by the men of the earth, and the Children of Israel chose it for building a House for the Lord.

76
THE FOUNDATION OF THE TEMPLE

For three hundred years before the Ottoman conquest of Jerusalem in the sixteenth century, travelers neither reported nor described the Western Wall. In this version of the tale, the Sultan who uncovered the Western Wall is not identified. But other versions of this story refer variously to two different rulers: Sultan Selim I (1512–1520), who conquered Jerusalem in 1517, and his son Suleiman "The Magnificent" (1520–1566), who built the wall around Jerusalem. Source: M. M. Reischer, Sha'arei Yerushalayim, No. 10, pp. 42–43.

In the year three hundred of the sixth millennium (1539/40) the foundations of the Temple, as much as were left, were discovered by accident. For when the sultan conquered Jerusalem, he chose as his residence the building which now serves for the judges of the Ishmaelites to the west of the Temple, which was in ancient times the Hall of Hewn Stone where the Sanhedrin used to hold its sessions. In their tongue it is called Makhima, the Seat of Wisdom, in memory of the wise men of the Sanhedrin.

One day the king saw an old woman fetching a sack full of rubbish and flinging it on a dunghill near his dwelling. He grew very angry to think that she dared to pollute the neighborhood of his dwelling place and ordered that she should be brought before him. She excused herself by saying: "I am descended from the Romans and dwell two days' journey from Jerusalem, but I carry out the commandments of my forefathers. For the leading Romans set up a practice that every person in Jerusalem must bring rubbish here every day, and all those who dwell in her outskirts must do so twice a week, while those who dwell up to three days' journey from her must do so once a month. For this was the House of the God of Israel. And since they were unable to destroy it to the foundations, they decreed that it must be covered with filth and street mud in order that no memory of it might be left."

When she ended her words, the king ordered her to be taken under guard until he investigated and found out whether she was telling the truth. He ordered his men to stand at a distance and arrest every person who brought refuse to this place, and every man whom they arrested said the same thing as the woman. When the king saw that they were telling the truth, he sent a proclamation throughout the land: "Whosoever desires to find favor in my eyes, let him come hither and do all that he sees me doing." Then with his own hand he took several purses full of gold and silver, together with a basket and a broom, and he went to that great heap and scattered the money all over it in order that the poor people should hurry to pick it up and shift the rubbish away from that place because of their desire for the money. He stood over them urging them on and worked himself, sweeping the rubbish away with his men and his ministers. This he did day by day for a whole month until he cleared the place, and the Western Wall and the foundations that can now be seen by all were revealed. As for the people who continued to bring their rubbish as before, he imprisoned them. Among them three women were cut to pieces and the parts of their bodies set aloft all around the town in order that they might see and hear. And he sent a message throughout his kingdom that no man should dare to come and pollute this place, nor even to spit there, since it was sacred to the God of Israel.

After that, he summoned the leading Jews who dwelt there and spoke to them of building the House at his expense. But they wept and answered him: "We must bless our lord the king and thank him for this kindness which he has shown us and this Holy Place. Yet according to the tradition we have at hand from our forefathers we cannot build this house until the Righteous Redeemer comes to restore its glory as of old." Then the king said: "In that case, then, I shall build it as a House of Prayer for myself, as Solomon said: 'Likewise for the stranger, who does not belong to Your people Israel. . . . When he comes to pray in this House, You shall hear him in the heavens which are Your seat and abiding place'" (I Kings 8:41–43).

Then he sent them back to their homes in peace and gave them freedom in his land.

77
THE TOMBS OF THE KINGS

This story was first recorded by the twelfth-century Jewish traveler Benjamin of Tudela, but it may build on earlier traditions. In Jewish Antiquities *Josephus describes a similar incident, and II Maccabees 3 tells about a similar encounter that Heliodorus had when he attempted to confiscate the Temple treasure. Source: Jacob Barukh ben Moses Ḥayyim, Shivḥei Yerushalayim, p. 22.*

There are great hills around Jerusalem, and on Mount Zion are the tombs of the House of David and of the kings who followed him, but the place is not known.

Once a wall fell from the church on Mount Zion and the chief priest ordered the local priest to build this wall, telling him: "Take the stones from the ancient wall of Zion and build the church with them." He did so. He hired maybe twenty workers at a fixed rate, and they took the stones from the base of the wall of Zion. Now among these men were two friends. One day one of them made a feast for his companion, and they went to work after they had eaten. "Why have you come late?" asked the man in charge. And they answered: "How does it harm you? When our comrades go to eat, we shall go on working!"

So they went on taking out the stones and set one stone erect and under it they found the mouth of a cave. "Let us go in," said one to the other, "and see whether there is any money there." So they went into the cave until they came to a magnificent chamber erected with marble pillars that were plated with gold and silver. In front of it was a table and a golden scepter and a golden crown; and that was the tomb of David, king of Israel. On his left-hand side was the tomb of Solomon likewise, as well as the tombs of all the kings of Judah who were buried there. Closed boxes stood there and no man knows what is in them. The two men wished to enter this chamber, but a great wind came from out of the cave and smote them so that they fell to the ground as though they were dead and lay there till the evening.

Then a certain spirit came and shouted in human voice: "Rise and depart from this place!" So the startled men hurried away and went to the chief priest and told it all to him. And the chief priest sent to Rabbi Abraham, the pious recluse who was known as al-Kostantini, the man of Constantinople, who dwelt in Jerusalem. He told him all this according to these two men who had been there. And then Rabbi Abraham told him that those were the tombs of David and the kings of Judah.

Next day they sent for the two men and found each of them bedridden. They were in great fear, and they said: "We shall not enter there, for the Lord does not desire to show it to any man." And then the chief priest ordered that the spot should be concealed and hidden from humankind until this day.

78
THE PASHA'S LANCE

This tale belongs to the narrative cycle about the Tombs of the Kings and has parallels in the folklore of other nations. Source: S. B. Ḥuzin, Ma'aseh Nissim, No. 2.

It is told that in bygone days the pasha of Jerusalem visited the tombs of the dynasty of David, and there he found a window giving on the cave. As he prostrated himself there, his lance fell through this window, and it was encrusted with precious stones and jewels of great price. He ordered that it should be brought back and they lowered an Ishmaelite by ropes to the floor of the tomb. A few moments later they brought him up and found that he was lifeless and dead. Then they lowered another and after waiting a long, long time brought him up as well, and he was dead like the first one, and so a third and a fourth. Then the pasha swore that this precious lance must be restored to him, even if all the inhabitants of Jerusalem lost their lives because of it. But the kadi told him: "Good sir, do not wantonly make an end of a large number of sons of the faith in your wrath! Yet I pray you to give heed to my word and to the counsel of your servant. Send one of your attendants to the hakham bashi (the chief rabbi), so that he should send you a Jew to bring up your lance. And if he refuses, then decree the destruction of all the Jews. Yet it is my assured opinion that your lance will be returned to you, for the Jews are held in high esteem by the Prophet David and he will fulfill their wishes and desires."

This counsel found favor with the pasha, so he sent to the hakham bashi, who was the chief rabbi in Jerusalem, and ordered that a Jew be sent him to return his spear from the tomb of King David, may he rest in peace. At this the rabbi trembled exceedingly, flinching from any profanation of so holy a place as the tombs of the kings by having any foot treading there, and he grieved for the destruction of his people.

So he burst into tears and entreated the governor for three days' time, and three days' grace were granted him. When he returned home, he gathered all the congregation together and ordered them to fast for three days, and each day in turn he proceeded with all the men and the children to the tomb of our Mother Rachel in order to pray for the Children of Israel, and there they wept and wailed aloud. On the fourth day he said to the members of his community who were with him: "One of us must risk this transgression and be given over to the executioners for the sake of us all, and go down to the tombs of the kings. Now which of you will go and atone for the Lord's congregation?"

When he saw that they were all silent and not a sound was to be heard, he went on: "In that case, let us put it to the lot and that will show!" And the lot fell on the attendant of the synagogue, an innocent and simple man, and he answered, saying: "I am the servant of the God of Israel!" So he prepared his soul and hallowed himself by immersing three times in the ritual pool before taking the deadly path. Then he parted from his household and family and all the congregation who stood weeping without ceasing as he set his feet to mount aloft to Zion and the place of the tombs of the kings of Judah. The pasha was already waiting there with a band of his companions and attendants, all bearing arms.

They lowered the synagogue attendant on a rope through the window. The pasha inclined his ear to the window and listened carefully, and the hearts of the accompanying Jews melted away within them. A few moments later they suddenly heard a thin voice crying: "Fetch me up!" They pulled at the rope and little by little the sword appeared together with the scabbard which was encrusted with so many precious stones. Then came the head of the attendant with a face as pale as death, and after that his whole body appeared. He held the spear out to the astonished pasha, and all the people there fell on their faces and cried: "Blessed be the Lord God of Israel!" And from that day forward the pasha held the Jews in very high esteem.

After that, the whole community rejoiced, and there was feasting and joy and gladness in every house. And people could be heard singing and playing with timbrels and drums all around. But the joy was greatest in the household of the synagogue attendant, for he was given gifts of food and drink and silver and gold beyond all measure. They all wished to know what the tombs of the kings looked like and what had happened to him there. But he remained silent.

Only to the hakham bashi did he reveal the secret that suddenly, while he stood in the gloom, an old man gleaming white appeared before him and gave him the lance in silence.

79
THE DEAD BEARS WITNESS

This tale appeared in print first in 1782. The identity of Rabbi Kalonymos is not clear, but apparently a rabbi by that name lived in Jerusalem in either the sixteenth or the eighteenth century. Until the thirties of the current century a heap of stone marked his grave at the boundary of the Jewish cemetery at the foot of Mt. Olives. Practically throughout history Jews were accused of performing murders in order to obtain the victim's blood for ritual purposes. There were documented blood accusations in Palestine during the nineteenth century, but this tale apparently alludes to an earlier case. Source: J. S. Farḥi, Oseh Pele 2:204–206.

This incident happened in the Holy City of Jerusalem, may she be builded speedily in our days, at the time of our Rabbi Kalonymos of blessed memory. The Gentiles in Jerusalem hated the Jews greatly and thought of bringing a false charge against them. Day after day they used to plan against them and bring charges of falsehood and trickery before the ruler of the city, so that he should wreak vengeance upon them. But he did not believe their words and would not incline his heart to their counsels until the distressers were sick of their lives. One night they gathered together in a special place in order to take counsel and prevail against him and decide what they could do to make an end of the Jews in the Holy City. "They decided among themselves to kidnap the very son of the king who ruled the city and slay him and fling him into the synagogue in the street of the Jews. That would undoubtedly cause the king to vent his fury upon them and slay them and all that was theirs without mercy. And so they did. They set a watch to trap the king's young son every day along the paths that he followed, until at length they tricked him one evening and began joking and playing with him. At length they brought him a long way from town to some desolate spot, and then they seized him and tied him up and slaughtered him and collected his blood in a vessel. They waited until it was very dark that night and took the body and flung it into the courtyard of the synagogue of the Jews and poured out all the blood in that courtyard in order that everybody should say that the Jews had killed him.

When the king saw that it was night and his son had not returned home as usual, he sent his attendants to seek him. They sought him all through the town and did not find him. That night he could not sleep because of his concern for his son, and he sent criers all through the city calling on anybody who had seen the prince to come and declare it. And the city was confused and at a loss all night long, as they sought for the prince without finding him.

And so they went on searching, going from one place to another and from house to house until they found his body in the courtyard of the synagogue of the Jews, and he was slain and lying in his blood. They raised him onto their shoulders at once and brought him before the king and said: "Live forever, our lord and king! With your own eyes you can see the evil deed done to your one and only son by the Jews you love so much. This is the reward they give you for your love. Now you can believe what we were always telling your august self, that there are no people in the world as bad as they are." And when the king saw his dead son lying before him and heard these words by all his subjects, a fire began burning within him and his fury blazed; and he sent at once and summoned all the sages and leaders of the Jews in the city of Jerusalem, and he said to them: "I demand that you should investigate and then inform me who this adversary of mine is that slew my only and beloved son, so that I may take vengeance upon him. But if you do not inform me, I shall make an end of all the Jews!"

When they heard this, their faces turned black as soot, and they could find no answer. Yet they replied gravely and falteringly: "Give us time to bring you our answer!" He allowed them time, and they went forth unhappily in order to gather all the people to the synagogue and proclaim a public fast and entreat the Lord.

Now when our master Rabbi Kalonymos of blessed memory heard of this great trouble and the exceeding danger in which all Israel found themselves, he rose and went to the king at once and said to him: "Your majesty! Believe me that I am in great distress at this sad thing that has befallen your son. But with the aid of our Almighty God you may rest assured that I shall reveal who it is that has done this thing to you in order that you may exact vengeance on him on behalf of your only son. Yet first allow me one hour's time to pray to the Lord our God that He may perform a sign and wonder and let us know who has done this wicked deed." And he gave him the permission.

So he departed from the royal presence and went and purified himself and immersed and changed his garments. Then he went to the synagogue where he opened the holy Ark and prayed to the Holy and Blessed One, weeping and entreating and saying: "Lord of all the Universe! Do not make a wanton end of Your people and Your heritage! For Your sake we are being slain every day and reckoned as sheep for slaughter!" And he continued in that fashion, uttering many verses of entreaty. Swathed in his prayer shawl he recited the thirteen merciful attributes of God, then bowed down before the holy Ark and kissed the Torah scrolls and went forth. From there he went up to the king and found him seated in council with all the leading men of the kingdom, to consider what should be done to the Jews. Bowing low before the king, he said to them: "Fetch me a piece of paper!" And they brought it.

Then he wrote a Holy Name on the paper and set it on the brow of the slain lad that lay before them. The lad revived at once and rose to his feet. And our master Rabbi Kalonymos asked him in the presence of his royal father and all the great men of the kingdom, who were seated before the king: "My son, I wish you to tell all that happened in detail before your royal father and these men who are seated here, and who wrought evil with you and all that befell you."

Then the lad who had been slain and killed responded by telling them all that had happened from beginning to end, and who the man was who had slain him. Among the evildoers who had come and helped to kill him, he pointed to three of those who were seated before them. When the king heard this, he was most startled at his words; but the lad said to his father the king: "Why are you so astonished and disturbed at what I say? If you do not believe what I am telling you, I shall give you a clear sign and full proof so that you should believe and my words enter your ears. Send one of your attendants to that given spot where they slew me, and there you will find a stone all bedabbled with blood, because when they slaughtered me the blood spurted on it. And tell him to dig it up and fetch it here before you."

And so it was. The king at once sent his attendants to the spot described by the slain lad, and they dug up that stone and brought it before the king. As soon as they had placed the stone in the king's presence and he had seen it, the lad fell dead again just as he had been.

In the king's abundant rage and fury he seized all those wicked men who had had a hand in this and set iron chains upon them and placed them in prison. After that, he sent for all the Jews in the city, great and small alike, and told them: "I wish you to know that those wicked men are my foes, and they were so evil as to lie in wait for my son and slay him in order to bring a false charge against you. Yet your rabbi had no rest in this matter until he revealed their shame and deceit and evil deeds and established your uprightness and honesty. Well, I hand over these cruel evildoers into your hands and you can do what you desire with them."

And so it was. The Jews seized those bastards and punished them with harsh and bitter punishments to their satisfaction, even more than they did to the ten sons of Haman.

Thus may the Lord take vengeance on all our foes who seek to do us evil and bring to naught the counsel of our enemies who rise against us to destroy us in every generation, and may He speedily redeem us and raise high our horn above all those that hate us, speedily and in our days!

80
THE SHEWBREAD

Rabbi Isaac Luria (1534–1572) was the leader of the Safed kabbalistic circle in the mid-sixteenth century. The preference for spiritual intention over rational explanation that the narrative conveys is in agreement with Luria's mystical teachings. Source: Anon., Ma'asiyyot Nora'im ve-Nifla'im, *pp. 3–4.*

"Y ou shall place shewbread before Me on the table at all times" (Exod. 25:30).

Now one of the Marranos left Portugal and came to Upper Galilee where he became a Jew: and he appointed his dwelling in the holy city of Safed, may she be builded speedily and in our days! In the synagogue he heard a sermon by the chief of the community's rabbinical court regarding the shewbread which was brought and presented in the Temple every Sabbath for the entire week. And the rabbi sighed in his sermon and grieved and said: "But nowadays by reason of our manifold sins we have nothing that is prepared and which should serve to bring plenitude down upon what is unprepared likewise."

After the Marrano heard this address, he went home in his innocence and told his wife that on the eve of every Sabbath day she should prepare him two loaves of bread from flour that had been sifted thirteen times and from dough that had been kneaded in purity. They were to be baked well and with all kinds of beautification in the household oven, because he wished to bring them as an offering to the Temple of the Lord. Perchance God would approve of this and accept them and eat this sacrifice. And as he instructed her, so his wife did. Every Friday he used to fetch the two loaves to the Temple of the Lord and pray and entreat before His Blessed Name that He should accept them with a good will and eat them and find them pleasant and fragrant. In this way he spoke and entreated like a son begging a favor of his father. Then he would leave the loaves in the holy Temple and depart.

Now the synagogue attendant used to come and take the two loaves without any questioning or investigation as to where they came from or who had brought them; and he would eat them and rejoice the way people rejoice at harvest. At the hour of the evening prayer at the close of Sabbath the God-fearing Marrano would hasten to the Temple of the Lord. And since he did not find the loaves he had left, he rejoiced greatly at heart. He would go home and tell his wife: "All praise and thanksgiving to His Blessed Name because He has not despised the offering of the poor and has already accepted our bread and eaten it hot!" And he went on urging her for His Name's sake not to be negligent in preparing them in future but to be very particular indeed about this. "We have no way of honoring God," he would say, "but we see that He finds this bread sweet and pleasant. It is therefore our duty to give Him pleasure through them!" And so he went on doing this for quite some time.

Now in due course it happened by chance that one Sabbath eve the rabbi of the congregation whose sermon had led the Marrano to bring the loaves to the Temple, stayed in the House of the Lord, where he stood on the almemar reading over the sermon which he was to deliver the next day.

And the Marrano came in accordance with his own worthy custom bringing the two loaves. He approached the holy Ark and began to order his words and entreaties before the Ever Present with the same fervor and joy with which he always brought his gift before him; but he did not notice that the rabbi was standing on the platform behind and could overhear him. The rabbi remained silent and watched and saw and heard all that the man was saying and doing. He grew exceedingly incensed and cried out to the man and rebuked him, saying: "You fool! Do you suppose that our God eats and drinks! The synagogue attendant must be the one who takes your loaves and eats them, while you believe and suppose that God accepts them! It is a great sin to attribute any kind of corporeality to the Blessed God who has neither physical shape nor body."

He uttered his words of reproof to him and went on until the attendant came as usual to take the loaves. When the rabbi saw him, he called him and said: "Thank this man for bringing what you have now come to take. And who else but you has taken the two loaves that this man has been bringing every Sabbath eve to this holy Ark?" And the attendant admitted it without shame.

When the Marrano heard all this he began to weep and lament and begged the rabbi to forgive him since he had misunderstood his speech and had wished to fulfill a commandment, yet, led on by his words, had only committed a transgression.

While he was still speaking, a special messenger came from the holy Rabbi Isaac Luria to the preacher. And he said to him in his master's name: "Go home and prepare a will for your household, for tomorrow at the time when you are due to preach you are doomed to die! And this has already been proclaimed on high!"

The preacher was greatly alarmed at these ill tidings and hastened to the holy rabbi; and he entreated him to explain what his sin and transgression had been. And the holy rabbi answered: "Ever since the destruction of the holy Temple, may it be rebuilt speedily in our days, the Ever Present has never had such satisfaction as He enjoyed at the hours when the Marrano from Portugal brought Him the two loaves in all his innocence to the Temple of the Lord, thinking that His Blessed Name accepted them from him. And now, because you have put a stop to his bringing them any more, death has been decreed upon you without any possibility of deliverance."

So the preacher went home where he declared his will and testament. And on the holy Sabbath day, at the hour that he should have delivered his sermon, he passed away and went to his eternal home as the man of God had told him.

Forebears and Descendants

81
NAHMAN KETUFA

This story was known among the kabbalists at the end of the fifteenth and the beginning of the sixteenth centuries. The narrative refers to events that, according to the dates that appear in the text, occurred almost a thousand years earlier. The destruction of the Second Temple, used here as a calendrical reference point, occurred in 70 C.E., and hence the dates mentioned in the story are 502 and 570 C.E. The first day of the month of Tishri is Rosh Hashanah, the day the world was created, according to tradition. The four beasts of the heavenly chariot refer to the vision in Ezekiel 1, which has a central place in Jewish mystical literature. Source: Anon., Nevu'at ha-Yeled, "Introduction," in Jacob Zemah, Sefer Nagid u-Mezaveh.

I n the year 432 after the Destruction of the Second Temple there was a man named Rabbi Pinhas who was very wise and knew the Great and Awesome Holy Name of God, but he never sinned and never made any use at all of that Name. Very often his heart impelled him to make use of the Name in order to go to the land of Edom (Byzantium) and destroy and uproot its government and power. Yet he would always change his mind, saying: "I am but a worm, and how can I transgress the decree of the Monarch of the Universe who has set an end to darkness. For when the proper time comes we shall find, as Isaiah wrote (24:21): 'The Lord shall command the host on high in the heights.'" And when he thought this, his heart would grow chill and he would weep and say in the words of the Psalm (135:6): "Whatever the Lord desires He performs in heaven and on earth."

Now the wife of Rabbi Pinhas was named Rachel. She was exceedingly beautiful and fair to look upon and was a God-fearing woman, but she was barren. After she married and saw that she did not become pregnant, she would expend much money on wise women to prepare medicines for her so that she might conceive, but they did not help her. Then she prayed to the Lord, and said, using the words of Jeremiah (31:15): "'Rachel laments her children, because they are not,' and I weep for myself." Every day when she rose she washed her face and placed a kerchief over her head and wept and did not eat. This she did for a long, long time; and when her husband Rabbi Pinhas came from the house of study, she used to wash his feet, and he went to sleep. And she ate food only at night. As for the holy Rabbi Pinhas, he never even looked in her face and did not show her tenderness.

Then Rachel prayed and said: "Lord of the Universe! By Your life and by Your living Name, I know that I have never sinned in all my days; and even if I have sinned, my husband has not sinned. Yet even if he and I have sinned, remember what You said in Your own Torah; in Exodus (34:7): 'Maintaining His loving-kindness for thousands of generations.' And remember the kindness of Abraham for our sakes!" And she fell on her face, saying: "For the sake of Your Name and Faith and Divinity and Royalty hearken now, I pray, to the prayer of Rachel Your maidservant!" And she wept and moaned, thinking her husband was alseep; but he heard her voice and outcry. Then he rose and said: "God of Israel, I pray you, hear the voice of Your maidservant Rachel!"

When Rachel heard this, she prostrated herself before Rabbi Pinhas her husband and seized his legs and said to him: "I conjure you by the Great Name you know that you should pray to the Lord to give us a son." Thereupon Rabbi Pinhas stood quivering and trembling and prayed. And the Lord favored him, and Rachel his wife conceived.

The child was in her womb for six months. One day in the seventh month on a Thursday, one hour after the rising of the Morning Star, when the planet rose in the signs of Jupiter and the Scales, on the first day of Tishri of the year 500 after the Destruction of the Second Temple, she gave birth; and she called her child Nahman, which means "the comforting one." When he came forth into the light of the world, he bowed down to his mother and said: "Above this dome of the heavens which you see there are nine hundred and fifty-five other heavens. Above them are the four Beasts of the Heavenly Chariot, and above them is the lofty and exalted Throne, and above the Throne is Consuming Fire, and His Precious Throne and all His attendants are fire!"

When his father Rabbi Pinhas heard these words, he rebuked and silenced the babe. After that the boy said nothing at all for twelve years. His mother wept all this time, saying: "I have a son, but if only I did not have a son!" And the boy Nahman was exceedingly handsome.

One day Rabbi Pinhas came from the house of study. His wife Rachel came and washed his feet as was her practice. After that, she brought her son Nahman to his father. Then she flung herself to the ground and gripped his legs and wept and kissed his feet and said: "I entreat you, permit him to speak, or let him be taken from the world!" Then Rabbi Pinhas uncovered the boy's face and saw how very good and handsome he was. Then he took him, and he kissed him three times. And when Rachel saw this, her mind was at ease.

"Rise up," Rabbi Pinhas then said to her, "why are you prostrating yourself?" Now she had never acted against him or disregarded his words, nor had he ever annoyed her or treated her lightly. When she rose to her feet, Rabbi Pinhas said to her: "What do you wish us to do with this boy?" "Whatever," she answered, "may give pleasure to our Maker." "I know," said Rabbi Pinhas to her, "that you wish me to permit him to speak." "Yes, my master," said she, and fell at his feet again and entreated him to do this.

"Alas for the boy," said Rabbi Pinhas to her. "Wise as he is and intelligent as he is, he has no length of days. You his mother entreat me to permit him to speak. Yet I know he will say things that will shock and shake all creatures."

"My master," answered Rachel, "permit him to speak in secret and not openly." Then Rabbi Pinhas placed his mouth against the boy's mouth and commanded him and adjured him not to speak openly but only in cryptic and obscure fashion in order that no man should comprehend him, not even the wisest, until his words came true. Then he said to him: "Now you may speak!"

Thereupon the boy opened his mouth and uttered five prophecies in alphabetic order. When he finished, his father said to him: "Be strong and brave!" And Nahman answered: "May your days be plentiful, father, and the days of my mother. I am your son, and in the end my father and mother will bury me."

When he said this, his parents wept from that day forth until he died. For he soon departed to live in the World to Come.

That is the story of Nahman Ketufa of Kfar Biram. And there are forty saints with him in a cave.

82

IBN EZRA AND JUDAH HALEVI

Rabbi Abraham ibn Ezra (1089–1164) and Judah Halevi (before 1075–1141) were poets, philosophers, and biblical commentators; both were born in Tudela (or, as some suggest in the case of the latter, Toledo) and traveled through a number of Spanish cities. They differed in their economic position, the former poor, the latter rich. While ibn Ezra mentioned Judah Halevi, his senior, in his biblical commentary, any relations between them, as the present tale accounts, are legendary rather than historical. Source: Ibn Yaḥya, Shalshelet ha-Kabbalah, p. 31.

I have heard it said that Rabbi Judah Halevi, who wrote the *Book of the Kuzari* was very wealthy and had only one daughter who was very beautiful. When she grew up, his wife urged him to marry her while he was still alive. So much did she importune him that once the old man grew angry and swore that he would marry her to the first Jew who came before him.

In the morning Rabbi Abraham ibn Ezra entered by chance, clad in rags and tatters. When his wife saw this pauper, she remembered her husband's oath, and her face fell. Still she began to question him as to his name and his knowledge of Torah. But he acted like a stranger and did not tell her the truth. Then the woman went to her husband in his study and wept. But Rabbi Judah said to her: "Have no fear. I shall teach him Torah and give him a great name." And he went out and conversed with the newcomer. But again ibn Ezra deceived him and hid his name from him. But later, after much entreaty on the part of Rabbi Judah, ibn Ezra pretended to begin to learn Torah from him and went on with his ruse and gave all the appearance of benefiting.

One night Rabbi Judah came late from his house of study, for he found it very hard to compose a verse in his hymn "Lord of Thy Grace," all the lines of which had to begin with the letter R. His wife called him to eat, but he did not come until she went and entreated him. Ibn Ezra asked what had delayed him so long. The old man laughed at him, but ibn Ezra insisted on knowing until the worthy woman went to her husband's study, for she too was wise. And she took her husband's notebook and showed it to ibn Ezra. Then ibn Ezra took hold of the pen and began to make corrections in two or three places. And when he came to the letter R he wrote the whole verse which begins, "Reckon He did, the One, to keep His troth twofold. . . ."

When Rabbi Judah saw this, he rejoiced exceedingly, embraced him and kissed him and said: "Now I know that you are ibn Ezra and my son-in-law!" And then ibn Ezra unmasked himself and admitted who he was. And Rabbi Judah gave him his daughter to wife, together with all his wealth.

83
A PRECIOUS JEWEL

Rashi (1040–1105) was the leading medieval commentator on the Bible and the Talmud. He was born in Troyes, northeastern France, and lived there all his life except for his years of studies. His textual commentary served as the foundation for traditional learning and he became the subject of folk legends. The present story follows a common narrative pattern in which the birth of a future scholar is a reward for some parental meritorious act. Source: L. Ginzberg, "Fragmentary Legends," pp. 239–240.

This is a story of Rabbi Isaac, the father of Rashi of blessed memory, who had a certain jewel which was worth thousands of gold pieces. Now it happened at that time that a similar jewel was lost from an eye of one of the emperor's idols. He sent to Rabbi Isaac of blessed memory to bring his precious jewel at once, since he had heard that it was fit to be placed in the eye of that object he worshiped; for he had already made inquiry in all parts of the world and had heard that no other jewel could compare with the second jewel in the other eye of his statue of worship. He declared that he would pay whatever he might be asked for it and would hold nothing back.

Thereupon Rabbi Isaac had to take the road and brought the precious jewel with him. But when he was on a ship in the heart of the sea his wisdom showed him, God-fearing as he was, how to ensure that idolatry would not be enhanced by him. He showed the precious jewel to a certain Gentile on deck of the ship. And as he showed it and held it out to place it in the hand of that Gentile, he let it fall into the sea. At once he flung himself upon the deck and tore his hair and plucked his beard and beat himself, weeping and wailing and moaning and crying: "Woe is me and alas, I have lost all I have toiled for, all the wealth I gained under the sun.

I was on my way to take it to the emperor who would have given me so much silver and gold for it, besides his lasting gratitude! Woe is me, I have no more hope, and what more can I do?"

All the people on board ship consoled and comforted him and reported the matter to the emperor, and explained exactly what had happened. And the emperor also regretted the loss of the jewel and said: "What a pity for what has gone and for the bad luck of the Jew who has lost so many thousands of gold pieces by losing that precious jewel which I would have loved like the apple of my eye!"

In this way the rabbi was saved, for the emperor brought no charge against him. And nobody felt that he had acted guilefully in order that he should do nothing that might aid idolatry.

When Rabbi Isaac returned from the ship and wished to go to his own land and city, Elijah, whom it is good to remember, found him and told him: "You made an end of that jewel in order to fulfill the will of your Maker. By your life, your wife will bear you a son in a year's time, and he will be a jewel beyond compare in the whole world!" And from him came Solomon, that perfect and precious and unique sage in his generation who is known as Rashi of blessed memory, who made a commentary on the whole Torah and the whole Mishnah and the whole six orders of the Talmud, and there has been no other like him.

To teach you that the Holy and Blessed One does not withhold the reward of any creature.

84
THE BREAKING OF THE BOW

Rabbi Judah ben Samuel he-Ḥasid (c.1150–1217) was the most prominent member of the medieval pietistic movement known as Ḥasidei Ashkenaz, and the major contributor to Sefer Hasidim. *The historical and biographical information about him is meager. The legendary information that fills the gap often follows the biographical pattern of rabbis—a period of ignorance preceding the attainment of prominence. Source: N. Brüll, "Beiträge zur jüdischen Sagen- und Sprachkunde im Mittelalter," pp. 32–33.*

Rabbi Judah the Hasid was more than eighteen years old but knew nothing, not even how to recite the morning and evening prayers. He was a complete ignoramus, but he was a bowman and archer. On one occasion his father our Rabbi Samuel was expounding law to his students, while Judah was shooting arrows and dashing about in his father's school. The students grew very angry and said to our Rabbi Samuel: "You and your father and your forefathers were all great men, yet you let your son grow up to be a savage with the skills of a robber." "You are quite right," said he to them.

After the students left, Rabbi Samuel called his son and said to him: "Judah, my son, if you wish to study I shall test you and see whether you succeed or not, for I do not wish you to have a robber's craft, which would shame me and you as well." "Yes," he answered his father, who took him up to his study and sat him down beside him; and Rabbi Abraham the brother of Judah also sat with him. Then our Rabbi Samuel uttered a certain Name and the whole study filled with light. Rabbi Abraham looked down at the ground, but Judah did not stir or move. When our Rabbi Samuel saw his son Judah sitting and not flinching at all, he uttered another Name. Rabbi Abraham did not have the strength to bear that light but wrapped himself up in his father's garment, while Judah looked down at the ground. Then his father said: "This is a favorable hour for your brother Judah. Know that you will be the head of the academy all your life, but your brother Judah will know what is above and what is below. Nothing will be hidden from him, and he will be a master of names and deeds."

When our Rabbi Samuel expounded law to his students, Judah began asking his father more difficult questions than all of them. The students were very surprised and said to one another: "Here is a fellow who never studied or made any use of Bible or Mishnah, yet he asks more pointed questions than any of us"; and they found it most remarkable. And after he had expounded law, and before he and the students left, our Rabbi Samuel said to Judah: "My son, fetch me your bow and arrows!" He brought them to him, and his father broke his bow and arrows in sight of the students and said: "You will no longer practice the skills of robbers. Henceforward the Torah will be your craft and skill."

From that day forward no bow was ever seen in his hand. But he studied and served his father until he became a man who was great in Torah and good deeds.

85

ROSE HONEY INSTEAD OF HOT LEAD

Rabbi Moses de Leon (1250–1305) was a Spanish kabbalist living in Gua-
dalajara and from 1290 in Avila. He is the author of the Zohar *which*
tradition attributes to the second-century tanna *Rabbi Simeon bar Yoḥai.*
Source: Anon., Ma'asiyyot Peli'ot, *pp. 21–22.*

There was a certain man who had been wicked all his life, and
he was well aware that it would be very hard for his repentance
to be received in heaven. On one occasion he jokingly asked Rabbi Moses
de Leon of blessed memory whether there was any remedy for his ailment.
And the great scholar told him: "The only remedy and atonement for you
is to accept the punishment of death as an atonement for your transgressions." Then the wicked man asked him: "If I do accept a sentence of death,
shall I have a share in the Garden of Eden?" "Yes," said the rabbi; and
the wicked man went on: "Swear to me that my place will be near you!"
Then Rabbi Moses swore to him that he would be near him in Eden. When
the man heard this, he gathered up his courage and followed him to his
house of study.

There the said rabbi ordered that (hot) lead should be brought to him.
They brought the lead, and he puffed air at it with the bellows until the
lead was glowing-hot. Then he sat the wicked man on a bench and tied
a cloth over his eyes and said to him: "Confess all your sins to our God
and accept your death as a return for the sins with which you have angered
your Creator all your life!" At this, the penitent burst into a great and
exceedingly bitter gush of tears. Round about him stood a large assembly
and session of elders and sages. And then the rabbi said to him: "Open
your mouth wide, and I shall fill it with glowing lead." And the man opened
his mouth exceedingly wide in the presence of all the people who stood
around about him, in order to accept the fullness of death and so gain
life in the World to Come.

At this, the said rabbi took a spoonful of rose honey and dropped it
into his mouth and said to him: "May your sin depart from you and your
transgression be atoned!"

But the penitent began to wail at once in bitter grief: "Rabbi! For the
honor of our Maker, the King who is King of Kings, the Holy and Blessed
One, slay me now indeed, so that I may not see the evil of losing my
soul; for why should I live. My sins have mounted higher than my head,

from the sole of my feet to the crown of my head, there is no sound place in me; so what have you done to me? Why have you deceived me?"

But the rabbi answered him: "Do not dread and have no fear, for God has already seen all your deeds."

Thereafter the penitent never left Rabbi Moses de Leon's house of study and spent his days in fasting and true repentance.

After all these things had happened Rabbi Moses de Leon was summoned to the assembly on high and departed this life. When the penitent saw that the rabbi was dead, he wept bitterly and cried out to the Lord to take him as well, since he no longer had a teacher who would guide him. Now after he had prayed and made entreaty, the Lord granted his wish, and he fell sick and took to his bed. When the hour of his death came, he began to shout: "Make way for Rabbi Moses de Leon, who is coming for me now to confirm and fulfill his oath and lead me to be with him in Eden!"

And after that the penitent died at once. But after his departure several elders and great scholars saw him in a dream, seated with his master in Eden and studying Torah together with him.

May their merits protect us and all Israel, Amen!

Kabbalists and Hasidim

86
Joseph Della Reina

Joseph Della Reina and the awesome experiences that befell him are mentioned and reported in manuscripts and books of the sixteenth and seventeenth centuries. They refer to events that took place toward the end of the fifteenth century when Rabbi Joseph Gabbai tried to hasten the coming of the Messiah by magical means; his failure delayed even further any hopes. The period that followed the expulsion of the Jews from Spain in 1492 witnessed a rise in messianic expectation, millennial movements, and individual attempts to end the suffering of Jews in exile. The history of these movements and the traditions that recount them are often bound with magic beliefs, demonology, and mysticism. The following story is one of the most prominent in this narrative tradition and was widely spread in Jewish societies, possibly orally and later in manuscript and in print. Source: J. Sambari, Sippur Devarim.

There is an awesome story of Joseph Della Reina who was a great man, versed in the skills of the practical Kabbalah, who dwelt in the city of Safed in the land of Galilee. One day he resolved to insist upon bringing the redemption and remove the rule of wickedness from earth. Now he had five disciples who stayed with him day and night and did anything he requested. He said to them: "My sons, I am resolved to use the knowledge God has given me in order to remove the pollution and idolatry from the world and bring our Messiah, who will release us from our oppressors." All five of his disciples answered together: "Master and rabbi, we are prepared for anything you may command us." "If so," he said, "do this: Purify yourselves and change your garments and be prepared within three days, and do not approach any woman during that time. On the third day we shall go out into the field, and we shall not return home until the Children of Israel are settled every man on his own farm in the Holy Land!" When the disciples heard these words of their master, they immediately rose up and energetically purified themselves and changed their garments. They took provisions and food, clean bread which they themselves had made in purity and which no woman had touched. On the third day they came to him and found him all alone in hallowed purity in his house of study, with his head between his knees. When they came, he lifted up his head and said to them: "May it be God's will that the Shekinah should inspire the work of our hands, and the Holy and Blessed One approve of us and aid us with respect to His glorious name." And they all answered: "Amen."

After all this, Rabbi Joseph took sundry spices and placed a scribe's inkhorn in his belt, and told them: "Let us go forth!" So they left the city of Safed and went to Meron, to the grave of Rabbi Simeon ben Yohai, at whose grave they prostrated themselves. Shortly before dawn Rabbi Joseph dozed, and Rabbi Simeon ben Yohai together with his son Rabbi Eleazar appeared to him in a dream and said: "Why are you getting involved in such a difficult task which you will not be able to carry out?" He answered: "God Himself knows my intention and will aid me for the sake of His profaned name." They in turn said: "May the Lord your God grant your wish!"

When morning came, Rabbi Joseph and his disciples proceeded to the city of Tiberias, passing through the open country till they reached a forest, and seeing neither man nor beast, but birds alone. There they engaged in the permutations of the holy names, and the contemplation of formulas which they knew. Every morning they went to immerse themselves in the Lake of Tiberias, twenty-six successive immersions in accordance with the numerical value of the letters of Havayah, the name of God the Ever Present.* This they did for three consecutive days and nights, likewise fasting by day and by night.

Toward evening when it was time for the afternoon prayers Rabbi Joseph and his disciples rose up and recited the afternoon prayers in pleasant voices with great devotion and closed eyes. When they reached the words "Hearken to our voices," they added "Answer us." And wherever the text mentions the holy name of God as "The Lord," they pronounced the great name as it is written with the proper vowels and the necessary formulas. The rabbi entreated in a long prayer and great conjurations of all the heavenly angels and finally he pronounced the name Havayah, combined

---

*Hebrew letters have numerical values, which are used, among other things, for magical purposes.

with the Name of Forty-two Letters, together with the words "Answer us." By the power of that great name he adjured Elijah the Prophet to appear. And, lo and behold, Elijah came at speed and suddenly appeared to them and said: "Here I am, and what can I do for you and what is your request to entreat so much in your prayers?" Then they bowed down to the ground and said: "All peace to our lord, 'My father, my father, the chariots of Israel and the horsemen thereof' (II Kings 2:12)."

And the rabbi began: "Let not my lord take it amiss that I have entreated to bring you hither. Indeed, I am zealous for the honor of the Holy and Blessed One and His Shekinah. Therefore let me entreat you to show me the way whereby I can subdue the powers of Satan and strengthen holiness." To which Elijah the Prophet answered: "Know that your purpose is welcomed. If you can fulfill your thoughts in action, happy are you and good is your portion. Yet my counsel is: Let it be and cease, lest Samael and his band strike you down, for you will not be able to prevail against him."

But Rabbi Joseph said: "I pray you, my lord, do not discourage me! For I have taken oath that I shall not return home until I bring the holy Shekinah to light and raise her from the dust!"

When Elijah the Prophet heard these words, he said: "This is what you must do. You and your disciples, go out into the fields far from any inhabited place, for twenty-one days. Do not eat your fill, but only what you yourself know will keep you alive. Reduce the amount you eat every night, and accustom yourselves to smell spices in order that your corporeality may be pure and clear, so that you may be capable of bearing the sight of the heavenly angels whom you will bring down to speak with you. Likewise immerse yourselves each day twenty-one times, that being the numerical value of the letters of the name Eheyeh (Exod. 3:13-14); and after the twenty-first day make an interval and fast for three days and nights. On the third day after the afternoon prayer mention the great Name of Forty-two Letters which you know, together with its permutations and intents; and also pronounce the great name which is derived from the verse 'Above Him stood the seraphim' (Isa. 6:2). When you do this, be wrapped in your prayer shawls and wear your phylacteries and cover your faces, and by those holy names summon the Angel Sandalphon and his host to appear before you. When they come, strengthen yourselves with the pleasant scent, for you will fear and tremble and grow exceedingly weak at the great commotion and the mighty fire. Request the said angel to strengthen you and give you the might wherewith to speak. He will tell you what you should do, for he guards the ways and paths to prevent Samael from entering the holy places, and he knows the spots where that one gathers his strength."

As soon as Elijah the Prophet went his way, Rabbi Joseph and his disciples gathered their strength and united their hearts. They added sanctity to their earlier sanctity, and they did all that Elijah had told them. When they had completed the term of days exactly as Elijah had commanded, they adjured the Angel Sandalphon to reveal himself to them at that very time. No sooner did they finish their conjuration than the heavens opened and Sandalphon the Angel suddenly came to them with all his host. And, behold, there was a fiery chariot with fiery horses and a great host, while flaming fire filled the whole countryside; there was a great commotion, but it did not continue. Rabbi Joseph trembled and shook exceedingly, and he and his disciples were left without any breath within them. They fell to the ground, and their hearts melted and a trembling possessed them. Still, they found the strength to smell the pure frankincense in their hands and came to themselves.

Then the Angel Sandalphon and his host came down to them and said: "Son of Adam, worm that you are, what gave your heart the audacity to set the upper and the lower worlds shaking? Have the self-respect to stay at home or my forces may strike you and burn you with their breath!" But Rabbi Joseph answered in a low and broken voice: "My lord, holy angel of God, what can your servant say in your presence? I am left without breath as though I were dead, so great is my fear and awe!"

As soon as the angel heard this, he touched him and said: "Stand up and say what you have to say, for I have strengthened you." Indeed, when the angel touched him, he rose up and gathered strength and prostrated himself, and then removed his shoes from his feet; but as for his disciples, they still had their faces to the ground and could not rise.

Then Rabbi Joseph spoke: "Welcome, peace be with you, angel of the Lord of Hosts and peace be with all your holy forces. I entreat you, give me the strength and courage to carry out my will! For it is not to honor myself or my father's house that I do this but for the sake of the Living God, the King who is King of Kings! I entreat you, holy one with all your holy forces, to agree to wage war against Amalek and his prince together with me, and instruct me as to what I must do to remove the rule of wickedness from the earth."

The angel answered Rabbi Joseph, saying: "Indeed, your words are good and proper, if only you might be heard, and God be with you! But you must know, son of Adam, that all you have done until now is nothing. If you were to know the high position which Samael with his forces has reached, you would not engage in this matter. For who can prevail against him except the Holy and Blessed One Himself until the time comes to fulfill His word. I have come to you now in respect to the great name you pronounced; but what can I do for you? For I am unable to learn what is the extent of the strength of Samael and his host and on what his fall and his rise depend. None know this except the great Angel Akhtariel and his hosts and Metatron, Prince of the Presence, and his hosts. Yet who can stand before such mighty angels? For if you were frightened by me, how will you be able to even exist in their presence?"

But Rabbi Joseph answered: "I am youthful and puny and I myself know that I am not worthy of doing this thing. Yet I also know that God will not despise a broken and depressed heart. I have made up my mind to sacrifice myself for the sanctity of the Holy and Blessed One and His Shekinah! Therefore, holy Ministering Angel of the Lord, instruct me as to what I should do to bring down Akhtariel and Metatron, and what further privations I must add in sanctity and purity, and what is the name by which I can conjure them."

The angel spoke again, saying: "Please hear my words and God be with you! Continue for forty days whatever immersions, fasts, and purification of thought that you have done until now. Let not your thoughts depart from the concepts even for a single moment by day or night. After forty days pronounce the holy name of power which consists of seventy-two letters (Exod. 14:19–21) with all intents and vocalizations and with its source which is known to you. Therewith you can conjure those two great and mighty angels, who shall instruct you as to the ways of Samael and how you can bring him down. May the Lord guard you from all evil and preserve your soul!" Then the angel of the Lord went heavenward in a tempest.

They rose up and went away from there through the wilderness to a certain mountain near Meron, where they found a cave in which they dwelt. For forty days they followed all their instructions in holiness and purity. They missed nothing until they could sense nothing corporeally of themselves; all those days they saw neither men nor beast. When they had completed the forty days, they went out into the wilderness to a place near the source of the River Kishon, for there they had been bathing all those forty days. They prepared themselves to pray the great afternoon prayer. They marked a circle on the ground and entered into it. Each one gave his hand to his friend, so that their hands were linked together in a circle. Then they cried unto the Lord after prostrating themselves and they pronounced the Expressed Name, and they conjured the Angel Akhtariel and his hosts together with the Angel Metatron and his hosts. When they pronounced the great name, the earth heaved and shook and there were lightnings and thunders, and the heavens opened; the angels with all their hosts came down and sought to smite Rabbi Joseph and his disciples. But they kept their hands together and strengthened their concentrations on names they knew in their minds though they did not pronounce them, because they did not have the strength to speak. They all fell to the ground but held their hands linked together and did not separate.

As soon as the said angels came down, they began to speak in a great fury, saying: "Who and where is the one who has had the audacity to use the royal scepter?"

When Rabbi Joseph saw this great vision, he felt as though he were dumb and slumbering with his face down, and he and his disciples were completely exhausted. But the Angel Metatron touched him and said: "Speak up, answer, you stinking drop, what is this great alarm which has brought us to you? And woe betide you because you have not been concerned for the honor of your Maker!"

Then, when the angel touched him, Rabbi Joseph opened his mouth and said in a faint voice with closed eyes: "What can this abject and worthless slave say in the presence of pure and holy angels if you do not strengthen me?" Then the Angel Akhtariel also stretched out his hand and touched him, saying: "See, I support you, say your say!"

At this Rabbi Joseph answered: "God Almighty assuredly knows that I have not done any of this in revolt or deceit, but to honor the Holy and Blessed One and His Shekinah. Therefore, I entreat you, Ministering Angels, by the power of the great and holy name, show respect to His name and instruct me where the strength of Samael and his hosts is to be found, and what I must do to bring him down."

The angels answered together: "This is a difficult request. Had you only known how mighty and powerful he has become because of the transgressions of Israel! None can bring him down, for his nest is amid the stars where his seat is surrounded by three barriers. You cannot prevail against him and none can do so except the Holy and Blessed One Himself when it is time to fulfill His word."

Rabbi Joseph went on again, saying: "I have already risked my soul for the honor of the Holy and Blessed One and His Shekinah. After I have seen the holy hosts and my soul has been delivered, I trust in the loving-kindness of God that He will aid me and I shall succeed, if your pure words will instruct me and tell me what to do. Whatever you may tell me I shall indeed fulfill."

Then the angels answered: "Joseph, hear the word of the Lord! He who spoke and the world came into being is aware that your intention is desirable; but the time is not yet come and the decree has already been made that 'You stir not up, nor awake love' (Songs of Songs 2:7). Yet nevertheless, in view of your wisdom and knowledge of hidden secrets which the Rock of the Universe has granted you, and by reason of them we are compelled to honor His great and holy name to tell you and instruct you as to the way you should go."

And after this the Angel Akhtariel began: "You should know that on one side, facing me, Samael has two powerful barriers, one is an iron wall which rises from earth to heaven and the other is a great barrier of ocean." Similarly, the Angel Metatron answered that on his side and facing him Samael had a barrier consisting of a mighty snow mountain, whose summit reached the skies.

"Now," said they, "pay careful attention to all we tell you, for you have to bring down these three barriers and eliminate them. This is what you must do: When you leave this place, make your way to Mount Seir; and we shall arrive before you to Mount Seir on high. Whatever you do below in accordance with our instructions to you, that we shall do above. The likeness of your soul would be on high with us; whatever actions you perform below your soul will perform above.

"When you go to Mount Seir, continue to be as holy as you have been till now in all your deeds; for your souls have already risen to such a height that you yourselves have almost attained the degree of angels and have forgotten the ways of the corporeal world; continue in this fashion.

"Along the way you will encounter a great horde of black dogs, these being the companies of Samael whom he will send to confuse you in your intention. But have no fear and pronounce the expanded name of HVYH in such a fashion that its numerical value shall be fifty-two (that being the numerical value of the Hebrew word for dog which is *Keleb*). Concentrate on its correct vocalization and formula and they will flee away from you. Go on from there and climb the mountain where you will find a great mass of snow up to the skies. Then mention the name which is derived from the verse 'Have you entered the treasuries of snow' (Job 38:22), and the mountain will be removed from its place. After that, pronounce the name derived from 'It snows in Zalmon' (Ps. 68:15), and the mountain will vanish entirely. Continue with these concentrations until you reach the other barrier of ocean, whose waves mount up to the skies. Pronounce over it the names that are derived from the Psalm (29:1): 'Ascribe to the Lord, O you sons of the mighty,' and it will dry up and you will pass dryshod through its midst.

"Go forward after that and you will encounter a great wall of iron rising from the earth to the skies. Take a knife in your hand and write upon it the name which is derived from the verse 'The sword for the Lord and for Gideon' (Judg. 7:20) and cut with the knife into the iron, make an opening and enter through it. But be careful to hold the opening fast until you and your disciples have passed through so that it should not close; for after you have all gone through the opening will close again. After that, go forward until you reach Mount Seir.

"At that very time we shall fling Samael from his place, and he will already be entrusted into your hand. And then let the holy name be prepared, written, and engraved by you on a plate of lead. Likewise prepare another plate on which you shall engrave the name which is derived from the verse in Zechariah (5:8), 'And he said, This is Wickedness. And he cast her down into the midst of the measure and he cast the weight of lead over its mouth.' After this, you may go wherever you desire in Mount Seir; and there you will find the wicked Samael and Lilith his mate in the form of two black dogs, a male and a female. On the male set the plate with the holy name and on the female set the other plate and put a rope around their necks at once to which the plates are attached; and they will follow you together with all their band. Then the Lord's desire will already have been achieved by you and you will bring Samael to judgment upon Mount Seir, which you have already passed. There a great shofar will be blown and Messiah will appear and will purify the earth from the spirit of pollution. The Holy and Blessed One will slaughter that spirit in the presence of the righteous and there shall be a full redemption. But be very cautious with the said intentions. Also take exceedingly great care, for when Samael and his mate are in your hands they will cry and appeal to you to give them something to eat or drink or any food to maintain their bodies. Pay no attention to them and do not give them anything. May the Lord be in your guide and guard your feet from snares!" And with that the two holy angels ascended to heaven in a tempest.

After the angels had ascended, Rabbi Joseph and his disciples rose and started toward Mount Seir. Bands of black dogs came toward them, but at once they uttered the name which they had been commanded, and the dogs scattered and disappeared. After this, they encountered a great mountain of snow, and immediately they strengthened themselves with the aforementioned names and combinations, and the mountain shifted from its place. And with the other aforesaid combination it vanished entirely. They went on two more days, and on the third day they saw before them a huge and spacious ocean. As soon as they mentioned the proper names, they passed through it dryshod.

At noon they reached the iron wall. Rabbi Joseph took the knife on which he had written the prescribed name, and he made an opening with it. They held the opening, but as they passed the last of the disciples was slow and the opening slipped away from Rabbi Joseph's hand and closed on the disciple's foot, so that it was caught. At once Rabbi Joseph took out the knife and cut the iron away round the disciple's foot, and he passed through. They climbed Mount Seir to its summit.

There they found a crater within which were several ruins, from where they heard dogs barking. They entered one of the ruins where they found two great black cowering dogs, a male and a female. When they approached, the dogs leaped at them to rend them. But Rabbi Joseph had the plates in his hand. Sensing at once that these dogs were Samael and Lilith, he stretched out his right hand and set one plate upon the neck of the male dog and with the left hand set the other on the neck of the female. His disciples had the ropes ready in their hands and tied them up with the plates upon them.

As soon as they realized what had befallen them, they put off the shapes of dogs and put on their own shapes like that of humankind, except that they had wings that were full of eyes, like flames. They entreated and begged Rabbi Joseph to give them food and water, but Rabbi Joseph refused as he had been commanded.

Then Rabbi Joseph and his disciples set out on their way, rejoicing and of good cheer with bright faces, while Samael and Lilith and all their hosts went weeping. Rabbi Joseph rejoiced and his mind was at ease, and he said: "Who could have believed our story? Upon this day the heavens will be joyful and the earth rejoice." Then Samael responded: "Indeed, we are all in your hands, for you to do whatever you desire, but let some little thing be given to us to maintain our spirits, otherwise how can we exist till we come there." But Rabbi Joseph answered: "I shall give you nothing!"

When they approached Mount Seir, Rabbi Joseph took a pinch of frankincense and smelled it. Samael said: "If you do not give me any food, let me at least sniff at a little of this frankincense of yours!"

Then Rabbi Joseph stretched out his hand and gave him a few grains of the frankincense he had; and Samael blew a spark of fire from his mouth and burned the incense while Rabbi Joseph was still holding it.

The vapor entered Samael's nostrils, and he snapped the bonds and ropes and flung the leaden plates from him, and he and his hosts began striking at the disciples. Two of them died at once upon hearing the mighty roar of Samael and his hosts, while two others were stricken and went out of their minds.

Rabbi Joseph remained alone with a single disciple, weary and exhausted and astonished. For he did not know that he had risked his soul when he gave the incense to the demon who turned it to vapor, and thus unwittingly was engaged in idolatry, thereby bringing all the holy forces in the leaden plates to naught.

At that very moment the whole mountain began to smoke amid gloom and darkness and a voice was heard, saying: "Woe unto you, Joseph and woe to your soul, because you did not observe what you were commanded but engaged in idolatry and offered incense to Samael, for now he will pursue you to drive you out of this world and the next!"

The single disciple remained together with Rabbi Joseph, weary and exhausted and weak, reaching the very gates of death. They stayed there under a tree and rested. Then they buried the two disciples. But demons had obsessed the other two who fled and finally came to the city of Safed, where they soon perished of the pains which the demons inflicted upon them.

After these events, Rabbi Joseph came to the city of Sidon where he settled and turned to evil ways. Since he saw that his intention had not succeeded, and particularly since he had heard the said voice, he gave up all hope of the World to Come, and made a covenant with the malicious Lilith and handed himself over to her so that she became his wife. He polluted himself in every way possible using the holy names and other names and conjurations that he knew in order to do evil. Every night he would conjure spirits and demons to fetch him whatever he might desire.

This was his practice for many a day until more than all other women he came to love the wife of the king of Greece; and he had her brought to him almost every night, and in the morning he would give orders to take her back.

One day the queen said to the king: "Every night in my dreams I find myself in a certain place where a certain man sleeps with me, but in the morning I find myself in my bed without knowing how it comes about."

When the king heard this, he summoned the magicians and set them on guard in the queen's house. That night the demons came by order of Rabbi Joseph, but the guardians noticed them at once and performed their works and conjured them in order to know what this was and how it came about. And the demons stated: "We are sent by Rabbi Joseph, who lives in Sidon." Immediately the king sent a certain minister with letters and a gift to the lord of Sidon, asking that Rabbi Joseph should be sent to him alive at once in order that vengeance might be executed on him. When Rabbi Joseph realized that his deeds were known and evil had finally fallen upon him, then even before the letter reached the lord of Sidon he went and threw himself into the sea and died.

As for me, the fifth disciple, I was left alone on a sickbed all my life, and there is no remedy for my ailment, nor do I have any reprieve from the demons. I have written this tale for a memorial.

87

THE MOCK MARRIAGE

In Jewish tradition this tale first appeared in Toledoth ha-Ari, *the legendary biography of the Safed kabbalist Rabbi Isaac Luria (1534–1572). In European tradition the tale appears much earlier, and textual comparison suggests even a direct influence of the European upon the Jewish tradition. The theme of marriage between a human male and a demonic female recurs in Jewish folk narrative. Source: E. Arakie,* Sefer ha-Ma'asiyyot, *No. 79.*

It happened on one occasion in Safed, may she be builded up speedily in our days, that some young men went out to stroll in the countryside. While they were seated, they saw a finger moving up and down to the ground. One of them said jokingly: "Who will place his ring on the finger as a wedding token?" At this, one of them rose and placed his ring on the finger, and the finger with the ring on it vanished into the earth. Then all of them went down to the town again, and in due course the matter was forgotten.

After many days had passed the young man was matched to a certain maiden. When the time of the wedding came, the congregation came together for the Seven Blessings. All of a sudden a woman began shrieking: "What has the bridegroom found wrong with me that he wants to marry someone else after he wedded me? If you arrange a trial according to the Torah for me, well and good; otherwise I shall slay the bridegroom and the bride. Here is his ring on my hand." She showed it to them all, and they recognized it because the bridegroom's name was engraved on it. The father of the bride at once took his daughter home, and joy was turned to sorrow and the shrieking woman remained with the bridegroom.

Then Rabbi Isaac Luria sent for the bridegroom and asked him privately: "Do you wish to marry this she-demon or not? Have no fear, for I can save you from her!" Then the young man answered: "Who would be fool enough to wish to marry a she-demon? Yet what can I do with my bad luck? If only I had broken my leg that day and not gone sauntering?"

"Sit down," said the rabbi to him, and ordered his attendant to summon the she-demon for trial before him. The attendant sought her in the whole house and could not find her. He came back to the rabbi and said: "I have not found her." "She is in the house," the rabbi told him, "but she keeps herself unseen because she is afraid. Go back until you reach the ladder, and say: I am sent by the rabbi. If you come with me, it is well; but if not, he will ban you and your family!" And the attendant did so.

No sooner had he ended his words than the woman came down and followed him and came before the rabbi, who said to her: "What do you have to do with this youth? Go and marry a demon of your own kind!" "Is that your judgment?" answered the woman. "Can I marry anyone else after he wedded me with his ring?" "That was a wedding in error," said the rabbi, "for he never saw your face and did not know that you are a she-demon; it was only as a joke that he placed his ring on your finger." Yet she went on answering him back at every statement until at length the rabbi berated her and said: "Even though the law does not require it I shall instruct him to give you a divorce; and if you do not wish to receive it, I shall put the ban on you and all your family."

He summoned the scribe at once. The scribe wrote her a bill of divorcement, and she accepted it. Then he made her take oath by a grievous ban that she would harm neither the bridegroom nor the bride nor anything that was theirs. Then the she-demon departed.

The rabbi sent for the father of the bride and prevailed upon him to restore the young man's betrothed to him; and he did so.

88

THE DYBBUK STORIES: THE FERRARA DYBBUK

These are three reports, among the first available, on the dybbuk, *a possession state and other forms of dissociative disorder that in Judaism are explained in terms of a belief in the transmigration of souls. It is believed that restless spirits of the dead seek to possess or cling to the bodies of the living, and when such an attachment or* dybbuk *occurs, a person exhibits the reported symptoms. These reports emanated primarily from kabbalistic circles, but later stories about* dybbukim *have been popularly told. Source: (a) Manasseh ben Israel, Nishmat Ḥayyim (Amsterdam, 1652), pp. 108a–108b. (b) Naphtali ben Jacob Elḥanan, Emek ha-Melekh (Amsterdam, 1648), pp. 16b–17a. (c) Nishmat Ḥayyim, pp. 109a–111a.*

Rabbi Eliezer Ashkenazi has written in his book *Helek Maaseh Bereshith*:

Likewise in the year 5337 A.M. (1577 C.E.) a widely told tale came from the mouths of men and women and infants and children. Their narratives did not vary and all told the same story, and that is a proof that they spoke truly.

Their story was that in the city of Ferrara a Jewish woman used to fall asleep, and a voice would come from her throat. Her lips would not move, but the voice would speak. Then people asked: "Who are you?" And the voice answered: "I am the Gentile So-and-So. I dwelt in such and such a place." He would give all the signs, so that all who heard him could recognize the said Gentile, who had died not long before. Then they asked him: "How did you enter the body of this woman?" And he answered: "Thus and thus did I enter and at such and such a place. . . ."

89
THE DYBBUK STORIES: THE SAFED WIDOW

See above note.

It happened in the days of that pure and holy rabbi, the godly Kabbalist, Rabbi Isaac Luria Ashkenazi of blessed memory. In the city of Safed a certain spirit entered a widow and distressed her most grievously. People came and spoke to it, and the spirit would answer each one according to his question. One day a sage named Rabbi Joseph Arzin, the disciple of Rabbi Isaac, came to it. "Blessed be the newcomer, my master and teacher and rabbi!" said the spirit to him. "Do you not remember that I was your disciple for a long time in Egypt? My name is So-and-So and my father's name is So-and-So and he lives in Egypt."

When the woman's kinfolk saw her exceedingly great pain and anguish, they went to the wise Rabbi Isaac Luria and entreated him to drive this spirit out of the woman. Now since he was otherwise engaged at the time, he sent his disciple Rabbi Hayyim Vital and entrusted certain holy names to him, and ordered him to decree that the spirit would be banned, and to drive it out against its will.

As soon as Rabbi Hayyim entered the room, the woman turned her face away from him to the wall. "Wicked creature," Rabbi Hayyim said to it, "why do you turn your face away from me?" And the spirit answered: "I cannot look at you because the wicked cannot gaze upon the Shekinah." At once Rabbi Hayyim ordered it to turn its face toward him, and immediately the spirit did so.

Thereupon Rabbi Hayyim asked: "What was your sin that you were punished so severely?" "I sinned," came the answer, "with a wedded woman and had bastard children. And now for the past twenty-five years I have been wandering hither and thither on earth and have no rest. For three punishing angels follow me wherever I go and punish me and beat me and proclaim: 'Thus shall it be done to a man who multiplied the number of bastards in Israel!'" And the spirit added to our master Rabbi Hayyim: "Can you not see, my lord, how one of them stands to my right hand side and one on my left hand side and proclaim this, while the third stands beating me murderously?" To which Rabbi Hayyim answered: "Yet surely our sages of blessed memory declared (in *Eduyyoth* 2.10): 'The wicked are punished in Gehenna for twelve months!'" "That means," explained the spirit, "after they have undergone all their punishment except that of Gehenna. Then they are taken into Gehenna where they are made white and cleansed in order to remove all the stains on their souls, so that they may be fit to enter Eden. It is like a skilled physician who first applies to a wound sharp and powerful drugs that consume the living flesh, and then places easing ointments and bandages to cool the wound and restore the flesh as at first. So it is with Gehenna. The sufferings of Gehenna are only one-sixtieth part of what the sinful soul must suffer ere it is admitted there."

"How did you perish?" Rabbi Hayyim asked; and the spirit answered: "I perished by strangulation, for although the four death penalties of the Sanhedrin have long been abolished, the sentences themselves were not done away with.* I left the city of Alexandria of Egypt to go by ship to the city of Rashet (Rosetta), and my ship came to the place where the Nile enters the sea and there it sank, and I was drowned." "And why," asked Rabbi Hayyim, "did you not say a confession before death when your soul departed?" "I did not even have the opportunity to say it," answered the spirit, "for the water choked me at once."

Then the rabbi asked: "What happened to you after your soul left your body?" To which the spirit answered: "The sinking of the ship became known in Rashet, and Jews of that city went at once to the seashore and drew out of the water all the Jews who had drowned, and they buried us. As soon as the Jews had left the graveyard, a cruel angel came with a fiery rod in his hand and struck my grave with it. The grave split open at once, so powerful was the blow, and the angel said to me: 'Wicked man! Wicked one! Rise for judgment!' He took me and set me in the pan of the catapult and flung me in one single motion from the city of Rashet

*The four death sentences were execution by stoning, burning, slaying by the sword, and strangulation.

to the very gateway of Gehenna which is in the wilderness. As I fell at the gateway there, thousands upon thousands of souls of those condemned to Gehenna came out, and all of them shouted at me and cursed me, saying: '"Depart, depart, you man of blood" (II Sam. 16:7), leave this place, you wicked troubler of Israel, you are not yet worthy to enter here, you have no permission yet to enter Gehenna.'

"So then I went from mount to mount and from hill to hill with these three angels of perdition always accompanying me, making their declaration and always thrashing me. Every single minute we have been met by other angels of perdition and evil spirits. When they hear the proclamation that is made, they too have added their blows and beaten me. One drags me this way, the other drags me that way, until my very soul is pulled apart.

"In this way I wandered through the world until I came to Hormuz, which is a great city near the land of India, lying beyond Babylon. It was my intention to enter the body of a Jew in order to escape all these blows and trouble. When I saw that those Jews were wicked and evil and sinned exceedingly before the Lord, lying with Gentile women and women in their courses and engaging in other transgressions, I could not enter into any single one of them because of the multitude of evil spirits that dwell within and around them. Furthermore, if I had entered any one of them, I would have magnified my own pollution and would have harmed myself even more.

"So I went back again from mount to hill and from hill to mountain for many a year until I came to the wilderness of Judah. There I found a pregnant doe. In my distress I entered her. This was after I had undergone much evil and anguish for seven full years. Yet when I entered the body of this doe I was in exceedingly great anguish because the spirit of man and the spirit of beast are not equivalent, since one walks erect and the other moves bowed over. Likewise the spirit of a beast is full of filth and abominable and has a stink that the human spirit cannot tolerate. Furthermore, I was greatly distressed by the unborn deer within her, and the doe herself also suffered exceedingly for three souls cannot stay together. Her belly grew swollen because of my soul, and she ran wild through the mountains and the crags in her suffering until her paunch burst and she perished.

"Then I departed from there and came to the city of Shechem in the Land of Israel where I entered the body of a certain Jew who was a *cohen*. That *cohen* sent at once for the holy man and priests of the Ishmaelites, and by their many spells calling on the powers of evil and the charms they hung around my neck, I could not withstand them and departed form there."

At this, the rabbi interrupted and asked: "Do the forces of pollution really have any power to work evil or good?" "No," answered the spirit, "but by their conjuration the priests introduced so many spirits of pollution into the body of that cohen that I realized that if I stayed there they would all attach themselves to me. I could not stay with them, so I fled from there at once and came to Safed where I have entered the body of this woman. It is now twenty-five years that I have been suffering in this fashion."

"How long must you suffer like this?" asked the rabbi. "And is there no hope for you?" "It will continue," answered the spirit, "until the bastards I begot have all perished. For as long as they are alive nothing can be done for me." At this, all the many people who were present began weeping sore, for the fear of judgment fell upon them. There was a great awakening of the spirit throughout the city and district because of this story.

"Who gave you permission," asked the rabbi, "to enter this woman's body?" And the spirit replied: "I stayed in her house one night, and in the morning watch she rose up and wished to strike a light from the flint and steel. But the sparks would not catch on the tinder. Then she grew angry and flung the flint and steel to the ground in her rage and said: 'Devil take it!' And because she mentioned the devil I had permission to enter into her, for the angels of wrath gave me that permission."

"Now was it because of this sin," asked the rabbi, "that they permitted you to enter her body?" To which the spirit answered again: "This woman is a hypocrite and does not believe in the exodus from Egypt at all. On Passover eve when all Israel rejoice and utter praises and tell of the exodus from Egypt, she regards it as nonsense and a mockery and a joke, and thinks to herself that this miracle never happened."

The rabbi at once asked the woman: "Do you fully and entirely believe that the Holy and Blessed One created heaven and earth and has the power to do whatever He desires, and there is none to ask Him what are You doing?" "Yes," she answered, "I believe it all." "Do you believe," the rabbi went on, "that the Holy and Blessed One brought us out of Egypt and rent the sea apart for us?" "Yes," she answered. And the rabbi asked again: "Do you believe all this with full and perfect faith, and do you repent and feel remorse for your earlier thoughts?" "Yes, indeed," she answered and began to weep.

Thereupon the rabbi decreed a ban upon the spirit, commanding it to depart, and to depart not by any limb or member except the little toe of the left foot. The rabbi also enunciated the names which his master had entrusted to him. At once the little toe grew as swollen as a turnip, and the spirit departed in that fashion and flew away.

After that, the spirit returned to the windows and the doorway of the house for several nights and alarmed the woman. Her kinsfolk returned to the wise Rabbi Isaac Luria. He at once sent his disciple, the aforesaid Rabbi Hayyim, to examine the *mezuzah* and see whether it was in order or not. He went and found that there was no *mezuzah* on the doorpost at all. At this the rabbi ordered that a *mezuzah* should be affixed there. They did so, and the spirit never came back any more.

Thus far runs the tale.

90
THE DYBBUK STORIES: THE MAN FROM TRIPOLI

See above note.

. . . I have therefore decided to record in a book for the benefit of others what I witnessed today (11th Adar I, 5331 A.M.– 1571 C.E.), in respect of a certain woman into whom the spirit of a man of Israel entered.

This was not a dream but it happened while I was awake and for everybody to see. I was in a large assembly where there were close to a hundred men including scholars and heads of congregations. Two men knowing conjurations and many such matters approached the woman in order that the spirit which was within her should speak. Under the effect of smoke, fire, and brimstone which they introduced in her nostrils the woman seemed to be out of her senses; for she did not remove herself or even her head neither from the fire nor from the smoke. Following the conjurations, the voice began to be heard, without any tongue movement or opening of the lips, a thick voice that sounded like the roar of a lion and the howl of a whelp. When this voice began to be heard, those two men began to strengthen and warm themselves swiftly and diligently, to do what they were doing nimbly. They began shouting at it at the top of their voices and said: "Wicked one, speak up and say who you are, in clear speech!" And then the voice became plain to all as being human.

They said to it again very loudly and in the fashion already mentioned: "What is your name, wicked one?" The answer came: "So-and-So." "And the surname?" And he answered: "So-and-So." They asked him: "How are we to know that you are So-and-So?" He answered that he had passed away in Tripoli and left a son named So-and-So. He had had three wives;

the name of the first had been such and such and the name of the second had been thus and thus and the name of the third had been this and that. He had passed away when wedded to the third and she was now married to who and what. In respect of all the signs he gave he spoke correctly, and with words that were veritable and true. Then all of us who were present there recognized that this was indeed the spirit of that man speaking.

They asked him: "Because of what sin do you undergo such transmigrations as these?" "On account of many sins which I committed in my lifetime," he said. Then they asked him to detail them. "I do not wish to," he said, "for what would be the use?" They urged him greatly at least to mention the greatest sin of them all, and he answered that he had been a disbeliever and had spoken against the Torah of Moses our Master, may he rest in peace. Then they asked him: "And what is your opinion now?" He answered moaning bitterly, crying aloud stormily, and said: "I recognize that I sinned and transgressed and was evil." And he asked forgiveness of the Holy and Blessed One and of His perfect Torah for his many transgressions.

Then the two men began to urge him and compel him to leave the woman and go to some desolate wilderness. They also told him that they would ask for mercy for him and would blow the shofar so that he should not continue to wander in this transmigration. They asked him: "Do you wish us to appeal for mercy and pray for you and blow the shofar?" "If only you did!" he answered. They asked him: "Who should blow the shofar?" And he said: "The honorable Sage and Rabbi Solomon ben Moses Alkabetz (c. 1505–1584)." But the sage said that he could not do that. They said to him: "Ask for another one." And he said: "Let it be the Sage and Cohen Rabbi Abraham Lahmi." They asked further: "Who should pray for you?" "Let it be Rabbi Elijah Falkon," he answered. Then we repeated the necessary prayers three or four times and blew the shofar, and everything was done according to the desire he had expressed.

After that, we called on him a second time to depart since his will had been done. "Let a little time pass," he said, "and then I shall depart." They asked him: "Do you wish us to perform any special service for your soul?" He answered that no special service could help. "Do you desire," they asked him, "that your son should recite the *Kaddish* or study Torah?" He answered that it would not help him in any way and his son was not fit or worthy to study Torah.

I also asked him regarding *Hibbut ha-kever* (the visitation of the dead soul in the grave by angels of wrath after burial). But one of those present there said: "This one was certainly never buried at all." Then the spirit answered in fiery words: "I was buried by day and that night I was taken out and have never returned again. Since then thirty-three years have gone by and I have wandered from mountain to mountain and hill to hill and found no rest in any place except for the time when I was in Shechem. There I also entered a certain woman who came here, and they drove me forth by the entire procedure that is described above, except that they placed charms upon her at once, and I could not enter her again." Now all this is true since we learned it from others that it was so.

And afterwards the spirit said: "I used to wander about the city and tried to enter synagogues in the hope that I might find rest and ease for my soul, but they would not permit me to enter any synagogue." "And who prevented it?" they asked him. And he answered: "The sages." Then they asked him again: "Were they alive or dead?" "Dead," said he, "and they would trample on me and tell me: 'Depart from here, wicked one!'"

91
THE BAAL SHEM TOV REVEALS HIMSELF

The Baal Shem Tov (1700–1760) was the legendary founder of the Hasidic movement, a religious Jewish sect that emerged in the middle of the eighteenth century in the Ukraine and spread throughout the Jewish population of Eastern Europe. Hasidic communities are flourishing today in the United States and Israel. The reference to a sect of great Hasidim in the text indicates its existence before the Baal Shem Tov became known. Hence the legend is a story about the assumption of leadership and not the establishment of the sect. The episode concludes the biographical part of the book about the Baal Shem Tov—a prefatory section that emanated from the Hasidic circle of Rabbi Shneor Zalman of Lyady (d. 1813). Source: Dov Baer ben Samuel, Shivḥei ha-Besht *(Kopys, 1814), pp. 4a–4b.*

About the time when Rabbi Israel revealed himself, it came about that a certain student went to visit his master, Rabbi Israel's brother-in-law, Rabbi Abraham Gershon of Kuty. He passed through the village in which Rabbi Israel lived and went to visit him. Rabbi Israel welcomed him, and he ate there. In the course of the meal the student asked him to prepare horses for the journey; and Rabbi Israel did so. Then he said to the guest: "What harm is it if your honor spends the Sabbath here?" The student thought he was joking, because it was then Tuesday. But when he had journeyed about half a league one of the wagon wheels broke, so he went back to the village, took another wheel to replace the broken one, but something else in his wagon also promptly broke. As a result he stayed over on Wednesday, Thursday, and on Friday as well, because there were so many delays that he actually did have to stay there on that Sabbath. This he regretted very much indeed, for what could he do there on the Sabbath day with a village Jew?

Meanwhile, he noticed that Rabbi Israel's wife was preparing twelve Sabbath loaves after the fashion of the Hasidim. The student was very astonished, and asked the woman: "Why are you preparing twelve Sabbath loaves?" To which she answered: "Although my husband may be ignorant, he is a proper Jew. And since I have seen that my brother hallows the Sabbath over twelve loaves I prepare the same number for him as well." Then he asked her whether they had an immersion pool and she answered: "We have." "Why do you need an immersion pool?" he asked further; and she explained: "My husband is a proper Jew and goes and immerses himself there every day." Yet in spite of this the student regretted that he was delayed in the village. When the time came for the afternoon prayers, he asked her: "Where is your husband?" "He is in the fields," said she, "with the sheep and the cattle." The visitor prayed the afternoon prayers alone and then welcomed the Sabbath. But Rabbi Israel had not yet come home, for at the time he said his prayers in his house of solitude.

After that, Rabbi Israel came home, his behavior, dress, and way of speaking all different, and he said: "A good Sabbath!" Then he turned his face to the wall as though he were praying. Then he turned back to his guest and said: "I told you that you would spend the Sabbath here, and so it is." Then he requested the guest to do him the honor of hallowing the Sabbath; for he told himself that if he should perform the hallowing he would achieve utter devotion, and then the student would realize the truth about him. So the guest hallowed the Sabbath, and they sat down to eat the evening meal. Then Rabbi Israel said to him: "Rabbi, let us hear words of Torah from you." That Sabbath the section that opens the Book of Exodus was being read in the synagogues, and the student began to tell plainly the whole story from the arrival in Egypt and the story of Pharaoh. After the meal they prepared the guest's bed beside the table, while Rabbi Israel and his wife went to their own bed.

At midnight the guest woke up and saw that a great fire was blazing on the stove. He ran there for he thought that the wood was burning over the stove. But then he saw that the master of the house was sitting there with a great light about him. He started back and fainted, and they woke him up. Rabbi Israel told him: "You should not have looked where you had no permission!" And the student could not make it out.

In the morning Rabbi Israel went to pray as usual in his house of solitude. When he returned home, he was very cheerful and walked hither and thither in his room with his head well back and sang the Sabbath hymns with true devotion. In the course of the second meal he requested the student to say some more Torah. But he did not know what to say for he was confused. He began to explain one passage of the Torah in its simplest significance. But Rabbi Israel told him: "I once heard another explanation of that passage." After the meal Rabbi Israel went back to his house of solitude and spent the whole day there. But after the afternoon prayer he returned home in full self-revelation, and at the third meal he declared secret meanings of the Torah such as no ear had ever heard. When that was done, they said the evening prayer and performed the *Havdalah*. And the student set out on his way.

He came to a city where he went to the great Hasidim of the congregation and also to the rabbi and told them: "There is a great light near your community. It would be fitting for you to go and fetch him to the city." When they heard what he said, they all agreed that he must be speaking about Rabbi Israel ben Eliezer of whom they had seen and heard many remarkable happenings. So they went to Rabbi Israel's village to ask him to move to their city. Rabbi Israel had foreseen this and he rose and made his way there, so that they met halfway. Thereupon they all descended from their carts and made a seat of tree branches in the forest; and they seated Rabbi Israel on it and accepted him as their rabbi. And he discoursed to them on the Torah.

92
THE PIPE

This story belongs to the narrative cycle of the simpleton's effective prayer. Source: [Isaac Dov Baer ben Zvi Hirsch], Sefer Emunat Zaddikim, *p. 6.*

A villager who was a friend of Rabbi Israel had a very stupid child who could not even learn how to read. His father never took him with him even when he went to town to pray on the Days of Awe. But when the boy was thirteen years old and became bar mitzvah, he took him to town for the Day of Atonement. The boy had a pipe on which he used to play when he sat looking after the sheep in the field. He took the pipe with him in his pocket, and his father did not know about it.

All day long the boy sat in the house of study and could say nothing. During the *Mussaf* prayer he said to his father: "I have my pipe with me, and I want to play it." His father was very startled and scolded him, saying: "Be careful and do not do any such thing." At the afternoon prayers he again told his father: "Father, permit me to play my pipe." His father warned him again that he should not dare to do any such thing. The boy asked him once again and his father saw how he longed to play, so he put his hand over the pocket to make sure he did not take it out. And so they went on through the whole final prayer, his hand covering the boy's pocket. But in the middle of the prayer the boy forcibly took out the pipe and blew upon it with all his might to the astonishment of the congregation.

At the end of the Day of Atonement Rabbi Israel declared that with his pipe the boy had sent all the prayers aloft to heaven.

93
THE DEATH OF THE BAAL SHEM TOV

The Besht died in 1760. The metaphor of life as time that appears in this tale is found in many folk traditions. Source: Dov Baer ben Samuel, Shivḥei ha-Besht, pp. 35b–36a.

R abbi Israel Baal Shem Tov departed from the world on the first day of the Feast of Shabuoth. On the evening before, his followers gathered together to remain awake all night long as provided by Rabbi Isaac Luria of blessed memory; and Rabbi Israel spoke Torah to them regarding the manner in which the Torah was given.

In the morning the rabbi summoned his followers and ordered two of his closest companions to attend to his burial. He instructed them concerning his body. He showed them signs of how the vital spirit was departing from each separate organ and member so that they should understand how things proceed with the sick; they also belonged to the burial society. After that, he summoned ten men to come and pray with him. He called for the prayer book and said: "I shall converse a little longer with His Blessed Name." After the prayer Rabbi Nahman went to the house of study to pray that Rabbi Israel might live. "It is in vain for him to disturb the worlds!" said Rabbi Israel. "But if he can enter by the door through which I usually entered his prayer will be effective."

Then the townsfolk came to greet the rabbi on the occasion of the festival, and he spoke words of Torah with them. When that was done, he said: "I have done you a kindness, now you do me one." And he gave them a sign, saying: "When I pass away, the two clocks in my room will stop working." And sure enough one of them stopped. Several men turned it away so that he should not see that it had stopped moving. But the rabbi said to him: "I know it has stopped going, but I am not concerned for myself, for I know that I shall merely leave one door and go into another at once."

The rabbi sat up on his bed and ordered the men to stand around him. He began to tell them of the pillar by which they ascend from the Lower Eden to the Upper Eden and also from one world to another. He ordered them to repeat the verse in Psalms (90:17): "And let the favor of the Lord our God be upon us; and establish the work of our hands upon us; and may the work of our hands establish it." Then he lay down and sat up several times and engaged in his concentrations, but they could no longer hear the clear pronunciation of the words. After that, he ordered them to cover him with a sheet and began to quiver and shake, and after that he rested a little. Then they looked and saw that the second clock had also stopped. And they saw that he had passed away.

It is said that one of the disciples standing beside the rabbi's bed saw his soul departing as though it were a blue flame.

Timeless Tales

94
THE STORY OF A WOMAN WHOSE UPPER BODY
WAS BEASTLIKE IN FORM

This tale is current in the folk tradition of several Jewish ethnic groups, and has parallels in the folklore of many peoples. The story involves a narrative gender inversion of the Beauty and the Beast theme. Source: J. S. Farḥi, Oseh Pele 2:152–160.

There was a rabbi who had a fine and wise only son. One day the son said to his father that he wished to go to other places in order to learn there with finer men and acquire more wisdom and knowledge and come to know the way of the world. He entreated him so much that at last his father agreed to send him to one of the large cities. His father made up his mind to send him to that praiseworthy city of Constantinople, may the All Highest establish it, amen, it being a great city full of sages and scholars and scribes. His parents ordered food for the journey on his behalf and said to him: "Depart in peace! But this we entreat you, that you come back to us to live well and peacefully at the end of a year, because your mother and I are aged and our eyes wish to see your pleasing face, and we wish you to be with us in our final days." Then they embraced him and kissed him and blessed him. He set out and made his way across the seas.

He arrived at the city of Constantinople, may God protect it. There he asked at once for the home of the chief rabbi. He went to his house of study, where he found him studying with his pupils and all his company. He greeted them with peace, each according to his station. Then he sat down to study with them, and they saw that God's wisdom was within him and he was capable in Torah.

It came about that the members of the academy found a certain matter difficult, and they could not understand it. At last it was time to eat and each one went his own way, south or north as the case may be. The said young man remained alone there, studying the text in order to comprehend its deep secrets. As he kept on repeating the passage in accordance with the principle "turn it over and over, for you will find everything there," in order to understand the true meaning, a slip of paper dropped on him. He looked at it and in it found written the full meaning of the matter and the explanation of all difficulties. At this he rejoiced, thinking that this must come from the Lord, and be a special gift from heaven. When the scholars returned, he said to them: "Praise the Lord for He is good, for I have merited to have a slip fall to me from heaven, clearly explaining the matter." When they heard this, they laughed at him, for they knew the secret of the slip and where it came from. But since the young man thought that heaven had taken pity on him to help him in his distress, he felt aggrieved, because they did not believe him and were laughing. He said to them: "By your lives, tell me the secret and the reason why you do not believe me. For wise and understanding men like you must have some cause for your behavior." He pressed them so much that at last they had to reveal the truth to him and told him: "You should know that in the attic above the academy dwells a daughter of the rabbi who is exceedingly wise. Whenever we find ourselves in difficulties about the true meaning of the text, she writes on a slip of paper and throws it down to enlighten our eyes and bring us a remedy."

When this young man heard their words, he was astonished and said to himself: "Can there really be so wise a woman as this who is so familiar with the ways of the Torah?" And he felt that he must speak about this woman, and he asked them to tell the rabbi, the girl's father, that he should give her to him for wife. But they answered him: "Choose a different way and do not speak about this for it is impossible." But when this young man had heard about her wisdom, he fell in love with her. He kept on entreating them to speak about it with the rabbi. Or if they would not do so, at least let them tell him the reason. "Do not press us so much," they answered, "for she is not fitting for you, and the Lord will bring you someone better who is destined for you." Then he insisted: "Tell me how she is blemished." But they answered: "We cannot reveal it and spread a bad report." "In spite of that," said he, "however she may be I am prepared to marry her. For my soul desires her on account of her wisdom."

He was so insistent that they had to speak about it with the girl's father, the rabbi. They told him the whole matter and how the young man's very soul was attached to the maiden; and although they had told him that she was not the right person for marriage, nevertheless he was prepared with his whole heart to accept any defect.

Her father felt distressed to wed his daughter without revealing her blemish, which would afterwards fill him with shame. But when he heard how much the young man liked his daughter he placed his trust in the Lord and accepted their words in spite of his own feelings. He decided to give her to him; and the young man rejoiced at his fate.

The rabbi's daughter heard and knew all that was being done, and she prepared herself and purified herself in sanctity and set a few days ahead for the wedding. When the day came, the canopy was set up in the presence of ten men without any great sound of joy and gladness, because her father and mother were filled with sorrow. When the bride came to the wedding, she wore a big mask which covered most of her body. The bridegroom thought that this must be the custom of that land, and he married her in accordance wtih the practice of Moses and Israel; and they read out all the conditions of the wedding contract in accordance with standard practice.

Now that night before the bridegroom entered her room, the bride prayed in tears before the awesome Lord God to see her distress and grief and permit her fine bridegroom to show grace and kindness and mercy towards her, and not to withdraw from her when he saw her face, leaving her alone and bereft. And when the bridegroom came to the bride's room and raised his hand to remove the cover from her face, he saw that she looked like an animal. So startled and shaken was he that he leaped backward.

But his bride said to him: "I beg you, do not injure me, for this is from the Lord who sent you to me; especially as it is due to your own desire, for you were told that I was not suitable for you, but you entreated my father and declared that you were ready to take me just as my Creator fashioned me. Now if you abandon me, you will have injured me grievously. Therefore I entreat you to show pity for me and fulfill your commandment. After that, if you wish to let me be and go away from me, I shall not compel you to remain and you will do whatever you wish. But this time you must compel your own desires and will in order to fulfill the commandment you have undertaken!" And she wept and entreated so much that he felt very sorry for her and approached her and had intercourse with her.

When he was about to leave her and go away, she held him back, saying: "I have one little request of you but you must fulfill it. Now that you wish to depart from me and go your way in peace to a good life, at least leave me some sign in order that I may have faithful witness that if I become pregnant it is from you." "What shall I give you?" he asked; and she answered: "Your seal and your prayer shawl and your prayer book." And he gave them to her.

Then he departed to his own country, for he simply did not have the heart to remain in that region. He went back to his city and his father and mother but told them nothing of all that had happened, since he felt it was a shameful matter and those who heard of it would mock him. In due course he married another wife, while that bride remained forsaken and sad at heart.

About three months after he had left his bride she recognized that the Lord had remembered her and she was pregnant. She told her father and mother, and she felt very much ashamed like any maiden of high degree in such circumstances. But they rejoiced very much at her words and consoled her and put heart into her. When her time was due, she gave birth to a son. Seeing how handsome he was to look upon, she embraced him and kissed him, then she swathed him in a garment and went to the house entry, where she left him. She felt very bitter since she was forsaken, being left all alone in her own separate room where nobody came to her not even her father and her mother, for they did not have the heart to see her from the time of her birth, and she had been brought up by a foreign wet nurse and a servant.

When her parents heard the baby weeping, they went out and took him. They saw how handsome and fine he was, and how radiant and bright his face, and they rejoiced with him very much, saying: "Great is the Lord and very much to be praised for He has not kept His kindness from us and has left us a remnant. He will restore our soul in our old age!" And they took a wet nurse who suckled him.

The Lord was with the boy, he grew well, and they hired a teacher to teach him Torah. The boy was sharp and clever and within a few days he learned the Hebrew alphabet and vowel signs and began to study the Bible. He advanced from day to day until he studied Talmud. By the time he was thirteen years old and could be counted among the prayer quorum, he was already studying the great authorities and the responsa, and had become like an ever-increasing fountain. He studied together with the members of the academy, pointing out difficulties and offering solutions to problems that went back to the days of the earliest Talmudists.

One day this boy was debating with another of his own age who envied him and hated him and said to him: "You fatherless and motherless brat. Be quiet and do not show your pride to me, for you are not as good as

I am!" When the boy heard this, he kept quiet and did not respond to the offense; but being very distressed and angry, he went home to his grandfather and grandmother, whom he thought to be his father and mother. "I have been very distressed today," said he to them, "more than I can tell you. I am distressed because I had to be silent while I was insulted and had no answer for the fool who offended me and said I had no father and mother. Yet I had been growing up and regarding you as father and mother. So now you must tell me the real truth." But they told him: "Do not be upset by the words of this stupid boy who is so jealous of you that he had to show his impudence and reveal his own shame. Indeed we are your father and mother, and you need have no fear for your ancestry."

But the boy could not believe them for he saw that they were old with white hair. And he reckoned that the other lad would never have the impudence to say such a thing and impute a blemish to such a holy pair, so there must assuredly have been a reason for his talking like that. So day after day he kept on persisting, for a fire burned within him that would not be put out. At length they had to tell him who and what he was and they said: "Your mother lives in this house!"

Without delay the boy knocked and entered her apartment without her knowledge, and since she did not know that he had entered she did not cover her face. He came in and found her unveiled to her great and deep distress, and she swiftly flung the veil over her face. But the boy said to her: "Mother, why do you feel ashamed and why are you so abased and distressed? I am your own son, and I wish to see your face. For no matter what your appearance is, I love you and owe you my respect!"

So saying, he approached and removed the veil and embraced her and kissed her, while the tears streamed from her eyes. She in turn fell on his neck and embraced him and kissed him and thanked the ever-blessed God because she had merited to see him again, for she had not seen him from the day of his birth. And now at last she rejoiced with her child.

Then the boy observed a table in front of her that was covered with books and manuscipts in which her wise thoughts were written. And he asked her: "Who comes here to read these books?" "My son," said she, "nobody comes here for this is a secret place which is hidden from all living creatures and daylight. But ever since I could think for myself and have recognized the blemish with which I was born I have sighed and wept. But I have accepted His blessed judgment as it was imposed upon me, and I have dedicated myself to His Torah. My consolation has been that the Lord has endowed me with some of His wisdom and I labor on the Torah by day and night. The Torah has enabled me to withstand my troubles and to spend my days and years devoted to it. For though I am alone I do not think of worldly pleasures and delights while I am engaged in the study of the Torah!" At this, the lad was very happy and told his mother that he would study with her by day and night. And so it was, and they sat studying together. He realized how well-versed she was in the Talmud and the Codes, how great her wisdom and understanding were, and he said: "This is a heritage from the Almighty above. Henceforward I do not need to go and study with any sage, since my mother knows far more than all of them together."

Yet the boy was not at ease, for he still wished to know who his father was. When several months had passed he said to his mother: "There is one thing which I ask of you, to give me a true answer and tell me who my father is and where he can be found, for I have seen no sign of him since I have been with you." To which she answered: "My son, do not ask me about him, for if I think of him my eyes grow dim with sorrow." "In spite of that," said he, "I entreat you to forgive me and do what I ask." And so much did he entreat her with his sweetness and charm that she had to tell him. She told him all that had happened from beginning to end, and showed him her *ketubah*. And the boy was very happy indeed to learn his ancestry and family. "Yet when he left you," said he to her, "did he leave you anything to remember him by?" And she told him: "I took his seal and prayer shawl and prayer book to keep him in my memory."

"You did wisely and well," said he, "and now I have to go to him and request him to return to you." "My son," she told him, "do not say something that is impossible for he is far, far away, and he certainly will not wish to come." "Nevertheless," said he, "I must go and get to know him!"

He went to his grandfather and said: "Please order me provisions for a journey as much as I may need, for I must go to my father's city and look for him, since I feel my soul is bound up with his." "How can you go to such a distant place," his grandparents answered, "when you are so young? And how can you go wandering and abandon us, old as we are? And why do you need him, since you lack for nothing and we are in his place to satisfy all your desires." But he paid no attention, saying that he was compelled to go and know his father, after which he would return to them. So they had to order him his needs, and he took his father's seal and book and prayer shawl and set out on his journey.

The Lord guided him successfully on his way and led him in the paths of righteousness to the place of his desire. He came to his father's city at the time of the morning prayers. There he asked where the rabbi's home was as he wished to go there first and pray there, for he heard that he had an academy at his home. After that, he wished to take counsel with him as to the proper way to go and see his father. He wrapped himself in his father's prayer shawl, holding the prayer book in his hand. And the rabbi stood before him.

The rabbi raised his eyes and saw before him a fresh young face of a youth who prayed with tenfold grace. He looked at the prayer shawl and saw that each corner was embroidered with the name of his only son. Then he looked at the prayer book he was holding and saw that the back was inscribed with his son's name, too. He was astounded by this and could not understand what it could mean. He longed to know how these could be in the hand of the lad who had come from a distant land. When the prayer was over, the rabbi approached the youth with all courtesy and said to him: "My son, where do you come from?" "Good sir," he answered, "from a great city of sages, called Constantinople." "Upon your soul," said the rabbi, "tell me your name." He answered: "Solomon, at your service." "Yet surely," said the rabbi, "that is not the name which is written on your book and embroidered on your prayer shawl?" "That," answered the lad, "is the name of my father." "Where is your respected father?" asked the rabbi; and the lad answered: "I do not know, and that is why I have come to seek him and to ask your advice how I can find him."

The rabbi was more and more astonished, wondering how and why his son had concealed so much from him. For he remembered that when he returned he had asked him what had happened to his prayer book and prayer shawl; and his son had told him that they had been lost on the journey home. Then, while he was still speaking to the young Solomon, he saw that he was wearing his son's signet ring on his right hand. "And what is that seal?" he asked. The lad answered: "This also belongs to my father who left it with my mother, when he went away."

Then the rabbi said to him gently and kindly: "My son, stay here a while and I shall send to find him. I think that this man must be in our city, so I shall bring him before you to see whether he is your father and you know him. But first, give me the seal, and the book and the prayer shawl. And rest assured, my child, that with the aid of His Blessed Name I shall bring him to you!" So he gave the rabbi the objects, and the rabbi left him by himself in a separate apartment.

Meanwhile, his son returned from his prayer and study, and his father asked him: "Where is your signet ring, my son?" He answered: "Father, you have been asking me about this for twelve years already, and I keep on telling you that I lost it on my way home." "And where," his father continued, "did you pledge your prayer shawl and prayer book?" "What are you dreaming about," said he, "to bear down on me like this? Please let me be!" "Then why not tell me the truth," said his father, "and if I show them to you, what explanation will you have?" And he promptly produced them from his bosom and showed them to him, saying: "These are your prayer shawl and book and seal!"

His son could find nothing to say but: "How did you obtain them?" "Your son has come here," then said the rabbi, "and brought them with him to look for you."

Thereupon his face turned black and he said: "Please forgive me! But if I mean anything to you, show him to me that I may see that it is so." "I have forgiven you," answered his father. Then he summoned the lad and said to him: "This is your father and I am your grandfather!"

When the lad saw his father, he threw his arms around him and embraced him and kissed him and wept. When his father saw this fine and handsome and clever-looking stripling, he too began weeping and embraced him and kissed him and rejoiced with him so greatly that he all but died; particularly since he had no children from the second wife whom he had wedded. So the lad restored his soul to him. The grandfather and grandmother also rejoiced when they looked at their grandchild and saw how wise and clever he was, perfect in good qualities and ample knowledge, fit to take his place in the heritage of their forefathers.

After a few days had passed the son said with much charm and entreaty to his father: "Father, I must go and fetch my mother to you so that you may dwell together, gladly and lovingly; for I grieve at heart to see you parted from one another." But his father answered: "My son, the delight of my eyes, this I cannot do for it will increase my grief, shame, and reproach. But you stay here with me and be my consolation." But his son repeated: "Father, forgive me, but this I cannot bear, that you should be parted from one another." And he refused to obey his father and his grandparents. At last he rose and went his way, trusting in the Lord.

Midway on his journey his thoughts distressed him and he began praying to the Lord God, entreating Him to perform a wonder and display a sign, turning thought into deed. So much did he weep as he prayed that he fainted and fell asleep. At that very moment his mother remembered her son who had gone afar to seek for his father and bring him back, though she herself knew that this must be wrong since he would never be able to look at her and there was no remedy for her distress; and so she sighed and uttered her prayer to God on high, weeping bitterly as she did so, and imploring that He might have mercy upon her and see her grief. And the joint entreaty of both mother and son came aloft before God at one and the same moment; and the quality of mercy was aroused before Him and He felt merciful toward her. So the Lord sent Elijah the Prophet, whom it is good to remember, who appeared to the youth in a dream and said to him: "What are you doing here, my young friend, weeping and sighing as you journey alone?" To which the young lad answered: "It is because I grieve so greatly at my parents who live apart, and I do not know what to do in order to bring them together again. God created my mother with a strange appearance which is the reason why my father left her. Oh how bitter I feel to see my mother suffering!" Elijah answered: "Take this full flask, for your outcry and hers have mounted on high. When you come to your mother wash her face with this water and she will be cured and become another woman, fair as the sun, choice as the moon, and bright for the eyes to see. But take great care that nobody in the world should see her, not even your grandparents; only you yourself. Until such time as her husband, your father, first sees her. After that her father and mother may see her and rejoice."

The lad woke up and saw before him the flask of which he had dreamed, actually there and not a mere vision; and he was still holding it in his hand. He rejoiced very much indeed and began reciting the Psalm (107:1): "Give thanks to the Lord for He is good, His loving-kindness is eternal!" As soon as he arrived home, he went to his mother and embraced and kissed her heartily. She too was so overjoyed that she all but fainted, so greatly had she longed for the sight of her delightful son. Then he told her: "Mother, do not weep or sorrow, for the Lord has seen your suffering, and I have full faith in the Lord that you will rejoice in the husband of your youth; for, praise the Lord, I sought and found him. Now we have to go to his place." "But how can I come to him," said his mother, "when he ran away from me and must hate me since he cannot bear to look at me." "Listen to me," he answered, "and may the Lord aid me." And he began to touch her on the head and hair, and asked: "How long is it since you last washed your hair and body like every respectable and clean and pure woman?"

"From the time you went away," she told him, "I did not have the heart to wash or clean myself properly, for I was forgotten as though I were dead."

"In that case," said he, "you have to wash your whole body now and I wish to serve you." And off he went at once and fetched her the water and the tub and began to bathe her. After that, she washed in the water of his dream from her head to her navel. Then he said to her: "Go and lie down and rest on your bed, and sleep well and may the Lord send and heal you."

So she went and slept, and when she woke up, lo and behold! she had been transformed into a different creature, a woman who was as beautiful as the moon at its full. But she did not notice this because of her heavy heart. Then her son told her: "Take the mirror and look into it." "My son, flesh of my flesh," she answered, "I have never wished to look at myself in order not to increase my grief." "I entreat you," said he, "to do what I ask you this time." He went and fetched the mirror and held it up before her, and she saw a charming person, white and reddish pink like a scarlet thread. "What have you done to me, my son?" she asked, and he answered: "Say not a word, mother, for the good God saw our distress and heard our prayer. But I cannot tell you the great and awesome feat of the Lord now, because we must all depart swiftly and go to my father." Then she opened her mouth with wise words in praise of the Lord, thanking him for the wonder he had wrought with her.

Then the youth went to his grandfather and grandmother and said to them: "Be swift and prepare yourselves to go to the dwelling place of my father, together with my mother and me." "That is impossible," they answered, "for we are well on in years and cannot take sea voyages." To which he said: "I shall give no ear to your words, but you must come with me and say nothing." And without their permission he went at once and brought workmen and packed and tied up the clothes and belongings. When he had finished and arranged everything wisely, he sent all the packages to the ship. He went and took his grandparents on his right arm and his left and conducted them on board. Then he returned to his mother and veiled her over from head to foot and brought a carriage to the entrance of the house. The mother and her son entered. He took a special cabin for her and himself on board, so that no stranger should approach while he served her in all respects. His grandparents rejoiced at this, for it meant that they would not be ashamed through others who saw their daughter.

When they came to his father's city, he closed his mother's cabin and went ashore to tell his father and his father's parents that all his family had come and that they should arrange a place for them to stay. And he ordered a special room for his mother, who would go upstairs with him and not come down. When his father heard that he had brought his mother, he became very distressed and shrank within himself, saying: "What has God done to me, for now my shame with my wife will become known and everybody will mock me. How can I look at the face of this monstrous woman?" Yet at the same time his father and mother rejoiced to learn that the father of their son's wife was one of the greatest of the rabbis. For they did not know that their son's wife was so outlandish a creature. Meanwhile, the lad went back to the ship and first took his grandparents there who were welcomed with great honor by their in-laws, who took them home. Then he returned and took his mother completely covered over and brought her to the room which he had ordered for her. Her father-in-law and mother-in-law longed to see her, but the lad would not permit them to approach, saying that she was confused and weary with the journey, so they must wait until she had settled down. Then he closed the door on her.

After that, he went to his father and said: "Father, come to see your lovely wife." His father trembled to hear this and said: "Let me be, for I do not have the heart to approach her." But his son caught hold of his coat and led him against his will, saying: "This time I must insist that you come to my mother in order to console her, for she is bitter and sad. After that, you may do whatever you desire, for I am your son and must obey you." So he led him to her chamber. He lifted up his eyes and saw her and, behold, she was a new creature, an exceptionally beautiful woman. The man cried in astonishment: "Can this be the wife whom I rejected?" His son said to him: "This is your wife, she is my mother, and you are my father and here is the *ketubah*." He told him all that had happened, both good and bad, and how the Lord had seen her distress and heard her prayer and had sent Elijah to heal her in order that they might dwell together peacefully, and bridegroom and bride rejoice and be glad.

At this, he was transformed and the love of her flamed up in his heart, and he embraced and kissed her, while she in turn was so moved that she fainted. After that, her father and mother came to see her, which they had rarely done since her birth. Her father-in-law and mother-in-law also came and rejoiced to look upon her, so wise and gracious and beautiful a woman whose like could not be found. When they learned all the awesome deeds of the Lord with her, changing her from the likeness of a beast to a beautiful woman, they all together gave praise to the One who brings about great wonders alone and who shows His loving-kindness as of old unto Israel. They set up the bridal canopy afresh to the sound of gladness and of joy. And all of them settled together in that city, living safe and secure.

And in this way, may the Lord perform some good work with us, and speedily gather our dispersed ones into the Holy City, Jerusalem the Golden, swiftly and soon, so may it be His will, amen!

95
THE STORY OF THE JERUSALEMITE

This story appeared in print first in 1510. In many versions the text contains an epigraphical attribution to Rabbi Abraham ben Maimon (1186–1237), Maimonides's son, who was a religious philosopher and community leader in his own right. The theme of marriage between a man and a demonic woman occurs in medieval Jewish folk narratives and is current in modern oral traditions. Source: Jehuda L. Zlotnik, Ma'aseh Yerushalmi.

I

There was a certain merchant who had only one son whom he taught Torah and Mishnah and Talmud, all the six orders. He gave him a wife and the son begot children in his lifetime. On the day of his death he summoned the elders of his city and told them: "I would have you know that I have ample property, and in accordance with the *ketubah* of my wife I have her jointure of a hundred sela of silver as is written in that document. All the rest is for my son if he obeys the commandment I give him in your presence. But if he transgresses my will, I here and now dedicate all my property to heaven and none of it shall be for my son."

Thereupon he summoned his son and declared in the presence of the elders of the city that he should never travel by sea as long as he lived. Then he said to him: "My son, I wish you to know that all my property and whatever I have, I gained through the journeys I made across the sea, where many mishaps and trials befell me. I entreat you that you should not run any risks in order to make profit by way of the sea, for I leave you ample property, so that even if you should never wish to trade or traffic at all, you and your children will have enough as long as you are on earth. Now I desire you to take an oath to me on the Torah scroll that you will never transgress this commandment of mine, not ever. But if you do transgress this commandment of mine, then I dedicate all my property to heaven before these honored gentlemen, in order that you should not be able to enjoy it at all." The son swore the oath he required in the presence of the congregation and the elders of the city; namely, that he would never set sail on the sea as long as he lived.

In due course the old merchant passed away and was buried, while the son remained at home and obeyed his father's behest. After a year or two a ship came to the port of that city, laden with gold and silver and precious jewels. When the ship's men came ashore, they asked whether that merchant was still alive and the townsmen told them: "He has died but his son has taken his place, and he is a very wealthy man and a scholar." "Please conduct us to him," said the ship's men, "or else show us where he lives." They showed them his home, and the ship's men greeted him and said: "Are you the son of So-and-So, the great merchant who was accustomed to cross the seas and travel with ample merchandise to the ends of the world?" "I am his son," said he, and they answered: "If so, tell us what your father's will was, when he departed from the world, about the property and pledges he had overseas." "In his will," answered the son, "he did not write that he had anything overseas, but he did make me take oath that I would never set sail on the sea as long as I live."

Then they told him: "Since your father never told you what he had left behind beyond the seas, he must have been out of his mind when he died. For you should know that the whole ship in which we have come is laden with gold and silver and precious stones, all belonging to your father who entrusted it to us. Now since your father has died, we shall not deny his property but shall give it to you, although he did not will it to you. For we are faithful men and God-fearing and do not covet your wealth, since we have everything we desire. God be thanked. Now come with these servants of yours and take whatever is on board, for it all belongs to you."

When the merchant's son heard this, he was very pleased indeed and went with them and fetched all that wealth to his home; and he brought the ship's men there as well, and they feasted and rejoiced together. Next day the ship's men told him: "We know your father to be a wise and comprehending man, therefore it seems to us that he could not have been in his right mind when he died, since he made you take an oath never to go to sea. In all truth you should know that there can be no validity in that oath because your father had so much property beyond the sea, ten times more than we have brought you. How could he have made you swear to lose all that wealth? So he must have been out of his mind.

"If you will listen to us," they went on, "obtain permission from the sages and come with us. We shall buy the goods that are required in our country and you will make a great profit on them, and you will bring back with you all the money your father left in our country and our place."

"I swore to my father," he answered, "that I shall not cross the sea, not ever, and I shall not break my oath or his commandment. For my father was in his right mind when he made me take the oath. If he did not inform me about those pledges and the money he left there, his purpose was that I should not imperil myself; and that was why he did not wish

to reveal the matter to me. Things being thus, I shall observe his commandment and abide by the oath I swore to him." "Did he love you more than
he loved his own self," they asked, "when he risked his life so many times?
It cannot be as you say, for he must have been out of his right mind,
so his commandment cannot be valid or binding. He could never have been
speaking with a lucid mind, and he made you take an oath without knowing
what he did. So it would be well for you to request an authorization and
cancellation of your oath on the grounds we give you."

Finally their words weighed with him, and he changed his mind and
agreed to accompany them to fetch the money back. What did he do? He
purchased goods and went aboard with them and they all set sail together.
No sooner had their ship reached the open sea than the Lord brought about
a great storm, since he had broken his oath and transgressed his father's
commandment. The ship was wrecked and all the people in it were drowned
because of the counsel they had given him. But the Holy and Blessed One
gave a sign to the Prince of the Sea, who flung that man ashore naked
and barefoot at the far ends of the world where there was no human habita-
tion, in order that he should suffer judgment for his transgression. When
he reached dry land and found himself naked and barefoot, he realized
that His Blessed Name was angry with him and this was the day of his
misfortune. And he raised his eyes aloft and accepted the judgment.

He began to walk along the seashore in the hope of finding some city
or something to eat or cover himself, for he was as naked as when he was
born. After walking for about a day, he found a tree whose branches hung
down to the seashore. Thinking to himself that this tree must have been
planted by men, he set out to look for the roots but could not find them.
Meanwhile, it grew dark so he covered himself with the twigs and leaves
of the tree for protection against the chill of night. At midnight he heard
a lion roaring. When he heard it approaching, he became very much afraid
that the beast might rend him apart because he had not kept his father's
commandment and had broken his oath. He raised his voice and began
weeping and praying for the Name to deliver him and be long-suffering
with him and spare him a savage and unnatural death. Meanwhile, he caught
hold of the boughs of the tree and climbed aloft, so that when the lion
came there it would not find him and would go back.

The man praised His Blessed Name who had delivered him from the
lion and decided to climb higher in the hope of finding something to eat,
for he was very hungry. When he climbed, he found a huge bird, a kind
of owl called Kipufa, which opened its mouth to eat him as soon as it
saw him. The man wished to flee, and His Blessed Name gave him the
wisdom to mount upon the bird's back and ride it. As soon as he did so,

the Kipufa became afraid of him and did not budge all night long. But
the man was also very afraid and gripped its feathers with both hands and
could not get off its back. And the Kipufa was just as frightened because
it did not know who was riding upon it.

When dawn broke the Kipufa looked around, saw the man, and became
even more frightened and flew off in alarm and fear all day long until the
evening fell. It took the man across the sea and carried him away to a
place at the ends of the earth. When the man saw the sea beneath him,
he was terrified and prayed to the Lord for deliverance. Toward evening
the Kipufa flew across a certain country and began to descend. The man
heard boys who were studying the portion of Mishpatim (Exod. 21:1–
24:18) which contains the verse (21:2): "If you buy a Hebrew servant. . . ."
When he heard this, he said to himself: "There are Jews in this country,
that is certain. I shall cast myself down. If I escape injury and they have
no pity on me, I shall sell myself to them as a slave." He flung himself
to the ground and fell at the gateway to the synagogue of that city, while
the Kipufa flew on.

When the man fell, he could not rise to his feet for about two hours,
for he was all but broken to pieces with the force of the fall, besides being
very weak because he had not eaten for two days. At last he rose to his
feet, went to the synagogue, and found that it was closed. Then he shouted:
"Open the gates of righteousness for me!" Out came a boy and asked him:
"Who are you?" And he answered: "I am a Hebrew and I fear the Lord."
The boy went to his teacher, who ordered him to open the door. When
they saw that he was naked, he told them all that had happened to him
from beginning to end. That teacher then said: "All that has happened to
you is far easier than what you are going to suffer now that you have
come here." "And are you not Jews?" asked the man. "I know that the
children of Israel are merciful sons of merciful fathers, and will certainly
be merciful towards a poor and naked and barefoot man like me." The
teacher said: "Do not speak so much, for you cannot escape death."

"My good sir," answered the man, "why should you say such things?"
The teacher replied: "Because this city is not of humankind but a city of
demons and she-demons. These boys who are reciting after me are young
demons. Now in a moment they will all gather together to pray, and when
they see you they will put you to death." When the man heard this, he
was terrified and fell on his face to kiss the feet of that rabbi; and he wept
and entreated him to aid him so that he should not die; since he was a
scholar and God-fearing and had sinned only through those men who had
misled him to transgress his father's commandment and break his oath.
When the rabbi heard his words, he felt pity for him and said: "Since you

are a scholar and familiar with the Torah and repent what you have done, you deserve to have mercy shown you. I shall try to see whether I can save you."

So the rabbi took him home and gave him to eat and drink. He stayed in his home that night and the demons were not aware of his presence. At dawn next day the rabbi said: "Come to the synagogue with me, and place yourself under my cloak and say nothing until I have spoken about you." So he led him to the synagogue, where he remained under the cloak of the rabbi.

With the break of day the demons came to the synagogue like flaming fire, and he heard a noise like thunder shaking the earth. He stood trembling and breathless because of his great fear and dread. He heard them reciting Psalms and prayers as though they belonged to Israel. One demon stood near the rabbi and said to the next: "I can smell the scent of a man." The word passed among them and they said: "There he is, standing by the rabbi." Now all of them respected the rabbi so they did not approach the man since he was sitting under the rabbi's cloak.

When the rabbi saw that the demons sensed that a man was there, then as soon as they finished reciting the Psalms he said to the cantor: "Do not pray until I have spoken." The demons answered at once: "Rabbi, say what you have to say to your servants and we shall listen."

Then he told them: "I request you not to harm this man for he had come under my rooftree." "What is this woman-born doing among us, and who brought him here?" Then the rabbi told them all that had happened to him from beginning to end. "How," they asked, "can we leave such a wicked man alive, when he has transgressed the commandment of his father and the oath of His Blessed Name? There can be nothing for him but death." The rabbi answered them: "He has already received his punishment by the suffering he has undergone, and he is versed in the Torah and deserves to have his Torah protecting him. For if he had been doomed to death the Lord would never have delivered him from the sea and the land and the Kipufa and the other troubles." "He is all the more worthy of death," insisted the demons, "because he did not keep his father's commandment though he is versed in the Torah, and he also broke his oath; so his errors have been willfully intended in his case, and the only reason why the Lord delivered him from all that happened to him was in order that he should die a cruel death at our hands." But the rabbi insisted: "He does not deserve to be killed by you but in accordance with a trial based on the Torah since he is a scholar. And now listen to me: Let the cantor announce that no demon will harm him until after the prayers. Then we shall fetch him before King Asmodeus, who will judge him, either to die or to live." "That is a good proposal," they all assented, and at once they ordered the cantor in the synagogue to proclaim that no demon was to injure him until Asmodeus, king of the demons, passed judgment.

After they had prayed, they brought him before Asmodeus and said: "Lord king, this man is among us because he sinned before His Blessed Name, by breaking his oath and not observing his father's commandment. This and that has befallen him, but we did not wish to put him to death until you pass judgment because he is well versed in the Torah." When the king heard this, he convened his court and said to them: "This man has done this and that and such and such has happened to him. He must be judged at once and I wish you to be careful in judging him, because he is well versed in the Torah. So judge him in accordance with the Torah of Moses." The judges went and considered his case properly and sentenced him to death because it is written in the Book of Deuteronomy (27:16): "Cursed be he who insults his father or mother." And this was major disrespect of his father and his commandment, and therefore he was cursed and being cursed he should be doomed to die. Furthermore, he had broken his oath, as it is written in Exodus (20:7): "For the Lord will not hold him guiltless that takes His name in vain."

They reported to King Asmodeus and told him how they had sentenced him to death for the given reasons. Asmodeus said to them: "Delay the sentence and keep him overnight, since it is written in Numbers (35:24–25): 'The congregation shall judge . . . and the congregation shall deliver.'" "Your majesty," they answered, "we shall do what you have said, for you are our lord and our eyes turn to you."

"Let the man go with me tonight," said the king to them, "in order that nobody should slay him until the judgment has been reconsidered." And he did so. At Asmodeus' palace he asked the man whether he had studied Scripture and Mishnah; and he ordered the Books of the Torah, the Prophets, the Writings, and the orders of the Mishnah and Talmud to be brought. He tested him and found that he was wise in all respects. Seeing this, Asmodeus said: "Now I know that you are a wise man and also you find favor in my eyes. Swear to me that you will teach my children what you know and I shall save you from the demons. For I know that they have approved of the sentence to slay you." He took a vow. Then the king said to him: "Come and I shall teach you the pleas you should make tomorrow. When they say that you are to be slain, you answer that you are a great and wise judge and wish to see the sentence and examine the arguments presented. They will come to me, and I shall save you from them."

Next day the court came to King Asmodeus and reported: "We have found no extenuating circumstances." To which the man answered: "I am a better judge than any of you. I wish to inspect your sentence." "It is appropriate to do what you say," they answered. They took counsel together and decided: "The best thing we can do is to bring him before King Asmodeus, who is always studying in the courts on high and then comes down and studies below. Therefore he is well versed in the laws of heaven and earth alike." They went and asked Asmodeus how he would judge, and he told them: "This man should not be sentenced to death, for there was neither revolt nor trickery nor evil intention in anything he did. Those ship's men beguiled him and misled him, and the Merciful One does not impose punishment on those who act under duress. And this you may know for it is plain that the Lord slew those other men in the sea but saved him." When the court heard this, they dismissed the case against him.

After that, Asmodeus brought the man to his home and gave him his son to be taught Torah and whatever else he knew, and treated him with great honor. Within three years the son of Asmodeus knew all that the man taught him, and indeed whatever else he knew as well.

II

In due course a certain country rebelled against King Asmodeus, and he gathered his forces to wage war against it. He took that man and placed him in charge of his household and all that belonged to him, and entrusted him with the keys of all his treasuries. Furthermore, he commanded his entire household that they should only do what that man ordered. Asmodeus showed the man all his treasuries, including one building which did not have a key. And Asmodeus told him: "You have the right to enter where you will except for this building."

Asmodeus went away to besiege that city. And one day when the man passed by the door to the building which Asmodeus had forbidden him to enter, he said to himself: "What can there be in this place that the king ordered me not to enter it?" He went to the entry and peered in and saw the daughter of Asmodeus seated on a throne of gold with many maidens dancing and rejoicing before her; and she was exceedingly beautiful to look upon. When she saw him, she said to him: "Come in here!" He entered and stood before her and she said: "You foolish man, how could you disobey the commandment of my father, King Asmodeus? Moreover, what do you desire among the women? Know in all truth that you will die today. For my father already knows that you have entered this building, and he will come at once brandishing his sword to slay you!"

When the man heard this, he prostrated himself and kissed her feet and wept and entreated her to deliver him from her father. For he had not en-

tered for purposes of fornication nor had he intended anything evil. When
the daughter of Asmodeus saw this, she said to him: "Since you are a
scholar, your humility will save you today. Now leave this building and
when my father comes and asks you why you disobeyed him and entered
my house, and wishes to slay you, then tell him: My Lord, I only went
there because I love your daughter very much and I wish to ask you to
give her to me as my wife! I know that he will approve of your words
and give me to you, for ever since you have been with us he has been
thinking of doing so because you are so well versed in Torah. But it is
not customary for the woman to ask the hand of the man, and it would
certainly be unworthy of a king like him to ask you to wed his daughter."

When the man heard her words, he rejoiced at heart. Barely had he
left the building when Asmodeus came, brandishing his sword, and said
to him: "Why have you disobeyed me? Now your day has come when
I shall settle accounts for all you have done." But he answered: "My lord,
I only entered because of my great longing for your daughter. I beg and
implore you, give her to me as my wife, for I find her exceedingly fitting."
When Asmodeus heard this, he was very pleased and said to him: "I shall
gladly give her to you, but wait until I return from the war." And he added:
"Henceforth I give you permission to enter the house where my daughter
is, and to be with her as much as you desire."

Asmodeus promptly returned and conquered that country and destroyed
it. Afterwards he said to his forces: "Come with me to my daughter's wedding, for I am giving her to a very wise man who is fully versed in the
Torah." What did they do? They gathered all the countless birds and beasts
that they found in the wilderness and brought everything to the feast. And
King Asmodeus gave prodigious wealth to that man, and they wrote the
ketubah, which the bridegroom signed together with all the great advisers
of the king. And the king made them a great feast on a truly royal scale.
In the evening Asmodeus gave his daughter to the man as is the custom.

Then two of them entered their chamber and the king's daughter said
to him: "Do not think to yourself that I am a demon while you are human.
You will find me to be a woman in all respects, with nothing lacking. But
be careful not to come to me if you do not desire me." He answered:
"I, too, love you like the apple of my eye and I shall never forsake you."
"Swear it to me!" said she, and he took an oath and wrote the oath down
in a document on which he put his seal. After that, he had intercourse
with her and begot a son whom he circumcised when he was eight days
old as provided by the Torah. He named his son Solomon after King Solomon, and dwelt in that land for two years more.

One day while the man was playing with his son Solomon in the presence of his wife, Asmodeus' daughter, he began to sigh. "Why are you sighing?" she asked him. He told her: "I sighed because of my son whom I left in my own country together with my wife." "But what do you lack?" she asked him. "Am I not beautiful in your eyes, or do you lack wealth or honor? Tell me and I shall do whatever you desire." "I lack for nothing," he answered, "but when I see my son Solomon, I remember my other children." "Did not I tell you," said she, "that if you do not love me wholeheartedly you should not take me as your wife? Now you are sighing because you remember your first wife! Never do it again!" "I shall take care not to," he assured her.

After some days the man began sighing again, and she said to him: "How long will you keep on sighing for your first wife and your children? If you continue to do so, I shall take you to them. But tell me how long you will go and when you will return." "You fix the time," said he; and she told him: "I shall give you one year to go and return to me." "I shall do what you say," he promised, and took oath and wrote his oath down, signed and sealed it, and gave it to her. She preserved the documents containing all the oaths he swore to her as testimony.

What did she then do? She invited all her servants and made a great feast. After they had eaten and drunk she said to them: "My lord and husband desires to see his first wife and children who live in such and such a place. Now which of you has the power to take him there?" To which one answered: "I can take him in twenty years," and another said: "And I in ten"; and a third: "And I in a year." But another who was at the end of the table and was a hunchback and blind in one eye answered and said: "I can take him there in a single day." "You are the one I choose," said she to him. "But take care of him and do not harm him or do anything at all to him but conduct him gently and easily, for he is your lord and is well versed in the Torah, and he does not have the strength to bear anything evil." "I shall act as you say," he assured her. But she found occasion to tell her husband in secret: "My lord, be careful not to annoy him for he is subject to furious rages and became blind in one eye because of them." "I shall not anger him in any way," he assured her, and she said: "Go in peace but remember your oath!"

What did the one-eyed hunchback do? He placed him on his shoulders and brought him to his city and set him down peacefully at the bridgehead outside the city. At dawn the demon assumed human shape, and they entered the city together. There they met a Gentile, who recognized him and said: "Are you So-and-So son of So-and-So, who went overseas and the ship sank?" "I am he," he answered, and the man said: "I shall run and inform your wife who has been sitting like a widow all these years, and your kinsfolk, too." He went and informed them to their exceedingly great joy, and all of them, friends and kinsfolk came to welcome him most happily. They asked him what mishaps had befallen him. He told them all that had happened from beginning to end until that very day and how the Lord had delivered him. Then he entered his home accompanied by the hunchback in human guise. He kissed his wife and children in the other's presence and made a feast for all his friends and kinsfolk and acquaintances.

After they had eaten and drunk, the man asked the hunchback demon who had brought him there: "Why are you blind in one eye?" The other answered: "There is a verse in the Book of Proverbs (21:23): 'Who guards his mouth and his tongue preserves his soul from distress.' Why must you shame me in public? Did not your sages declare in Tractate *Babba Metzia* (59a): 'He who shames his friend in public has no share in the world to come!'" But the man went on annoying him and asked: "Why are you a hunchback?" He answered again in the words of Proverbs (26:11): "'As a dog that returns to his vomit, so is a fool that repeats his folly.' And yet I shall tell you the truth as to why I have only one eye, since I am hot-tempered. One day I quarreled with my friend, who struck me with a knife and put my eye out. And as to why I am a hunchback, remember that in Tractate *Ta'anith* (20b) another such as I told one of the rabbis to go and ask the craftsmen who made him!" Then the man said: "You have answered me fully, now please forgive me." But he said: "I shall never forgive you for shaming me." Then the man told his household: "Give him something to drink." But he replied: "I shall never eat or drink anything of yours. But call for the blessing after meals, and then I shall return to my own place."

After they had said the blessing after meals, he asked him: "What do you wish me to inform my lady, your wife?" And he told him: "Go and tell her that I shall never go back to her again, and that she is not my wife and I am not her husband." "Do not say that," warned the demon, "and do not break your oath!" "I have no fear," said the man, "with regard to any oath I swore to her." He brought his first wife and kissed her and embraced her in his presence and said: "This is my wife, since she is a woman and I am a man while your lady is a demon. So you can tell her that I shall never return to her again."

When the demon saw this, he went away and returned to his mistress in a fury. As soon as she saw him, she asked him: "What did my lord and husband tell you?" He answered: "You are asking about a man who does not love you but despises you and says that he will never come back to you again, since you are not his wife and he is not your husband." He told her everything that had happened. To which she replied: "I cannot believe you or what you say, for whatever he did say was in order to annoy you. But I know that he is well versed in the Torah and would never transgress his oath. So I shall wait for the length of time we arranged, and we shall see what happens."

So she waited for a year. Then she summoned the same demon and said to him: "Go and fetch me my lord and husband." "But I told you in his name," said the demon, "that he told me that he would never come back to you." "When he said that," she declared, "the time had not yet arrived to keep his oath. But now go and tell him that the time he swore to has come, and that he should return to me." So the hunchback demon went as she ordered and came to the man and told him: "My lady asks after your well-being and demands that you should return to her because the time to which you swore has come." "Go and tell her," answered the man, "that I do not wish for her inquiry as to my well-being, and I never shall return to her." And the demon returned and told her what her husband had said.

She went and reported the whole matter to her father Asmodeus, and asked him what she should do. "Maybe," he answered, "it is because he quarreled with your one-eyed servant that he does not wish to travel with him, and what is more, maybe he does not find it fitting to come with a one-eyed hunchback. So this is what you should do: Send him worthy and honorable messengers to warn him about his oath."

She did so. They came and gave him due warning, but he said to them: "I shall never go back to her again." "Now you are a scholar and well versed in the Torah," said they, "so how can you break your oath? For the time you specified has long passed, and you are transgressing the negative commandment in Leviticus (19:12): 'You shall not swear falsely by My Name.'" But he gave them the same answer as before. So the messengers went their way and brought his reply back to her.

She sent more numerous and honorable emissaries than those, thinking in her heart that maybe he did not think the first messengers to be worthy of him. They went to him and made their demand as the others had done, but he answered: "Do not talk so much, for I shall never return to her at all." They returned and told her: "Do not send any more emissaries, for he does not desire you but despises you!"

When she heard this, she went and told her father and asked his advice. Her father said: "I shall gather my forces and go to him. If he wishes to come, good. If not, I shall slay him and all the people in his city." "Heaven forbid, my lord," said she, "that you should go to him. But instead send as many of your servants with me as you may see fit, and I shall go. Maybe he will be prepared to return with me."

So he did. He sent forces with her to her husband's place, and she also took her son Solomon. On the night they arrived there her soldiers wished to enter the city and kill him together with the inhabitants, but she would not permit them to enter, saying: "It is night now, and they are all asleep. You know that before they go to sleep they entrust their souls to the Holy and Blessed One, and we cannot do them any harm as long as they are in the hands of the Lord. But this we shall do without sinning: We shall wait for them till morning and enter the city then. If they are prepared to do what we desire, that is good; but if not, we shall know what to do to them." They all responded: "Our lady, do whatever you see fit."

"Solomon, my son," said she to her son, "go to your father and tell him that I am here and that he should not break his oath but should return with me." The boy went, found his father asleep, and woke him up. The man stood trembling and asked him: "Who are you to rouse me from my sleep?" He said: "I am your son Solomon, and the son of King Asmodeus' daughter."

As soon as he heard this, he rose apprehensively and embraced and kissed him and asked him: "Why have you come here?" His son answered: "Your wife, my mother, has come here for you to go with her; and she sent me to inform you that she is here." "I shall not go with her," said the man, "and she will never be my wife again nor I her husband, since I am human and she is a demon and the two cannot properly unite."

To which his son replied: "With all due respect, you do not speak properly, for all the time you were with her nobody harmed you in any way, nor was anything that was not proper done to you; and if the demons treated you so honorably, it was only on her account. My mother also honored you very greatly, while her father Asmodeus appointed you a prince and leader of all his ministers and ordered them to do what you desired. This being so, why do you fling her away and despise her, never remembering the kindness they showed you. For my grandfather Asmodeus saved you from the demons when they wished to put you to death, that being the sentence they passed. Also my mother saved you from her father when he wished to slay you for disobeying him. What is more, why are you breaking the oath you swore never to forsake her? Did you not say as well that you would not remain here more than one year and would then return to her? Now, father mine, listen to me in your own interest. Return with mother and fear no evil."

"Solomon, my son," answered his father, "do not go on speaking to me about this matter and do not prolong your words, for I shall not listen to you, and I shall never return with her anymore. All the oaths I swore to her were because I feared and dreaded that they would slay me. Therefore the oaths were sworn under duress and are not valid." "I shall not say anything more to you about this," replied his son Solomon, "since that is your command; but you should understand that you are making an end of yourself on this account."

The boy returned to his mother and told her all their conversation. Rage flared up within her when she heard his words and she said: "Still I shall not slay him until I have spoken to him before the congregation and have heard his plea and see how the congregation behaves and how they adjudge this matter." So she waited until the morning.

When she learned that the congregation had gathered in the synagogue, she went there with all her ministers and notables, but told them: "Wait for me outside the synagogue, I shall enter and hear what his answer is and what he wishes to do."

She entered, and after they had finished the Psalms, she said to the cantor: "Wait and do not pray until I have spoken." And he replied: "Speak."

Then she said to the congregation: "Hearken all ye peoples and do justice between me and the man against whom I complain, who is named Dihon son of Shalmon. This man fell among us because of his transgressions, and my father showed him kindness and saved him from the demons who wished to slay him. I also saved him from my father who wished to put him to death because he had disobeyed him; but he gave me to him for wife and appointed him a minister and leader of his forces. He took me as a wife according to the practice of Moses and Israel and wrote me a *ketubah* providing a large amount for my jointure, and swore to me that he would never abandon me all his life long. When he wished to take leave of me in order to return to his first wife here, he also swore that he would not remain more than one year and would then return to me. Here are the oaths written in these deeds which bear his sign and seal. Now he wishes to pay me evil for good and does not wish to return with me. And I request of you to ask his reasons for his behavior, and you be the judges in respect of these deeds of oath."

The judges of the congregation asked him: "Why do you not return with her after she has treated you so well? Furthermore, how can you break the two oaths which you signed and sealed with your own hands?"

"Whatever I did and whatever I swore," he replied, "was done under duress and out of fear, for I knew that if I would not do what they wished they would slay me. Therefore I have already asked about the oaths and they had been annulled for me, and I do not wish to go back with her. For it is not customary for a man to marry a demon and beget demons.

But I wish to stay with my wife who is of humankind as I am, as is written in our Torah in Genesis (2:18): 'I will make a helpmeet for him.' This one is not a helpmeet for me, and that is why I do not wish to return to her. Let her go and take a demon like herself so that they are two of a kind, while I remain with my first wife who is the wife of my youth."

Then the daughter of Asmodeus said to the judges: "Surely you admit that whoever wishes to send his wife away has to write her a bill of divorcement and place it in her hand and pay her whatever is provided in her *ketubah*?" "That is perfectly true and correct," responded the judges, "for that is what the law requires." "In that case," said she to them, "let him write me a divorce and pay me what is prescribed." She produced her *ketubah*, in which they found written a vast and countless sum of money. The judges said to him: "Pay her what is prescribed in the *ketubah*, or else return with her." He answered them: "She has all the money, I forgive her everything and shall give her a divorce, but I shall not return with her, not ever." And the judges said to him: "Consider that this is what has to be done according to the law: You must either go with her or else allow her to go free and pay what is prescribed in her *ketubah*. If you do not do this, she has the right to do whatever she may desire with you."

She said to them: "I see that you have recognized the law and have stated his duties in accordance with it. That being so, I do not wish him to accompany me under duress after he has made a mockery of me. But if you please, tell him to kiss me and I shall return to my own place." "Do what she wishes," they said to him, "and kiss her, for then she will set you free from all we have imposed upon you." So he went and kissed her, and she choked him with her kiss so that he died.

"That is your recompense," said she, "for swearing falsely in the name of the Lord and disobeying the commandment of your father and making a mockery of me and wishing to abandon me to living widowhood. Now it is your wife who will remain a widow and alone."

Then she said to the congregation: "If you do not wish me to slay you, take my son Solomon and give him the daughter of your leading notable for wife, and set him over you as your chief and leader, for he comes from among you, so let him dwell with you. For now that I have slain his father I do not wish him to dwell with me so that he should not always be a reminder and a cause of distress. I shall leave him a vast amount of money so that he shall never lack for anything. You should issue an order to give him a larger share of his father's property than any other of his brothers!"

The congregation did so. They set him over them as leader and commander, and he ruled over them while she returned to her father and her own place.

96

THE STORY OF A WOMAN-LOVING KING

This is a version of an international tale, known as "Leo" in the medieval narrative cycle of "The Seven Sages of Rome." The metaphor comparing a woman to a garden in the brother's allegory is rooted in the biblical verse a garden shut up is my sister, my bride *(Song of Songs 4:12). Source: J. S. Farḥi,* Oseh Pele *3:371–375.*

There was a king who loved women very much. Every day he went walking in his capital city with his eyes roving in all directions at the houses and the windows. Whenever he saw a beautiful woman he would try every manner of trick to catch her. Since he was a king and all powerful there was not a beautiful woman who could escape from him. All the people in his kingdom knew about him but they did not dare to open their mouths and protest.

In his capital city there was a pious Jew who had an exceedingly beautiful wife; and she had three wealthy brothers who were leading citizens. This pious man knew of the king and his evil reputation, so he kept his wife as secluded as possible. His modest wife was also careful not to appear in public; for she knew that if the king were to see her she would be unable to escape him. But one day she glanced forgetfully out of the window, and by chance the king was just passing by with his eyes roving over the upper floors of the houses. He saw this woman, and he became excited and was possessed by a great desire to sleep with her.

She felt that he had already seen her and was much distressed. She concealed herself at once and closed the door. The king wished to enter but could not find an open door. For though he was king and there was none to say him nay, still he knew that his behavior was worthless and disgusting even though his desire was so powerful; and so he did his wicked deeds secretively as far as he could, and would not use force for his actions. And day after day he promenaded in front of the courtyard where this woman's house stood in order to find a favorable opportunity, an open door, to enter.

The woman being a good Jewess told her pious husband what had happened in sheer forgetfulness. From that day forward they were both very careful to close the door behind them. But one day it chanced that the pious man went to his yeshiva and forgot to close the door. Since the woman knew how careful her husband was about this, she paid no attention but went about her affairs as usual. But the king passed by and found the door open and entered.

When the woman suddenly saw that the king had come in, she trembled and quivered and shook and all but perished away. But since he was a king, she could not say anything and certainly could not shout, and had to receive him most politely, albeit unwillingly. So she invited him into the large chamber of her home with all due honor. Then she went and fetched a small gilded book to read and gave it to him and said: "Your majesty, your maidservant is in your hands to do with as you see fit. Yet I entreat you, my lord, to permit me to go to another room for a quarter of an hour in order to cleanse and adorn myself and then return to you as is fitting. Meanwhile, take this book and read it in order to pass the time until I return." "Good, my child," said he, "go in peace and prepare yourself and come back swiftly." And he took the book from her.

Out went the woman and ran away to her neighbor in the next courtyard, where she waited and watched the entrance of her home until the king departed. The king began to read the Bible and read the ten commandments: "You shall not commit adultery; . . . you shall not covet your neighbor's wife (Exod. 20:13, 14); If a man commits adultery with another man's wife, . . . the adulterer and the adulteress shall be put to death" (Lev. 20:10). He went on reading in this way until he settled down to study. His mind cleared and he recognized how foolish he had been, and that he had strayed from the path of wisdom with his worthless and contemptible urge to pursue what his eyes desired, losing the strength of his body and all his soul and merely gaining shame and reproach. He sat as though astounded for about two hours, considering what he had learned.

At last he himself realized that two hours had passed, and he started up as though he had been fast asleep and told himself: "Most certainly this woman has done this in her wisdom and has gone and concealed herself. If I stay any longer her husband may come and find me in his home and I shall be a subject of mockery and shame and reproach." He quickly rose in order to flee away. But under the cushion he left a purse full of gold coins for the distress he had caused her. He was in such a hurry to leave before the woman's husband might come that he forgot the scepter encrusted with pearls that he had with him. But he slipped the book into his pocket and fled away.

The woman had her eyes fixed on the entrance, waiting for the king to leave her home in order that she might return before her husband came, so that he would not know what had happened to her. When she saw the king leaving her home at last, she rejoiced very much and praised the Holy and Blessed One who had done this miracle and delivered her from trouble. She returned home at once and swiftly prepared a meal for her husband. She was in such a hurry that she did not even think of entering the room where the king had been.

When the mealtime came her husband returned from his yeshiva and entered the room to take off his coat. There he saw the royal pearl-encrusted scepter lying on the cushion and the pillow nearby pushed to one side. He lifted it up and underneath it he found the purse with the gold coins. At this, he grieved and sighed and said to himself: "Here are two clear signs of a successful wicked deed. I forgot to close the door and the king found it open and entered and satisfied his desire with my wife against her will and agreement." He kept the matter to himself and said nothing to her, neither good nor bad. But he turned his face away from her and did not approach her anymore.

When the poor woman saw how her husband was behaving, she began to grieve and sigh. He would not speak to her, while she did not have the heart to tell him of the wisdom the Lord had set in her heart, by means of which she had been delivered from transgression and remained pure; for she felt that he would certainly not believe her. Her heart broke with her grief, and she became very ill and took to her bed and all the beauty and radiance of her face vanished and she became greenish, while her flesh withered away, so that those who saw her could not recognize her. Her three brothers came to visit her every day, bringing notable physicians, to heal her. But the physicians could not diagnose her illness nor could they know what had caused it. Her brothers loved her like the apple of their eye and were greatly distressed on her account and entreated her to tell them what was weighing down her heart; for her grief and sorrow was so great that she was nigh to death. They went on entreating her day after day until she told them the cause of her grief and what had happened to her and how her husband had turned his face away; for ever since that day he did not approach her or show her any love and affection as before, but in his heart there were now hatred and enmity in ample store. When her brothers heard her words, they told her: "Rest assured that with God's aid we shall seek and find a remedy for you."

So the three brothers rose and went to the king; and they bowed down and prostrated themselves and said to him: "Long live your majesty! We entreat you to hear our cause and judge the dispute we have with So-and-So." Since they were wealthy and respected men, among the most important in the city, he agreed, saying: "I shall do so in your honor." He summoned all the ministers and judges of the kingdom and ordered that the pious man against whom they had the claim should be brought. And he told them: "State the claim that you have against this man!"

Then the brothers wisely used a parable because of the honor of royalty, in order not to shame him in the presence of his ministers. They said: "May your majesty live forever! Be it known to your exalted highness that our aged father was wealthy. He had much property, gold and silver, houses and land, fields and vineyards. He also had one little garden of rare beauty, set with trees and flowers, and he loved it and took particular care of it at all times. Now before his death he summoned us three brothers and divided his property into three parts. To the first he gave all the gold and silver, to the second he gave the houses and the land, and to the third he gave the fields and vineyards. He did it all with good measure, and each of us received his share from him with great gladness and love. But he kept the little garden in his own possession because that was all his delight, until this man came and persuaded and enticed him. Our father agreed to let him have the garden without money and without price, although it could not be valued in gold for it was invaluable. The only condition which this man undertook was to till it and guard it and look after it carefully, to maintain it and to do whatever might be required therein in order that it might not suffer loss or be spoilt, but should always retain its beauty and splendor. In all truth, this garden remained in the man's possession for several years after our old father passed away, and this man kept faith and did as he had promised, so that the garden became absolutely glorious, even more than it had been. Yet now for several months this man has turned his face away from it and takes no steps to look after it or till it or safeguard it or do therein whatever it requires. So naturally this garden has been spoilt, and instead of producing grapes it has produced sour and worthless fruit. So now we make our claim of this man, who has betrayed it and has not observed the express condition and undertaking in accordance with which our father gave it to him."

To this the woman's husband answered: "Your majesty! Every word they say is true and there is nothing warped or twisted in their evidence. Yet be it known to your majesty that it is far from me to play false. Since they have told the truth as to the way I behaved toward it from the day I took it, all my aim and purpose being to do whatever was required therein with love and affection. But be it known to your majesty that once I forgot to close the entry to the garden as I usually did. When I returned I found it was open. I entered and saw the tracks left by your majesty's lion, which had escaped from his own place and entered there. I suspect that it must have eaten the fruit and been sated with all its goodness. Since the lion has already tasted what is there, I fear to enter lest it return while I am within and finds me there and slays me."

When the king heard all their wise words, he understood they were talking of him in parable and metaphor in order to show honor to his royalty, so that the others should not understand and feel that he was being mocked. The king said to the husband: "Your words are correct. In truth, the lion once escaped from his cage and entered your garden where it saw the fruit hanging as high as the heavens with the fragrance of a field that is blessed by the Lord. It tried very hard to reach the fruit and sate itself on it but could not. But in its mouth it took one fruit as a souvenir and came back to its own place."

Then the king sent for that book and showed it to him and said: "I swear by the king's life that the lion did not touch or injure anything apart from this fruit, and had no advantage from your garden at all. Indeed, ever since that day I have set up a fortified wall so that the lion can no longer come out. Neither into your garden nor into any other in the world. Therefore you may be at ease in your heart, for no man has touched your garden and you may return to it and till it and guard it and do whatever may be required in order to restore it to its earlier beauty and splendor as was provided in the agreement with you."

When the man heard the words of the king and his oath, he felt assured and his honor was at ease. For he knew in all sooth that his worthy wife was pure and no stranger had approached her. He bowed down and prostrated himself before the king and said: "I shall act as you have counseled." Then the brothers also bowed down before him and said: "You have restored us to life." They all departed from the king glad and rejoicing, and the three brothers and the pious husband of their sister kissed one another.

Then he returned home and kissed his wife and said to her: "Blessed you are, my love! Now I know that you are a worthy wife and your wisdom sustained you in your distress and the Lord came to your aid."

And they became man and wife again in love and affection. And little by little she was consoled and was fully and wholly cured.

[*Translator's Note:* In the Hebrew the parable shines through the words because the term used for "little garden" is in the feminine, with corresponding pronouns all the way through. Unfortunately I could see no way of rendering this in English.]

97
THE FALSE WIDOW

This tale, still current in Jewish oral tradition, dates back to classical litera-
ture. It has been a part of the medieval cycle "The Seven Sages of Rome"
and of the Jewish medieval fable literature, in each case serving as an
example of female fickleness. Source: Babylonian Talmud Kiddushin 80b,
"Tosafot," commentary attributed to Rabbi Ḥananel (c. 990–c. 1055/6).

A certain woman wept and wailed over her husband's grave. There was a man nearby who had to guard the corpse of someone hanging from the gallows, by order of the king. He went to the woman and seduced her, and she gave way to him. When he returned to the hanging corpse, he did not find it and grieved very much for fear of the king. But the woman said to him: "Have no fear! Take my husband from his grave and hang him there instead!"

98
THE KEYS TO THE MISER'S TREASURES

In Jewish narrative tradition the mohel, *the religious functionary who*
performs circumcisions, is substituted for the midwife who delivers ba-
bies in the land of the fairies that appears in European tales. Source:
A. Jellinek, ed., Bet ha-Midrasch 6:143–146.

There was a very rich man who had whole treasures of gold and silver and precious stones, but he was the most miserly man in the world. He did not go to synagogue on Mondays and Wednesdays, for he was afraid he would have to put a coin in the charity box. There was only one commandment that he fulfilled, and that served to deliver him from the Day of Judgment, and there after that he became very generous. This man was a mohel. If there was any occasion to perform a circumcision, even at a distance of several leagues from his home, he would go there in order to fulfill the commandment; and he would never take any pay, neither from a poor man nor a rich one.

One day a certain demon came to him in human form and said: "My wife bore me a son and the circumcision will be on such and such day, and I request you to come and circumcise my son." The mohel went home at once, took the circumcision knife, and then took his seat on the cart to accompany the man who had come to him; for he supposed that this was a human being, and did not know that he was a demon. So they both went in the cart, and when they reached the forest the demon led him through a country where no man ever passed, a land of hills and valleys and wilderness, for two days. On the third day he fetched him to his home which was in what seemed to be a little village containing about twenty houses; and the houses were very beautiful indeed. When the mohel entered, he saw that the master of the house was very wealthy, and it was full of good things, with meat and large dishes. The master of the house took the horse and gave it to his servant to be fed. And the mohel did not realize that the householder was a harmful demon.

The householder went about his affairs while the mohel went to the room where the mother was. When she saw him, she rejoiced exceedingly and greeted him, saying: "Come over to me, sir, and I shall reveal a great secret to you." Then she went on: "My husband is a harmful demon but I come of humankind. When I was small, the demons took me away and so I was lost and done for, since all their deeds are vanity and emptiness and trickery. Now I warn you to circumcise my son who is born to me of them. I further warn you to save your soul and be careful not to eat any food or drink any liquor or take any gift, neither from my husband nor from any one of them." When the mohel heard these words, he became very frightened indeed.

Toward evening many men and women came from the villages with horses and carts in human fashion; but they were all destructive demons. The time of the feast arrived, and they urged the mohel to wash his hands and sit down and eat with them at this feast in honor of the commandment. He refused to do so, saying that he was weary from the journey, and he neither ate nor drank that night. Next day they went to the synagogue and prayed there, and the mohel had to recite the special prayer that the mohel recites on such occasions. After the prayer they brought the infant whom he circumcised in accordance with the custom of Israel. Then, as was the practice of the country, the sandak* honored the congregation with brandy and sweetstuffs. The mohel had to go to the home of the sandak, but neither ate nor drank there, saying that he was fasting on account of a bad dream. In the afternoon the householder said that since the mohel had come more than a dozen leagues for the sake of the commandment,

---

*The man who holds the baby on his lap during the circumcision.

he, the householder, would make a feast on his account that night after his fast was over. Of course, the whole purpose of the householder was that the mohel should eat something of his, after which he would be within his power. For he did not know that his wife had revealed that he was a demon.

That evening they made the circumcision feast. Yet still the mohel neither ate nor drank with them, saying that his head and limbs felt heavy. So they ate and drank all kinds of good food. When they were merry with wine, the householder said to the mohel: "Come with me to one of my rooms." The mohel was very frightened, thinking that his time had come, but he accompanied him to the room. There the householder showed him sundry vessels of gold. "Take one of these," said he, "to remember me by." But the mohel answered, "I have my own gold and silver and all the goods in the world: Jewels and pearls and rings and bracelets and necklaces." "But take one of the rings," said the householder, "or anything else you may wish for." Yet the mohel refused to take anything and answered that he had quite enough jewels and pearls of his own.

After that, the master of the house conducted him to a room in which there were many keys which hung on a great number of hooks. The mohel was astonished at this, for among them he seemed to see a bundle of keys which were the same as what he had at home for all his rooms and all his chests. And the master of the house asked him: "Good sir, I have shown you so many fine vessels of silver and gold and so many jewels and precious stones, which did not impress you at all. Yet you wonder at this store which is only iron!"—For the keys were all of iron. And the mohel answered: "I am surprised at this bunch of keys, which are all like the keys of my houses and treasures and rooms, which I see hanging on this nail here."

Then the householder said to him: "You have shown me your kindness and have accompanied me for more than twelve leagues to circumcise my son. Also I see that the Lord is with you because you have not eaten or drunk or taken anything of my belongings. Therefore I shall now tell you that I am appointed over those demons who are set over the men who are misers by nature. All their keys are entrusted into our hands in order that they should have no power or authority to perform any kind of charity or kindness; while they themselves are not entitled to have any pleasure or purchase any good food or dainties. But since you have done me this great favor, take that bunch of keys and have no fear. By the living God, no evil will befall you!"

So the mohel took the bundle of keys and went home rejoicing. When he arrived home he became quite a different person. He at once erected a stone building to serve as a magnificent synagogue. He performed much charity, sustaining the poor and clothing the naked, and he went on in this fashion until he died, leaving a good name behind him when he passed away.

99
THE JEW AND THE IDOL WORSHIPER

Although this tale has a talmudic source in the Babylonian Talmud Berakhot 18b, it is rather rare in the literature of the period. However, it is an internationally known tale that is very popular in current oral traditions of Jewish ethnic groups. Source: M. Gaster, The Exempla of the Rabbis, *No. 29, pp. 59, 21–22.*

The rabbis told this tale: Once upon a time a Gentile and a Jew were walking together and the Gentile said to the Jew: "My faith is better than yours." But the Jew answered: "No, indeed, my faith is better than yours, as it is written in Deuteronomy (4:8): 'And what great nation is there that has statutes and ordinances . . . like all this law?'" Then the Gentile said to him: "Let us ask others. If they say my faith is better than yours, I shall take your money. But if they say that your faith is better than mine, you shall take my money." The Jew answered: "I agree."

So they went on walking. Satan came their way in the shape of an old man. They asked him, and he said: "The Gentile's faith is better." They went on walking and met the same Satan in the likeness of a youth. They asked him and he said: "The Gentile's faith is better." They went on walking and the same Satan assumed the likeness of another old man. They asked him and he said: "The Gentile's faith is better." So the Gentile took the money of the Israelite.

So that Israelite went on vexed and lodged in a ruin. When a third of a night had passed he heard demons speaking to one another, and two of them said to one: "Where were you today?" "I found a Jew and an Aramaean," said he, "and I had my sport with them and I gave false witness to the Gentile." Then they asked the second one: "And where were you?" "I," said he, "prevented the emperor's daughter from giving birth, and she has been wailing in her birth pangs for seven days. And if they were just to take some of the leaves of the tree which is beside their lavatory and press them into her nose, she would give birth at once." "And where were you?" they asked the third, who told them: "I blocked the spring of such and such a city; but if they were to take a black ox and slaughter it over the water, it would flow again."

Of course, the Jew took these things to mind. Early in the morning he went to the emperor's city, where he found that his daughter was suffering in the pangs of a difficult birth. "Take the leaves of the tree beside your lavatory," said he, "and squeeze them into her nostrils." And she gave birth at once. The king at once gave him much money, for she was his only child.

Then he went to the city where the water had ceased to flow and told them: "Take a black ox and slaughter it over the water and it will begin flowing again." They slaughtered the ox and the water flowed indeed. Then the townsfolk gave him much money.

A day or so later the Gentile who had taken his money met him and wondered and said to him: "Why, I took all your money away. Where does this wealth come to you from?" He told him the whole story. Then the Gentile said: "I shall go to that ruin and try to hear what I can."

So he went and spent the night in that ruin. But the three demons came and slew him, as it was written in Proverbs (11:8): "The righteous is delivered from distress, and the wicked comes in his stead."

100
The Righteous Is Delivered from Distress

In Jewish folklore this narrative theme about a victim substitution often takes an ethnic dimension, reflecting the conflict between Jews and non-Jews. Source: I. Lévi, "Un recueil de contes juifs inédits," No. 12, pp. 81–83.

There was once a pious man who was wealthy and of the king's company. He had a handsome, fine-looking, and wise son. Before he passed away, he told his son not to leave the synagogue from the moment the cantor rose to pray and began to recite the *Kaddish* prayer until the whole service was over. Also, if somebody who had not heard the prayer were to rise and recite the evening prayer he should stay there until he had finished as well. The dying man added: "I have done this all my life and I have prospered. And if you pass through a city where there is a synagogue and you hear the cantor, enter and do not leave until he has finished his prayers." Then the pious man passed away.

Now the son was well thought of by all who saw him. He served the king and was the wine bearer to the king and queen and sliced them their bread and meat. They loved him very much and praised him to the skies. But the king's vizier saw this and envied him. He came to the king and said: "Your majesty, you have eyes yet you do not see that this young man loves the queen, and they fornicate together." But the king rebuked him and did not believe him, yet he repeated it day after day until the king grew jealous.

One day the king went to inspect the workers who were preparing a limekiln, and he said to the master of the workers: "Take the first man who comes here tomorrow and throw him into the kiln at once. If you do not do so, you will pay for it with your own life." "Your majesty," answered he, "I shall obey your orders." Then the king returned home. That night while the young man was serving him, he called him and ordered: "Rise early tomorrow morning and go where they are preparing the lime and tell the man in charge to make a great fire." "I shall carry out your orders," answered the young man.

In the morning he mounted his horse, but as he passed the synagogue he heard the cantor's voice. He dismounted, entered the synagogue, and prayed. When the cantor had finished, another man who had not heard the prayers rose and began to pray, and he waited until he finished as well. And so he was delayed until it was broad daylight. Meanwhile, the king summoned his vizier and ordered him: "Go to the place where they are making the lime and ask the man in charge: Have you obeyed the king?" Then the vizier mounted his horse and rode off and asked the man in charge: "Have you obeyed the king's orders?" Thereupon they seized him and tied him up and threw him into the kiln. The young man arrived just then and saw them throwing the vizier into the kiln, and he said to them: "If the king knows this, he will slay you." But the man in charge answered: "Yesterday the king ordered me: 'Take the first man I send to you tomorrow, and throw him into the kiln.' And this is the man who came first."

Then the young man returned to the king and said: "Your majesty, why did you order the vizier to be burned?" At this, the king shuddered and shook with astonishment and said to the youth: "Now I know that you are God-fearing, and your Creator loves you. This is what the vizier said about you and the queen. So I ordered that the man whom I first sent to the limekiln should be thrown into the fire; and it was you I first ordered to go. After that I told the vizier to go and see whether my orders had been obeyed. But you were delayed, so they threw him in instead. Now

I know that you are innocent." That is as the Book of Proverbs declares (11:8): "The righteous is delivered from distress, and the wicked comes in his stead."

101
SEVEN GOOD YEARS

Elijah the Prophet is the most popular figure in Jewish folklore. As in this tale, he offers rewards to worthy needy people, bringing to them the blessing of fertility, prosperity, and health, and demanding in return observance of cultural and religious Jewish values. Source: S. Buber, ed., Midrasch Suta (Berlin, 1894), "Ruth," 4:11, pp. 54–55.

Once there was a pious man who became poor, and he had a worthy wife. Finally he became a hired man. On one occasion he was plowing in the field. Elijah, whom it is good to mention, chanced by him in the likeness of an Arab and said to him: "You have seven good years: When do you desire them, now or at the end of your days?" "Are you a wizard?" said the pious man to him. "I have nothing to give you but go away from me in peace."

But he returned to him three times. On the third occasion the man said to Elijah: "I shall go and take counsel with my wife." He went to his wife and told her: "Somebody has come bothering me three separate times saying: 'You have seven good years: When do you desire them, now or at the end of your days?'"

"Let them be today," said she to him. He avoided his children and returned to Elijah and said: "Let me have them now." "Go home," said Elijah, "and before you reach the entry to your courtyard you will see the blessing awaiting you at home." Now there his children were sitting, digging down in the earth, and they found a treasure on which they could maintain themselves for seven years, and they went and called their mother. So before the pious man even reached the gateway his wife came out to meet him and told him. He praised the Holy and Blessed One at once and felt at ease. But his worthy wife said to him: "The Holy and Blessed One has already drawn a thread of kindness down for us and has given us a living for seven years. So let us engage in deeds of charity during these seven years, and then maybe the Holy and Blessed One will add to us of His bounty." They did so; and whatever they did, she told her little son: "Write down whatever we did!" And he did so.

After the seven years were over Elijah the Prophet, whom it is good to remember, came and said to him: "The time has come to take back what I gave you." "When I took it," said the pious man, "I only did so as my wife desired. So when I return it I shall return it only with my wife's knowledge." He went to her and said: "The old man has already come to take back what is his." "Go and tell him," said she to her husband, "if you have found people more faithful than we are, I shall give you your pledge." The Holy and Blessed One observed their words and deeds and the acts of charity they had performed and added more goodness for them, thus fulfilling the words of Isaiah (32:17): "And the work of righteousness shall be peace."

102
THE LOAN

In this Elijah story the person whom he helps neglects his pious conduct and hence his good fortune is reversed. Source: I. Lévi, "Un recueil de contes juifs inédits," No. 3, pp. 58–60.

Once there was a pious man who used to pray three times daily. His prayers ascended before the Glory Seat like the daily offering that was once sacrificed on the altar. Now this man undertook that he would accept no gift from any man. Every day he made the rounds of the rubbish heaps and picked rags which he placed before him and behind to cover his nakedness. And that was his practice.

When the Holy and Blessed One saw his shame and suffering, He said to Elijah: "Go and give him four gold coins." So Elijah went and found him praying after his fashion. He waited until he had finished his prayers and said: "Peace be with you, rabbi!" And he answered him in kind. And Elijah wished to give him the four gold coins as the Holy and Blessed One had commanded him. But he did not wish to take them until he persuaded him, and then he accepted them.

He went to the market and bought himself a garment for his own needs. But a man came to him who desired those clothes and said to him: "Sell me this garment." "For how much?" he asked, and the other said: "For twenty-four gold coins." "Take them!" said he. And through those twenty-four gold coins he grew wealthy, so that he could purchase himself men and women slaves and beasts, while ships set sail for him upon the sea. Once he grew rich he stopped praying and forgot his earlier custom. Then the Holy and Blessed One said to Elijah: "See how that saint to whom I gave so much wealth and property and honor has ceased to pray. Go and take back what I gave him."

So Elijah went and found him seated on a gold seat in the synagogue. "Peace be with you, rabbi," said he. And he answered in kind. Then Elijah said to him: "Do me a kindness and give me back what I deposited with you." "What did you deposit with me?" he asked. Elijah answered: "The four gold coins I placed in your hand." "I do not recognize you," said he. Whereupon Elijah told him: "Such and such is my name and I gave them to you while you were praying in the synagogue." "You have reminded me well," said he, and he wished to give him four gold coins at once. But Elijah said to him: "Give me the same four and not any others." "Why," said the man, "who could know them and who could pick them out!" "Fetch me your wallet," said Elijah, "and I shall find them." A wonder befell, for he found the very coins and took them and went away.

Thereupon the pious man began to dwindle away. All his sons and daughters and maidservants died, and his ships sank at sea. He returned to his original practice and used to pick up rags in the rubbish heaps and prayed three times a day. Then the Holy and Blessed One stayed His anger and said to Elijah: "That pious man is very dear to Me and I cannot bear to see his sufferings. Go and lend him ten gold coins and make him swear by My Name that he will never cease his prayers as is his habit!"

Elijah went to him at once and found him praying. He waited until he finished and then greeted him with peace. He said to him: "Take what I am giving you, but swear to me by the Lord that you will never again miss your prayers."

103
THE THREE BROTHERS

The respective choices of the three brothers represent three basic values in Jewish society: prosperity, learning, and family. In another version a continuation of the narrative suggests the preference of good family over either economic success or learning. Source: Anon., Mayseh Bukh *(Basel, 1602; Amsterdam, 1723),* No. 46.

Once there was a pious old man. When his time came to die, he summoned his three sons and commanded them that they should never quarrel with one another in order that they should never come to take an oath. For he himself had never taken an oath all his life long.

When he died he left a garden of spices behind, which it was their duty to guard in turn against thieves. During the first night when the oldest son was lying in the garden Elijah the Prophet came and asked him: "My son, do you wish to study Torah, to be wealthy, or to wed a beautiful woman?" This son answered: "I desire much wealth." So Elijah gave him a coin, and he became very wealthy.

On the second night the second brother lay in the garden and Elijah came and asked him the same questions. He said that he wished to study the whole Torah. Then Elijah gave him a book, and from it he knew the whole of the Torah.

On the third night the youngest brother slept in the garden. Elijah came to him and asked what he desired. He desired a beautiful wife. "In that case," said Elijah, "you must travel with me." And the two of them set out on a journey.

They spent the first night at a house belonging to a wicked man. During the night Elijah heard the chickens and geese saying to one another: "What sin did this young man do that he should take the daughter of this householder as his wife?" When Elijah heard this, he understood and they journeyed farther.

Next night they lodged again in a house where Elijah heard the chickens and geese speaking together and saying: "How did the young man sin that he should take the daughter of this householder, when they are all so wicked!"

Next day they rose early in the morning and journeyed farther. That night they stayed at a house whose owner had a beautiful daughter. And Elijah heard the chickens and the geese telling one another: "How does this young man merit to marry a woman who is so beautiful and God-fearing!"

So when the morning came Elijah rose early and arranged a match between them, and they made the wedding and returned home in peace.

God gave him all this because he had observed the last will and commandment of his father.

104

THE SCHOLAR, THE RICH MAN, AND THE GOD-FEARING MAN

This is a Jewish version of an internationally known tale. The characters in the narrative represent three classes in Jewish society: merchants, scholars, and pious people. The preference is for the latter. However, piety does not stand by itself; its appropriate performance is dependent upon family support. Source: Anon., Ma'aseh ha-Keddoshim, pp. 15–21.

I n a certain great city there were three men. The first was very wealthy and the second was an outstanding scholar of the Torah, while the third was exceedingly God-fearing. Now we shall tell what happened to them.

Everybody knows that all times are not the same but that they make up a wheel turning round and round in the universe. So it happened to the rich man. All his life long his star had been in the ascendant and he had succeeded in all his affairs and bought himself houses and fields and vineyards and lived a good life. But suddenly his star was reversed and he lost all his fortune and became very poor. His wife and little ones cried for food but he did not have even a single coin with which to buy bread for them. Indeed, all he had left were the clothes he was wearing. The man could not bear to see the sufferings of his wife and little children and he said to his wife: "I can see how great our distress is. It occurs to me that I shall go wandering through the world. Maybe the Holy and Blessed One will take pity on me and send me His holy aid so that I shall find a living. For the men of old said: 'Change your place and change your luck,' so I shall change my place." His wife said: "Do whatever seems proper to you and may the Ever Present take pity on you and send you Elijah the Prophet so that your road may prosper." The man took leave of his household and went to the city street where he stood sad and at a loss, hoping that he might join some company and they would all take the road together.

The second was a great scholar, deeply versed in the Torah of the Lord, which he studied day and night. But where there is no food there is no Torah. The scholar was very poor indeed and did not have even a loaf of bread in his home. He had to sell all his household belongings in order to maintain himself and his household and so that he should be able to engage in the study of the Torah. Now when the man saw that there was no more money in his pocket and his children were wailing for food, he had to sell his books in order to supply his household. Not even a single book was left him for studying. Then the man said to his wife: "I have sold everything we have at home, and I do not even have a single book left for studying. I am afraid that I may forget all I have learned. So I propose, if you agree, to set out on the road and seek a living, maybe His Blessed Name will take pity upon me and allow me the grace and mercy of those who see me, and give me a living." The worthy woman answered: "May the Ever Present be merciful to you from on high and cause your path to prosper." She added: "Go in peace!" So the man left his home and went out into the street of the city, where he found the aforementioned rich man. So they both stood by the wayside and waited there for others to come so that they might proceed in company.

The third man feared God and kept His commandments. But there was no rest in his home because he had a disobedient wife. This woman gave him no rest but kept on cursing her husband savagely every moment, shaming him in public. It is of such women that King Solomon said in Ecclesiastes (7:26): "I find a woman more bitter than death." Now the man could not bear such treatment by his wife and at last he had to leave his home. So without her knowledge he fled away and went out. In the street he found the rich man and the scholar, and he joined them. Then they said to one another: "Let us repose our trust in the Lord and set out, and maybe His Blessed Name will be merciful and prosper our path."

The three men went together from city to city and from village to village, hungry and thirsty, with none to show them pity. Three years passed and the men had not yet found any livelihood. Their clothes became torn and tattered. Once when they were on the road they came to a large open field where they stood still under the heavens and raised their voices and wept. "We pray Thee, O Lord," they cried, "aid us now!" They prayed with great devotion and intensity. And the Lord heard their prayer.

For lo and behold! an old man came to them and greeted them with peace. Then he asked them why they were so sad and wept. The men told him: "Even so, supposing we tell you, good sir, can you aid us? Surely if the Lord does not aid us, who can?" But the old man urged them to tell him of their distress, and each of them began to tell him of his own troubles. The rich man told him how he had left his household three years earlier because he could not make a living, and during all this time had not found any livelihood. The second told him how he had stayed at home engaging in Torah by day and night and studying the two Talmuds; but since he had no livelihood he had had to sell his books. "Now," he went on, "you can see for yourself, sir, that even the clothes I am wearing are falling apart, so that I am ashamed to go among people and tell them that I am a bookman." The third one told with bitter weeping how he had nothing whatsoever, while even at home he had had no rest because of his spiteful wife who was prepared to shame him in the presence of others. "Now, good sir," he finished, "what can I do?"

The old man heard their words. He was Elijah the Prophet, whom it is good to remember. And he said to them: "Listen to me, my masters, and have no fear. I have come to deliver you from your misery and sighing. You will return home most honorably and find everything peaceful and everybody alive and you will be delivered from your distress. But you must listen to my counsel and not turn aside after your hearts' desires; and then all will be well with you, both here and hereafter."

And Elijah gave a coin to the rich man and said to him: "Listen to what I tell you. When you come home place this coin in a chest, and the chest will be filled at once with a great treasure. Then build a house of study at once and let ten men do nothing else but stay there constantly and engage in Torah by day and by night. And also give alms to the poor. If you do what I am telling you, all will be well with you, and the wealth will remain in your hands, and the chest will always be full with ample silver and gold. But be strong and of good courage and observe these words of mine."

Elijah also gave the scholar a remedy to aid him in his distress. "Take this book from me," said he, "and when you come home place this book in a cupboard. Every time you open the cupboard you will find it full of books. So you can sell books at any time and maintain your household with the price. You will also be able to study Torah as of old. And if you do not neglect the Torah, you will merit to bring up your children in ease and wealth."

To the third of them Elijah said: "Here is a ring for you. When you come home, hang the ring on the wall and then you will no longer hear curses from your wife, for she will improve her behavior and no longer be spiteful and malicious as of old. For your wife is wayward and restless at home because a dybbuk has entered into her. But once you hang the ring upon the wall the dybbuk will no longer rule over her, and there will be peace and quiet at home forever!"

The Man of Truth flew away, and the three men went their way in peace.

Now let us first tell about the rich man. When he came to his town, his wife was standing waiting for him. When she saw her husband coming naked and empty, his clothes torn, with one patch over another and walking barefoot, she raised her voice and wept bitterly, saying: "Consider, husband, you left me and our little children three years ago and I supposed that you would come home and support me, and now I see in how bad a state you are. But may the Lord be our aid and help us." Then the man said: "Listen to me. Elijah the Prophet himself came to meet me and gave me this coin which I hold in my hand and told me to place the coin in a chest, for it will fill at once with ample gold and silver. But Elijah told me that I should give alms every day and also build a house of study for ten men who will do nothing but study Torah by day and night; and then the wealth will remain with us." The rich man placed the coin in a chest which filled up at once with a vast treasure, just as Elijah had told him. When the man and his wife saw all this great wealth, they rejoiced very much.

Then the man built a great and beautiful mansion like a royal palace containing many rooms. He also gave alms to the poor every day. But he did not fulfill the entire command of Elijah as he had ordered him; for he did not build a house of study and did not support ten men to do nothing but engage in Torah. For he said: "Why build a house of study and why engage in Torah? I have a great deal of money and now I shall engage in business and earn more." So the rich man began to engage in business and grew even wealthier and his fame spread far and wide. For the poor and wayfarers told one another: "In such and such a city there is a very wealthy man who gives ample alms." So poor people came to his house every day and he gave them of the best.

One day a certain lord came to his house to discuss some matter of business with him. And the lord said: "I see that you are a wealthy man and you share out ample alms to the poor. But that is not a good thing, for you must wither away. Consider, that because of those poor you cannot engage in business properly." The rich man felt ashamed to look the lord in the face and went to his room in a fury. "I pray you, husband," said his wife, "what has made you so angry?" The man told his wife what the lord had said, and she answered: "Listen to my advice and you will do well: Build yourself a separate mansion where you will do your business and the poor will not disturb you. When they come to me, I shall give them alms as before."

The rich man did so and constructed a special building for his transactions. The poor came to his first house, and his wife gave them alms. But when the poor saw that she begrudged them and gave them only paltry sums unlike the practice of her husband, they asked that the rich man himself should give them the charity as before. Then the woman ordered the servant to drive the poor away empty-handed. When her husband returned home she said to him: "I do not have the strength to stand those poor. When they gather here I cannot eat even a slice of bread. So I ask you to go to the governor of the city and request him to give you two soldiers to guard the entrance and drive the poor away." The rich man did as his wife asked. He thought that he would find some quiet, but forgot that man is like a passing breath. A man is distressed when his money is lost but not at his days that are wasted.

The end of the rich man will be told later, and now we shall speak of the scholar. When he came home he took the book that Elijah had given him and placed it in a cupboard which filled up with books. He sold the books and the cupboard filled again, and he gained much money. He built himself a large house and bought himself fields and vineyards and men and women slaves. Indeed, he prepared himself a special room for studying, but did not study or engage in the Torah as of old. When a poor man came to his home he went away empty-handed, and his servants mocked at the poor. So the scholar also did not obey Elijah.

Now let us tell about the God-fearing man and his nasty wife. When he came home, the woman closed the door in front of him and would not let him in. So the man went to his neighbor and asked him to go to his house taking the ring that Elijah had given him, and hang it on the wall. The neighbor did so, and the moment the ring was hung on the wall the woman abandoned her evil ways and began to honor her husband. They gave alms to the poor who came to their home, and continued doing so for a number of years.

The time came when Elijah arrived in this city. First he went to the home of the rich man to whom he had given the coin. Elijah saw a guard standing in front of the rich man's courtyard driving away the poor. Then Elijah entered the house, and the rich man recognized the one who had given him the coin, and trembled at the sight of him. Elijah said: "Did I give you the coin in order to build yourself houses and buy yourself fields and vineyards and men and women slaves? Indeed, I took pity on you and wished to deliver you from your manifold distresses, and I gave you the coin on condition that you too should take pity on the poor and needy. I also told you to build a house of study where ten men should learn Torah. But you have disregarded my words. Now I have come asking you to return the coin."

The rich man entreated Elijah not to take it from him, but Elijah was zealous for his God and said: "What you have done I am now doing. I have spoken and I shall not change." So Elijah took the coin from him and went his way. And as soon as the Man of Truth had departed, all the rich man's wealth simply vanished and the rich man remained naked and bare.

After this, Elijah went to the home of the scholar. He entered the house and found the scholar and his household eating and drinking and not lacking for any of the delights of the world; but they drove the poor away. Then Elijah said to the scholar: "Return to me the book I gave you!" And the scholar gave the book back to Elijah, who went his way. Suddenly the cupboard was bare of books just as the money had disappeared from the chest. So the scholar was once again as poor as he had been.

After that, Elijah went to the God-fearing man whose wife had formerly cursed him in public. Elijah entered his home, but he was not there and only his wife was in the house. As soon as the woman saw the old man, she set the table for him and showed him hospitality; for it was her practice to honor all the guests who came to her house. When her husband came home, he recognized Elijah the Prophet, who had given him the ring, and the man showed Elijah even more honor than his wife had done.

Then Elijah said to the God-fearing man: "The rich man and the scholar did not pay attention to my words but went their own way, and so I have taken the coin and the book from them. But now I see that you are indeed God-fearing. Take the book and the coin from me and may His Blessed Name aid you. But hearken to my words and support the poor. Build a house of study where ten men do nothing but study Torah by day and night. And if you hearken unto me, all will be well with you."

Then Elijah went his way. As for the God-fearing man, he became very wealthy indeed and followed the ways of the Torah and the fear of God. And His Blessed Name helped him to bring up his children with pleasure and satisfaction. May the merits of Elijah be of avail to all Israel, amen!

105
ELIJAH THE CRAFTSMAN

This story serves as the narrative basis for a popular Sabbath hymn, Ish Ḥasid Hayah, *"There was a pious man," composed in the twelfth or thirteenth century. Source: Rabbi Nissim,* Ḥibbur Yafeh, *p. 24.*

Our sages of blessed memory told that there was once a very poor man who had five children and a wife. One day he was very much distressed because he did not even have a farthing to support them. His wife said to him: "Go to the market place, for maybe the Holy and Blessed One will provide you with some livelihood and we shall not perish of starvation." "Where shall I go?" he asked. "I have neither kinsman nor brother nor friend to help me in my distress, nothing but the mercy of heaven." The woman had nothing to say but the children were hungry and wept and wailed for food. So she spoke to him again, saying: "Go out to the market place instead of watching the children die." "How can I go out naked and bare?" he asked her. But she had a ragged garment and gave it to her husband to cover himself.

He went out and stood at a loss, not knowing which way to turn. He wept and he raised his eyes to heaven and prayed: "Lord of the Universe! You know that I have nobody to look upon my suffering and poverty and take pity on me. I have neither brother nor kinsman nor friend. My little children are starving and shrieking with hunger. Show us now Your kindness or gather us to You in Your mercies and let us rest from our miseries!" And his outcry went up to God in heaven.

Then came Elijah, whom it is good to mention, and said to him: "Why are you weeping?" And he told him his story and misery. Elijah said: "Do not be afraid, just take me quietly and sell me in the market place and take my price and live on it!" "Good sir," said the other, "how can I sell you when people know that I have no slave? Why, I am afraid that people would say that you are my master and I am the slave!" But Elijah repeated: "Do what I tell you and sell me, and after you have sold me give me one little coin of all the money."

So he did so and led him to the market place, and all who saw them were sure that the poor man was his slave while Elijah was his master until they asked Elijah, who said: "He is my master and I am his slave."

One of the king's ministers passed by and saw him and decided that he was good enough to be purchased for the king. So he stood there while they auctioned him and his price mounted to eighty dinars. Elijah said to the poor man: "Sell me to this minister and do not take anything more for me." The man did so. Then he took eighty dinars from the minister and gave one dinar to Elijah, who returned it to him and said: "Take it and live on it, you and your household, and may you never know poverty or lack all the days of your lives!"

So Elijah went off with the minister, while the man went back home where he found his wife and children weak with hunger. He placed food and wine before them, and they ate and drank their fill and left what they did not eat. Then his wife asked him and he told her all that had happened. She said: "You did what I advised and it has worked out well. For if you had been lazy we would have perished from hunger."

From that day forward the Lord blessed the man and he became rich beyond compare and saw no more lack or need all his life, nor did his children after him.

Meanwhile, the minister brought Elijah to the king. The king intended to build a great palace outside the city, and he had purchased many slaves to drag stones and cut down trees and prepare all the needs of the building. The king asked Elijah: "Which is your craft?" Elijah answered: "I am skilled in all the planning and preparing of buildings." The king was very pleased indeed and said to him: "I wish you to build a large palace outside the city, of such and such a form and size." "Be it as you say," said the prophet. And the king told him: "I wish you to hurry and finish the building within six months, and then I shall set you free and show you my kindness." To which Elijah answered: "Order your slaves to set out all the materials required in the building." And he did so.

Then Elijah rose and prayed to the Lord and requested Him to build the palace in accordance with the king's desire. And God heard his prayer and fulfilled his request, and the palace was built within a few moments just as the king desired. Indeed, the work was all completed before the dawn. Then Elijah went his way. The king was informed and went to see the palace which he approved of exceedingly; and he rejoiced very much. Still, he was exceedingly astonished and sent in search of Elijah, who could not be found. The king was sure that he must be an angel.

But Elijah went his way and met the man who had sold him and who now asked: "What did you do with the minister?" "I did what he asked of me," said Elijah, "and I did not disobey him, and I did not wish him to lose his money. Indeed, I built him a palace which is worth a thousand times as much as what he gave you."

Then the man blessed him and said: "Good sir, you have restored us to life!" Elijah answered: "Give praise to the Creator who has done you this great kindness."

106

IF HIS NAME DECREES

The expressions im irzeh ha-shem, *"if His Name decrees," or* be-ezrat ha-shem, *"with the help of His Name," are current conversational expressions in modern Jewish society. The tale, which has parallels in the folklore of many peoples, advocates their use. Source: M. Steinschneider,* Alphabetum Siracidis, *pp. 9b–10a.*

Once there was a certain man who was very rich indeed and had much land, but he had no oxen with which to plow it. What did he do? He took a bag of money amounting to a hundred dinars and went off to a city in order to purchase oxen or cows with which to plow his land. On the way he met Elijah, whom it is good to mention, and he said to him: "Where are you going?" "To a village," said he, "in order to buy oxen or cows." "But add," said Elijah, "if His Name decrees!" "Whether His Name decrees or does not decree," said the man, "I have my money with me and I shall do what I need." "But without success!" said Elijah.

He went on the way to do what he needed and his bag of money fell. When he came to the village of the oxen to do his business, he stretched out his hand to take the bag in order to pay the money and found nothing. So he went back home in great annoyance and took more money, and he went to another village in order that Elijah should not meet him. On the way Elijah met him in the likeness of an old man and asked him: "Where are you going?" "To buy oxen," he answered. "But add," said Elijah, "if His Name decrees!" "Whether His Name decrees or does not decree, I have my money with me and am afraid of nothing!" And he hurried off on his way. As he was walking along, Elijah made him feel very tired and he lay down by the wayside and slept. Then Elijah took the bag of money from him, and when he woke up he found nothing. So he went home very annoyed and took money a third time and set out again.

Elijah, whom it is good to mention, met him and asked: "Where are you going?" "To buy oxen, if His name decrees," said he. "Go in peace and be successful!" said Elijah. And the prophet, whom it is good to mention, restored him all his money, replacing it in his bag, and the man knew nothing. So he went on to buy his oxen and found two red cows which were without blemish. "How much are these cows?" he asked their owners, who told him: "A hundred dinars." "I do not have a hundred dinars with me," said he, but he thrust his hand into his bag where he found three hundred dinars. So he bought the cows at once and did all he needed, likewise purchasing oxen to plow his lands, and afterwards he sold the cows to the king for one thousand gold dinars.

So let every man who wishes to do anything be careful to say: "If His Name decrees." For he cannot know what may happen from evening to morning. Indeed, Ben Sira remarked in this connection: "Between morning and evening the world may be destroyed."

Tales of Wisdom

107
DO NOT TELL YOUR WIFE ANY SECRETS

The association between women and speech is one of the dominant features in the image of women in Jewish folklore. They appear in tales as talkative and unable to refrain from letting out secrets that could harm their own husbands. The present story makes use of a worldwide known test of confidentiality that the wife fails. Source: S. B. Ḥuzin, Ma'asim Tovim, No. 24, p. 26.

There was a certain man whose father instructed him not to tell any secrets to his wife, not even a trifling word. Once he decided to test whether his father's words were true, for he held that his wife loved him boundlessly and her soul was entwined with his. And he said to her one night: "Stay at your father's home tonight with the children and come in the morning. For my partner is coming today from such and such a place and wishes to make up the accounts with me so I need a very clear head."

She went to her father's home, and what did he do? He fetched a sheep and slew it and dragged it over the cushions and pillows and then buried it in the garden. In the morning his wife came and asked: "Where is this blood from? And whom have you hurt?" He answered: "For heaven's sake, speak to me quietly so that the neighbors and others should not hear, and do not tell anyone the secret. I made up the accounts with my partner and I have thought that he had several thousand of my money with him, but it turned out to be the opposite for I owe him ten times as much. When I saw this, I flew into a rage and shed his blood with a knife I had, and I dug a hole in the garden and buried him there, for I do not have the money to pay and I cannot obtain it."

A month later he began to grow angry and scolded her. When she an-

[256]

swered him back, he slapped her and beat her. Then she began wailing bitterly and ran out of the house and shouted to every passerby: "Look at this wicked, ugly husband of mine and what he did to his partner whom he murdered and buried in the garden!" The matter came to the governor of the city, who summoned him and asked: "What is this you have done, shedding innocent blood? For she who shares your bed has borne witness against you and what she says seems true, and you buried him in the garden." "My lord," said the man, "this is what has happened to me and the rest is false. If you do not believe me, please go and you will see that it was a sheep I buried in the garden."

When the governor saw that he was telling the truth, he dismissed him, saying: "Be careful to do what your father said, for his commandment was very sound."

108
Cast Your Bread upon the Waters

This is a very popular tale in Jewish folklore, appearing both in medieval literary tradition and in current oral traditions. The last advice of a dying father serves as a narrative framing device for the unfolding of a story that is associated with the widely known theme of knowledge of animal languages. Source: M. Steinschneider, Alphabetum Siracidis, *pp. 4b–6a.*

A certain man used to teach his son every day the words of Ecclesiastes (11:1): "Cast your bread upon the waters, for you shall find it after many days." In due course the man died, and the young man remembered his father's words. He used to take bread every day and throw it into the sea.

On one occasion Elijah, whom it is good to mention, met him in the form of an old man and asked him what he was doing. He answered: "My father ordered me to cast my bread into the water." "Yet surely you have learned," said Elijah, "when you cast your bread upon the water, that bread is like salt. Just as bread cannot be eaten without salt, so the world cannot exist without bread." So from that time on he used to take only a piece of bread every day and went to the river and threw it into the water.

There was a certain fish at that place which used to eat the bread, and it did so every day until it grew very big and distressed the other fishes in that place. At last all the fish in the sea gathered and went to Leviathan and said to him: "Your majesty, there is a certain fish which has grown very big so that we cannot live together with him, and he is so strong that he eats twenty or more of us every day." When he heard this, Leviathan sent for him, saying: "These live out at sea and have not grown so much, yet you have grown so large at the sea's edge. How is that?" "Indeed," answered the fish, "it is because a certain man fetches me a piece of bread every day and I eat it morning and noon; and in the morning I eat twenty fish and in the evening thirty."

"Why do you eat your companions?" asked Leviathan, and he answered: "Because they come to me and I consume them; and the words of the Prophet Isaiah (58:7) apply to them: 'And do not disregard your own flesh.'" "Go," said Leviathan, "and fetch that man to me." "Tomorrow," answered the fish.

He went at once and dug beneath the spot where the young man used to come, and he made a tunnel there, and placed his mouth in that tunnel. Next day the young man came as usual and wished to stand in that spot, but fell into the water. The fish opened its mouth and swallowed him up and carried him away through the sea to Leviathan, who said: "Spit him out." He spat him out of his mouth, and the man fell into the mouth of Leviathan, who said to him: "My son, why have you cast your bread into the water?" and he answered: "Because my father taught me from childhood that I should cast my bread upon the waters."

And what did Leviathan do then? He released him from his mouth, kissed him and taught him seventy languages and the whole Torah, and flung him a distance of three hundred leagues onto the dry land. He fell in a spot where human foot had never trodden. Lying there exhausted, he raised his eyes and saw two ravens flying above him. One of them said to the other: "My father, see whether that man is alive or dead." The father replied: "My son, I do not know." "I shall go down," said the son, "and eat his eyes because I enjoy picking out the eyes of human beings." But his father said: "My son, do not go down in case he is alive." The son insisted: "I shall go down and pick out his eyes," and down he flew.

This man understood what they had been saying to one another, and when the raven settled on his forehead he seized him by the legs. At once the raven cawed to his father: "Father, father, the Lord has delivered me into his hands and I cannot rise." When his father heard this, he croaked and wept and said: "Alas for my son!" And he cried: "You, human being, let my son go! May it be His will that you understand my language! Rise and dig down where you are standing, and you will find the treasures of Solomon, king of Israel."

He let the raven go at once and dug down and found the treasures of Solomon, with many jewels and pearls, so that he and his sons after him remained wealthy. It was of him that Ben Sira said: "Offer your bread and your table and give to whomever may come."

109
THE TWO RAVENS, THE LION, AND THE WAYFARER

Several versions of this tale occur in midrashic literature. The opening scene reverses the relations that initiate the "father's advice" tales. In contrast the proverbial conclusion is typical of the fable form that often functions in advice stories. Hence the present text playfully pits themes and forms against each other. Source: M. Steinschneider, Alphabetum Siracidis, pp. 7a–7b.

A certain man who was on his way to the Land of Israel raised his eyes and saw two ravens, father and son, which were quarreling. The father said to the son: "Why did you not listen to my words about the man wandering in the fields, when you told me that you wanted to eat his eyes and I told you, keep away from him and do not eat his eyes for he may be alive; and every human being is very cunning indeed. But you said he was dead and would not listen to my words and went down to him; then he took hold of you and you cried as loudly as you could to me, and I took pity on you. And because I saw how greatly you were distressed, I showed him the hidden treasure as you saw. There are so many other things about which you refuse to listen to me." The raven rebuked his son about this, but the son paid no attention to him. His father grew so angry that he went and killed his son and voided all his fury on him. But when his fury had died out, he regretted what he had done. He swiftly flew away and fetched back a herb in his beak. He placed it on his son and brought him back to life, and they flew away together.

This man saw all that the raven had done. He went and took that herb and concealed it with him and continued on his way. Then he raised his eyes again and saw two birds quarreling with each other until one attacked the other and slew it. The living bird flew away at once, while the man sat where he was to see what the living bird would do to her dead companion, and whether she would revive her as the raven had revived his son.

He waited there for up to two hours until he saw the living bird hurrying back with the herb in her beak. She placed it on the dead bird and restored her to life; then they both flew off peacefully into the air.

When the man saw what the bird had done with the herb, he said: "I shall go and take this and see if it is the same kind as the herb I took from the raven." He went and took that herb and saw that they were like one another. Then he said: "Why am I standing here? I shall take this herb since I have seen it tested twice, and with it I shall revive the dead who are in the Land of Israel."

As he went on, he found a dead lion by the wayside, and said: "Now I shall take this herb and place it on the lion and see if he comes to life." So he took part of the herb and placed it on the lion and revived it. The lion rose at once and slew him and ate from him until he was full. The two ravens stood over the rest of the body and said: "Alas for you, alas for you. You took the herb and brought disaster to yourself!"

And this supports the saying of Ben Sira: "Do no good to the bad, and you will bring no harm on yourself."

I 10
THE HUNTER AND THE BIRD

This is an eighteenth-century text that was discovered in a Yemenite manuscript. However, the tale is much older and is part of the Oriental, classical, and medieval didactic literature of fables. Source: L. Ginzberg, "Fragmentary Legends," pp. 228–229 (Hebrew).

A certain hunter once caught a bird that knew seventy languages. The bird said to him: "If you set me free, I shall teach you three wise sayings." "Teach them to me," said the hunter, "and I shall let you go." "Swear to me," answered the bird, "that you will let me go after I have taught them to you." The hunter took an oath and the bird said to him: "The first wise saying is: 'After a thing has been done do not regret it.' The second is: 'If a man tells you something that cannot be done, do not believe him.' And the third is: 'If you cannot climb up, do not weary yourself trying to climb up.'" Then it said to the hunter: "Let me go," and the hunter set him free.

The bird flew off, perched on a tree that was loftier than all the other trees and laughed at the hunter, saying: "You set me free, and you did not know that in my crop I have a pearl that is worth more than a thousand dinars, and it is the only thing that makes me wise." At this, the hunter regretted what he had done and ran to the foot of the tree and started to climb it. But when he had climbed halfway, he fell and broke his legs and twisted all his joints.

Then the bird mocked him indeed and said: "Fool of the world, you did not act according to the wise sayings I taught you even for a few moments. I told you that once a thing is done you should not regret it—yet you regretted having let me go! And I told you that if anybody tells you something impossible do not believe him—yet you believed that I have a pearl in my crop! Yet I am only a bird that flies and seeks food all day long. I told you that where you cannot climb you should not tire yourself out trying—and yet you had to run after me till you fell and broke your legs and twisted your limbs! It was said about you in the Book of Proverbs (17:10): 'A rebuke enters deeper into a man of understanding than a hundred stripes into a fool.' Many men are wiseacres like you."

Then the bird went its way to seek its food.

III
THE WISE VILLAGE MAIDEN

In the original Hebrew this tale is in rhymed prose. It is a medieval rendition of the theme of the clever peasant's daughter that has worldwide distribution. A brief rendition of the opening story of Thousand Nights and a Night *serves as the concluding episode of this story. Source: I. Davidson, ed.,* Sepher Shaashuim: A Book of Mediaeval Lore *by Joseph ben Meir ibn Zabara, pp. 36–40.*

There was a certain great and wise king who had many wives and concubines. One night he dreamed that he saw an ape from Yemen leaping and dancing over the necks of his womenfolk. When morning came his spirit was restless and he lost his strength and said to himself: "This can only mean that the king of the Yemen will drive me out of my kingdom, and will sleep with my wives and concubines on my bed." When he rose, one of his attendants appeared before him and saw that he was moaning and disturbed and in an uneasy mood. "My lord king," said he to him, "why are you so ill at ease? Tell your secret to your servant and maybe I can aid you." "I dreamed a dream," answered the king, "and it gave me a taste more bitter than death. Do you know any wise interpreter of dreams in these parts?" "I have heard," answered he, "that there is such a man who dwells three days' journey away. He is wise and understanding, they say, and understands the meaning of things, and also he can interpret every dream, no matter how deep and confused it may seem. Tell me your dream, and I shall visit him." So he told him and said: "Go in peace."

So the courtier went home and mounted his mule and set out for his destination. In the morning he met a villager who was riding on his ass. The courtier said to him: "Peace be with you, tiller of the soil, who is soil and who eats the soil." The villager laughed at his words, and the courtier asked him: "Whither away?" "Home," said the villager. "Old man," said the courtier, "shall I bear you or will you bear me?" "My lord," said the villager, "how can I bear you when you are riding on your mule and I am riding on my ass?" So they went along together quite a distance till they saw a field that was full of wheat, and the villager said: "See how good this field is with all the ears of wheat so full!" And the courtier said: "If they have not all been consumed."

They rode a little farther and saw a lofty, fortified tower that was well built and stood on a rock. "See how handsome and fortified this tower is," said the villager, and the courtier answered: "It is fortified from outside but is it not ruinous within?" And he added: "There is snow on the hill." The villager laughed because it was the height of summer and there was no snow anywhere. They journeyed on and saw a path with wheat on either side, and the courtier said: "This path has been traveled by a horse that was blind in one eye and was carrying a load of oil on one side and vinegar on the other." They journeyed farther and came near a town, where they saw a dead man who was being taken to burial. The courtier asked: "Old man, is he dead or alive?" At which the villager thought to himself: "How can he appear so wise and sensible when he is only a great fool!"

It began to grow dark and the courtier asked: "Is there any place to stay nearby?" "There is a village just ahead," said the villager," and there I have my house and home. Please do me the honor of coming to my house, where I have plenty of straw and fodder for the beast." The other answered: "I shall be honored indeed to do what you say and come to your house at the end of this day." So he came to his home where he ate and drank and so did his mule, and they gave him his bed to rest, while the villager and his wife and two daughters also went to sleep.

At midnight the villager woke up and said to his wife and daughters: "What a fool this guest of ours is! He met me on the way and tired me

out with his words all day and exhausted me with the things he said."
"How did he show his foolishness?" asked his wife. So he told them about
the burden, and the field, and the tower, and the snow, and the path, and
the dead man, and the food of the soil. Now he thought that the courtier
slept, but he was awake and he grew angry and disturbed. But the little
girl said—and she was only fifteen years old: "This man is very wise indeed,
but you did not pay attention, father, to what he said, and you did not
understand how wise were his words. Everything he said was shrewd, and
those phrases of his each had their purpose. When he said 'tiller of the
soil and eater of the soil,' he meant that everything a man eats comes from
the soil. When he said that you are soil, it is true, 'for dust you are, and
unto dust you shall return' (Gen. 3:19). And he spoke truly about the
burden, for everyone who travels with another and speaks to him and tells
him riddles and parables bears him along and conducts him and eases him
of the hardships of the way and keeps him away from all kinds of thoughts.
Of the field he also spoke the truth, because maybe the owner is a poor
man who has sold the wheat in the ear or borrowed a loan before he harvests
it. He also spoke truly about the tower, for every house that has no food
and bread is ruinous and has nothing but the fear of famine. When he
said there is snow on the hill he only wished to say that your beard is
white, and you should have answered: It is the work of Time. As for the
horse that was blind in one eye, he may have known this because it had
been browsing on one side of the path and not on the other. Then he could
have recognized the oil and the vinegar because the vinegar scorches the
earth and the oil does not. And in his question about the dead man he
spoke the truth, for if he has left a child he is alive, and if not he is dead."

In the morning the girl said to her father: "Father, before this nobleman
departs give him what I prepared to eat." She gave him thirty eggs and
a bowl full of milk and a whole loaf. Then she said to him: "Go and tell
this lord how many days are missing in the month, and whether the moon
is at the full and the sun is complete." So the old man went and ate two
eggs and a little of the bread and drank a little milk. He gave the rest
to the courtier and asked him all the questions of his daughter. The courtier
answered: "Tell your daughter that the sun is not complete nor is the moon
at its full, and the days of the month are short of two." So the villager
laughed and said to his daughter: "Did I not tell you that this lord is a
fool? For we are halfway through the month and he says that it is two
days short." "My father," said his daughter: "Did you eat any of what
I gave you?" The villager answered: "I ate two eggs and a little bread and
I drank a little milk." "Now," said the girl, "I know that he is a wise
and intelligent man."

When the courtier heard how the words of this maiden fair struck the mark to a hair, he was surprised at her intelligence and rose at once without delay and to her father he did say: "I wish to speak to the daughter who was conversing with you tonight." So he brought his little daughter to him, and he spoke to her kindly and asked her many questions and found that she was wise and full of good sense. Then he told her about the king and his dream. When she heard him tell this, she said: "I shall explain it to the king if I see him but not to anyone else." So the minister entreated her father and mother to permit her to accompany him, for that would bring honor and glory upon them. He revealed that he was the courtier on a journey by order of the king. The villager who was in awe of the king his master said: "Let my lord do what is good in his eyes."

So the maiden accompanied him, and he brought her to the king whom he told all that had happened and how she had said that she would tell the king the meaning of his dream if she saw him on his throne. The king looked at her and she found favor in his eyes and he led her to the chamber and spoke to her in secret and told her of his dream. "Have no fear, your majesty," said she, "of all that seemed to be in your dream for all is well with you and there is nothing to fear. Yet I feel ashamed to explain the meaning for I may reveal your majesty's shame to you." "Why should you be ashamed," said he, "to tell me what my dream must be when there is nobody here with me?" Then she said: "Your majesty, seek among your women and wives and concubines, for among them you will find a man wearing female dress and he mounts them and lies with them, and he is the ape whom you saw in your dream."

Then the king searched among all his concubines and wives, and amid them he discovered a handsome and seemly youth who was head and shoulders taller than all and so handsome he made the silver and the gold look dull. He took him and slew him before their eyes and flung his blood in their faces, and then he slew them all. After that, he took the maiden to wife and placed the royal crown on her head and swore that as long as she lived he would take no other woman to his bosom but she would remain his daily lot and portion.

112

THE HE-MOUSE AND THE SHE-MOUSE

This tale appears in Indian, classical, midrashic, and medieval fable literatures, as well as in modern oral tradition. Source: Berechiah ben Natronai ha-Nakdan, Mishlei Shu'alim *(written end of twelfth or early thirteenth century; Mantua, 1557–59), No. 28.*

Thus said a mouse: "What good is a male without the female who is his house? I have seen every kind of thing that is alive, yet among all these I have found none that is fit to be my wife." And he did greatly desire to seek for himself a wife most fair and he could find none to suit his thought and aim except the sun, who was fair beyond all compare. So he said: "If all who dwell on earth are in darkness when she is not there, the good sun brings healing with her when she comes." And when the sun began shining again, she found much favor in his eyes, and he said to her: "I love you with an everlasting love, therefore I beg you to come down from above and I shall pay your bridal price and wed you in a trice." And the sun answered with guile and deceit: "Surely it would not be meet to take the light which grew dark yesterday and shines again today and then sets in the evening. As soon as you look at it, it will pass away and clouds can conceal it anyway, and so I am but a servant to the cloud for whenever it desires I am clad in darkness. But if you should offer your pleas to the cloud, I am sure that it will not turn you away."

The mouse thought it over and hastened away to seek the cloud and said to her: "Indeed, I have toiled and found, O cloud most fair and fine, and by counsel of the sun I wish to make you mine, and I shall never forsake you." But the cloud answered and said: "He who is high above the high has placed me in the hands of the wind which bears me wherever it finds to be best, whether north or south or east or west. With might and main it carries me away. Now if a wife like me you desire, you will be wandering to and from on earth until you tire. Forsake the maid and the lady take, for the wind can make me or it can break. Go to the wind and dwell with her, entice her if you can."

So the mouse went away to the wind and found her in a desolate land and to her he did say: "Have no fear. But haste away to the hills with me for of all the females I did see in these times and our present age you are the best and most fit for me, so you be mine and I shall be yours." But the wind answered: "Why do you come to take me? You do not know how abject I be for I have no strength or power to blow down a wall at any hour, whether of stone or earth it be. I am not strong at all, you see, when a wall is stronger than me. So if it should seem fit to you and you can persuade her to be faithful and true, let her be your citadel and stay."

So he went to the wall and this did say: "Listen to me, for I would have you know the counsel of the sun and the cloud and the wind and they advise that I should ask you to be sweet and kind to me, so that we may wed, you see." But the wall answered in rage and wrath: "They sent you to me to display my shame and reproach. You have come to remind me that they are all of them free to rise up and go down while my stone and wall cannot move at all, and I have neither strength nor power and any mouse or worm can make me bare and dig into my base and make themselves a ladder and a stair. Though I may be an upthrust wall, they injure me with their mouths and feet as though I had no strength at all, and the mice come here with all their kin and dwell in me, the mothers and their litters. And they have many a hundred nests, and I cannot stand against them at the best. And do you desire a wife like me?"

So when the mouse saw that his hopes were in vain, he took a wife of his own kith and kin who had been born not far away, and she became his helpmate on that day.

113
A King for a Year

This is one of the most popular ethical parables occurring in Indian, Islamic, European, and Hebrew literature. The year on the throne is compared allegorically to the span of human life. During his lifetime a man is admonished to adhere to moral behavior in order to ensure his reward in the afterlife. Source: Bahya ben Joseph ibn Paquda, Hovot ha-Levavot 3:55–56.

At the far ends of the isles of India the inhabitants of a certain city decided to appoint a stranger over them as king every year. When the year is over, they send him away and he goes back to whatever he was before he was appointed. Now when they would appoint a foolish man, he did not know their secret but would gather wealth and build palaces and strengthen them and take nothing out of their city and do his best to bring there whatever he had which was in other places, such as wealth and wife and children. And when his year was over, the men of the city would throw him out naked and empty-handed and without anything, and part him from all he had built and purchased. So when he left he would find nothing of all he had in the city and outside it, and he would sorrow and mourn for all his toil and efforts and for all he had built and gathered which now belonged to others.

But one day they chose a stranger who had a wise and understanding heart to rule over them. When he was appointed to his office, he chose one of them and treated him well, and asked him about the customs and laws of the people and how they had treated those who had preceded him. The man revealed their secret and what they intended to do. Now when he learned of this, he did not engage in any of the things that earlier kings had done but did his best to remove everything precious from that city to another, placing all his riches and treasures elsewhere and not trusting their reverence and the honor they showed him. And as long as he was in the city he was between joy and sorrow, mourning because he would leave them so speedily and because of the small amount, in his opinion, that he could take away of their precious things, for if he could stay there longer he would have taken more. Yet he rejoiced when he departed, going away to settle in a place where he had placed his treasures and where he used them as he himself desired with a whole heart and assured soul. When his year was over he was not concerned because he left them, but swiftly and joyously departed, praising his own deeds and efforts to himself. For he went away to much benefit and great honor with conscious joy, rejoicing at both matters, since he had fulfilled his desire in both places.

Bibliography

Abraham ben Elijah of Vilna. *Rav Pe'alim.* Warsaw, 1894.

Adler, Elkan-Nathan, and M. Seligsohn, eds. and trans. *Une novelle chronique Samaritaine.* Paris: Durlacher, 1903.

Albeck, Ch., ed. *Midraš Berešit Rabbati: ex libro R. Mosis; Haddaršan.* Jerusalem: Mekizei Nirdamim, 1940.

Anon. *Ḥibbur Ma'asiyyot. First edition unknown; Ferrara, 1554; Venice, 1605; Verona, 1647.*

———. *Likkutei ha-Ma'asim.* Verona, 1648.

———. *Ma'aseh ha-Keddoshim.* Lemberg, 1905.

———. *Ma'asiyyot Nora'im ve-Nifla'im.* Cracow, 1896.

———. *Ma'asiyyot Peli'ot.* Cracow, 1896.

———. *Mayseh Bukh.* Basel, 1602; Amsterdam, 1723 [English translation: Moses Gaster, trans., *Ma'aseh Book: Book of Jewish Tales and Legends Translated from the Judeo-German,* 2 vols. Philadelphia: The Jewish Publication Society of America, 1934].

———. *Midrashot u-Ma'asiyyot.* Venice, 1543.

———. *Nevu'at ha-Yeled.* In Jacob Zemaḥ, *Sefer Nagid u-Mezaveh.* Amsterdam, 1712; Constantinople, 1726; Isaac ben Moses Satanow, ed., Berlin, 1793.

———. *Sefer ha-Yashar.* Venice, 1625; many editions. Eliezer Goldschmidt, ed., Berlin: Hertz, 1923; Joseph Dan, ed., Jerusalem: The Bialik Institute, 1986.

Arakie, Eliezer ben Aaron Sa'adiah ha-Kohen. *Sefer ha-Ma'asiyyot.* Calcutta, 1842; Bagdad, 1892.

Bahya ben Joseph ibn Paquda. *Ḥovot ha-Levavot.* Written in Arabic, 1080; translated into Hebrew by Judah ibn Tibbon in 1161; Naples, 1489; Venice, 1548; I. Benjacob, ed., Leipzig, 1846 [English translation: Menahem Mansoor, Sara Arenson, and Shoshana Daunhauser, trans., *The Book of the Direction to the Duties of the Heart, from the Original Arabic Version of Baḥya Ben Joseph Ibn Paquda's al-Ḥidāya ilā Fara'id al Qulūb.* London: Routledge and Kegan Paul, 1973].

Berechiah ben Natronai ha-Nakdan. *Mishlei Shu'alim.* Written at the end of the 12th or in the early 13th century; Mantua, 1557–59; Mantua, 1587 [modern edition: A. M. Habermann, *Mishlei Shu'alim.* Tel-Aviv, 1946]; Moses Hadas, trans. *Fables of a Jewish Aesop.* New York: Columbia University Press, 1967; Haim Schwarzbaum, *The Mishle Shu'alim (Fox Fables) of Rabbi Berechiah ha-Nakdan: A Study in Comparative Folklore and Fable Lore.* Kiron: Institute for Jewish and Arab Folklore Research, 1979.

Breithaupt, (Johannes Fridericus), ed. *Josippon.* Gotha, 1707 (Latin translation).

Brüll, N. "Beiträge zur jüdischen Sagen- und Sprachkunde im Mittelalter," *Jahrbücher für jüdische Geschichte und Literatur* 9(1889):1–45.

Buber, Salomon, ed. *Midrasch Suta: hagadische Abhandlungen über Schir ha-Schirim, Ruth, Echah und Koheleth.* Berlin: Mekizei Nirdamim, 1894.

———. *Midrash Tanḥuma.* Vilna, 1885, 1913; reprinted 1946, 1964.

———. *Midrash Tehilim: Shoḥer Tov.* Vilna, 1891; Jerusalem, 1966.

David, Moritz. *Das Targum Scheni zum Buche Esther, nach Handschriften.* Cracow, 1898.

Davidson, Israel, ed. and trans. *Sepher Shaashuim: A Book of Mediaeval Lore by*

Joseph ben Meir ibn Zabara. New York: The Jewish Theological Seminary of America, 1914.

Dov Baer ben Samuel. *Shivḥei ha-Besht*. Kopys, 1814 [English translation: Dan Ben-Amos and Jerome Mintz, eds. and trans. *In Praise of the Baal Shem Tov* [Shivḥei ha-Besht]: *The Earliest Collection of Legends About the Founder of Hasidism*. Bloomington: Indiana University Press, 1970; New York: Schocken, 1984].

Epstein, Abraham, ed. *Sefer Eldad ha-Dani*. Pressburg [Bratislava], 1891; reprinted in A. M. Habermann, *Collected Writings of R. Abraham Epstein*. Jerusalem: Mossad Harav Kook, 1950. Pp. 1–211.

Farḥi, Joseph Sh. *Oseh Pele*. 4 vols. Livorno, 1845, 1869, 1870; Jerusalem: Bakal, 1959.

Gaster, Moses. *The Exempla of the Rabbis*. Leipzig: The Asia Publishing Co., 1924; reprint ed., New York: Ktav, 1968.

Ginzberg, Louis. "Fragmentary Legends," pp. 220–250 in *Al Halakhah ve-Aggadah*. Tel Aviv: Dvir, 1960 (H).

Grünbaum, Max. *Judisch-deutsche Chrestomathie*. Leipzig, 1882.

Grünhut, Lazar. *Sefer ha-Likkutim: Sammlung älterer Midraschim und wissenschaftlicher Abhandlungen*. 6 vols. Frankfurt a.M: Kauffmann, 1894.

Günzberg, David, and Abraham Kahana, eds. *Josippon: According to the Edition of Mantua, 1480*. Berdichev: Shiftel, 1896–1913.

Ḥuẓin, Solomon Bekhor. *Ma'aseh Nissim*. Bagdad, 1890.

———. *Ma'asim Tovim*. Bagdad, n.d.

Ibn Daud, Abraham. *Sefer ha-Kabbalah*. Written 1160–61; Mantua, 1514; quoted from Ad. Neubauer, ed., *Mediaeval Jewish Chronicles and Chronological Notes*. 1:47–84. 2 vols. Oxford: Clarendon Press, 1887–1895. [English translation: Gerson D. Cohen, ed. and trans. *The Book of Tradition* (Sefer Ha-Qabbalah) *by Abraham Ibn Daud*. Philadelphia: The Jewish Publication Society of America, 1967].

Ibn Ḥasdai, Abraham ben Samuel ha-Levi. *Ben ha-Melekh ve-ha-Nazir*. "The Prince and the Hermit." Constantinople, 1518; Mantua, 1557. The second edition serves as the basis for many reprints and editions.

Ibn Verga, Solomon. *Das Buch Schevet Jehuda*, ed. M. Wiener. Hanover, 1856 [Modern edition: Azriel Shoḥat and Yitzḥak Baer, eds. *Sefer Shevet Yehudah of Shlomoh ibn Verga*. Jerusalem: The Bialik Institute, 1947 (H)].

Ibn Yaḥya, Gedalyah. *Shalshelet ha-Kabbalah*. Venice: 1587; Zolkiew, 1804.

[Isaac Dov Baer ben Ẓvi Hirsch]. *Sefer Emunat Ẓaddikim*. Warsaw, 1900.

Israel ben Sasson. *Likkutei Ma'asiyyot*. Jerusalem, 1909.

Jacob Barukh ben Moses Ḥayyim. *Shivḥei Yerushalayim*. Livorno, 1785; Warsaw, 1840; Zhitomir, 1860.

Jellinek, Adolph, ed. *Bet ha-Midrasch. Sammlung kleiner Midraschim und vermischter Abhandlung aus der ältern jüdischen Literatur*. 6 parts. Leipzig: F. Nies, 1853–1877; reprint ed., Jerusalem: Wahrmann Books, 1967 (H).

Judah Halevi, *Sefer ha-Kuzari*, ed. A. Tsifrinovitch. Warsaw, 1911 [English translation: Isaak Heinemann, trans., *Kuzari: The Book of Proof and Argument*. Oxford: East and West Library, 1947; Recent editions: David H. Baneth, *Kitāb al-Radd wa-'l-Dalīl fi 'l-din al Dhalīl (al-Kitāb al Khazarī) by Judah Ha-Levi. The Book of Refutation and Proof on the Despised Faith (the Book of the Khazars) Known as the Kuzari*. Jerusalem: The Magnes Press, 1977; Yehudah Even Shmuel, *The Kosari of R. Yehudah Halevi*. Tel-Aviv: Devir, 1972 (H)].

Krauss, Samuel. "A Moses Legend," *Jewish Quarterly Review* 2 n.s. (1911–1912):339–364.

Lévi, Israel. "Sefer Alexandros Mokedon," pp. 142–163 in *Festschrift zum acht-zigsten Geburtstage Moritz Steinschneider's*. Berlin: Otto Harrassowitz, 1896.

———. "Un recueil de contes juifs inédits," *Revue des Etudes Juives* 35(1897):65–83.

Manasseh ben Israel, *Nishmat Ḥayyim*, Amsterdam, 1652.

Margulies, Mordecai, ed. *Midrash Haggadol on the Pentateuch: Genesis*. Jerusalem: Mossad Harav Kook, 1957.

Midrash Tanḥuma. Attributed to the Palestinian *amora* Tanḥuma bar Abba, 4th century C.E.; a middle period midrash, 7th–10th centuries. Constantinople, 1522; Venice, 1565; Mantua, 1563; frequently published.

Naphtali ben Jacob Elḥanan. *Emek ha-Melekh*. Amsterdam, 1648.

Nissim ben Jacob ben Nissim ibn Shahin. *Ḥibbur Yafeh me-ha-Yeshua*. Ferrara, 1557; Amsterdam, 1745 [English translation: William M. Brinner, ed. and trans., *An Elegant Composition Concerning Relief After Adversity*. Yale Judaica Series, Vol. 20. New Haven: Yale University Press, 1977; Modern editions: Shraga Abramson, *R. Nissim Gaon Libelli Quinque*. Jerusalem: Mekiẓei Nirdamim, 1965; H. Z. Hirschberg, ed. and trans., *Ḥibbur Yafeh me-ha-Yeshu'ah*. Jerusalem: Mossad Harav Kook, 1954].

Pirkei de Rabbi Eliezer, "The Chapters of Rabbi Eliezer" [8th century]. Constantinople, 1514.

Reischer, M. M. *Sha'arei Yerushalayim*. Zhitomir, 1860.

Rosenberg, Yodel. *Nifla'ot Maharal im ha-Golem mi-Prague*. Piotrkow, 1909.

Sambari, Joseph. *Sippur Devarim*. Constantinople, 1728.

Sasportas, Jacob, Ẓevi Ashkenazi, and Moses Ḥagiz. *Me'ora'ot Ẓevi*. Lemberg, 1804; Warsaw, 1838.

Steinschneider, M. *Alphabetum Siracidis cum expositione antiqua (narrationes et fabulas continente). In integrum restitutum et emendatum e Cod. Ms. Biblioth. Leydensis*. Berlin, 1858.

Zlotnik, Jehuda L. *Ma'aseh Yerushalmi (The Story of the Jerusalemite)*. Studies in Folklore and Ethnology, Vol. 1. Jerusalem: The Palestine Institute of Folklore and Ethnology, 1946 (H).

EDITOR   Nancy Ann Miller
BOOK AND JACKET DESIGNER   Sharon L. Sklar
PRODUCTION COORDINATOR   Harriet Curry
TYPEFACE   Stempel Garamond/Stempel Garamond Initials
COMPOSITOR   European American Graphics
PRINTER   Maple-Vail Book Mfg.